T0313801

Fighting Free to Become Unfree Again

The Social History of Bondage and Neo-Bondage of Labour in India

Fighting Free to Become Unfree

Again The Social History of Bondage and Neo-Bondage of Labour in India

JAN BREMAN

 Tulika Books

Published by
Tulika Books
44 (first floor), Shahpur Jat, New Delhi 110 049, India
www.tulikabooks.in

First published in India in 2023

ISBN: 978-81-956392-6-7 (hardback)

Printed at Chaman Enterprises, New Delhi

Contents

Glossary

aatmanirbhar	self-reliant
adivasi	tribal
anna	money coin
ashram	(here) Gandhian institution of social action
bagayat	garden land
basti	slum
bhata	grain ration
bharku	gruel
bhoodan	land gift
bidi	country cigarette
chiku	fruit: sapodilla
crore	ten million
dhaniyamo	master
garibi hatao	remove poverty
ghar jamai	son-in-law
gulam	slave
gulami	resembling slavery
gur	jaggery
hal	plough
hali	bonded labourer
hali pratha	labour bondage
harekwali	maid
Hindutva	ideology and politics expressing high-caste Hindu supremacy
jajmani	exchange of commodities and services
jarayat	dry land

kali paraj	dark-complexioned people
kaam	work
khandeshi	people from Khandesh
khavathi	allowance for eating (lit., in order to eat)
kaim major	permanent labourer
khedut	peasant/landowner
kisan	peasant
kisan sabha	peasant union
koyta	work team of two to three members
kyari	low-lying wetland
mela	meeting/fair
mukadam	jobber
olkhan	recommendation
paisa	money coin
panch	council
panchayat	village council
rajah	lord
ryotwari	system of land taxation
rupee	16 *annas*
samara	'true' democracy
sarpanch	village headman
satyagraha	Gandhian campaign of non-violent resistance
sevak	social worker
shram phal	wage bonus
swaraj	self-rule/freedom
udhad	contract work
ujli paraj	fair-complexioned people
vasiduvali	housemaid
vavla	land plot
vibagh	region
wadi	garden
zimrakha	field watchmen

Climbing Up and Out of
Poverty, Derogation and Discrimination

A Footloose Livelihood

Lolkje, my mother, was born in 1906, the last but one child of a bargee's family. Her father plied a *hektjalk*, a traditional sailing barge carrying cargo along the inland waterways of Holland. Although bargees led a footloose existence, they did belong somewhere. For the Bergsma family, home was the southern part of the province of Friesland, in the north of the Netherlands. Lolkje's parents, father Haitze and mother Trijntje, brought up their twelve children as they went around rivers, lakes and canals in their barge. Not all the children came of age, however. An older brother was knocked overboard during bad weather and drowned – bargees never learned to swim; a second brother got pneumonia and by the time a doctor saw him at the next mooring place, it was already too late; a little sister died of typhoid, caught from drinking polluted water drawn from the river.

Life aboard the barge was one of abject poverty. The boat had a capacity of a little less than 100 tons, so it could not load much cargo. It accommodated mostly agrarian goods, like potatoes, grain, apples, or inputs to produce them such as fertilizer; or gravel, shells and sand for building; and lastly, peat from the east, sold all over the country for use as domestic fuel. My mother had many memories of the times she travelled to and through the peat colonies in the faraway hinterland when she was young. The cutters lived in self-built huts of peat without doors or windows, and their children wore no socks or clogs. They were shy folk who avoided contact with outsiders.

By the end of the nineteenth century, there was a rapid fall in the number of wooden barges. Lolkje's father's vessel must have been one of the last cargo sailing ships that remained operational into the second decade of the twentieth century. To start with, water transport declined rapidly with the rise

The kind of sailing barge carrying cargo on which my mother and father were born and passed their early childhood

of mechanized rail and road transport. But the fiercest competition came with the changeover to larger boats made of sheet metal and driven by steam. Their bigger holds could carry more freight and they took less time to get from place to place. In the sailing barge, if the wind blew the wrong way, the main sail had to be lowered and the barge had to be towed. On the most navigated sections, this was done by horses specially rented for the purpose. But if there was no cash to pay for this, the bargee, his wife and/or their children had to man the ropes themselves. Lolkje remembered that, once, when she was pulling the tow line together with one of her brothers, a constable stopped them and her father had to pay a fine for trespassing the ban on child labour.

Life on the barge was not without its dangers. Sailing over the inland sea or to the islands off the coast was especially perilous. My mother told me how the barge would set sail even though there was a storm raging. At such times Haitze would tie himself to the helm when they left the harbour to cross the sea, while Trijntje and the children huddled in the lower deck.

At the end of the First World War, there was a shortage of food in the cities. The government started rationing imported grain which was stored in ships requisitioned for this purpose. That was the only time Lolkje had a chance to go to school. At age nine or ten she spent almost a year in the fourth grade. Her classmates were way ahead of her, but she still managed to learn to read and write a little.

When the rivers and lakes froze during severe winters, traffic on the waterways came to a halt. No cargo meant no income, and so, as soon as the ice melted, Haitze would go to the bargees' exchange set up in every port. This was a pub where tradesmen with cargo to be transported negotiated prices with the bargees. The complements and bids were accompanied by strong drinks, and the bargees used to return to their ships tipsy or simply dead drunk. And even as he did so himself, Haitze would apologize, saying that it was customary and unavoidable to get a load.

The *tjalk* had the additional disadvantage of higher maintenance costs: a wooden board, rudder or a ripped sail that had to be replaced. That vulnerability was intensified by the need to keep moving, even in bad weather. Throughout the country, there were shipyards along the rivers to carry out essential repairs. As there wasn't always enough money to cover the bill, they sometimes had to take a detour to avoid an angry wharf boss with whom an outstanding debt had not yet been settled. The payment that would eventually follow meant that their own household expenses had to be covered from what was left. It was difficult to meet even the most basic needs. Food was scarce and had to be shared, clothes were passed down from child to child, and birthdays couldn't be celebrated.

Even the Nicholas festivity passed unnoticed. Assembled in the deck house with their mother, the children sang their hearts out but their clogs remained empty. Father explained the saint's failure to show up by saying that he had forgotten to place the gangplank down to the shore. The girls slept in the deck cabin with their parents, where the meals were also prepared, and the boys spent the night in the lower front deck. But the barge was too small to accommodate both adults and all the children at the same time. The solution to this problem was to find the girls a position ashore once they reached the age of eleven or twelve years. The boys would be apprenticed to a larger boat-owner, preferably a family member, in exchange for board and lodging. The low cargo capacity of the *tjalk* meant that the parents could do the work themselves, since the limited space did not allow them to keep all the children with them as they grew up.

The barge had been in the family for generations. Grandfather had inherited it from his father shortly after he married my grandmother. When bargees grew old – which would be after the age of fifty – they went to live ashore. My great-grandfather Lolke Douwes and his wife Trijntje had gone to live in the Frisian town they originated from, and started a little business selling peat from a dog-cart around town and in the countryside.

Going Ashore

Lolkje was the last but one child to come ashore, when she was eleven years old, and become a live-in maid in Amsterdam. Her older sisters had also gone to the city and one of them helped find this job for Lolkje, in a household that ran a store. Later, employing full-time domestic help would become a privilege of the wealthy upper class, but at the beginning of the twentieth century a much larger social segment could afford to engage a maid. The pay was bad and, for the younger ones, comprised only board and lodging. Being a *skivvy* also meant a frequent change of employer. Sometimes, a maid would search for an employer who would treat her better.

Lolkje was unfamiliar with housework as it was all so different ashore than on the barge. She had never needed to clean a toilet because such comforts were unknown on board. She meant well but did not come up to what was expected of her. She didn't last long in her first job. How many positions she had in the early years is hard to guess, as are her reasons for leaving. But at least in one instance, it was because the master of the house or one of the sons was unable to keep his hands to himself. My mother told me this when she was quite old, and said how thankful she was that she had somehow managed to keep out of harm's way.

It was not easy for Lolkje, who had been brought up speaking Friesian, to become accustomed to the urban Dutch spoken in Amsterdam. It was part of a far-reaching change of identity. Loneliness was a yoke that the young girl had to bear. She had only sporadic contact with her parents, largely because they sailed around the whole country and only came to Amsterdam if they had cargo that brought them there. Lolkje gradually got used to living in the big city, knew where to go and what to avoid. The dependence that marked the life of a housemaid decreased a little when she and an older sister decided to rent a room together. They earned a living by working from home, sewing and mending clothes or going out to work on a casual basis.

It was five years since Lolkje had arrived in the city, and she was gradually becoming an adult. When she had just turned seventeen, she met my father, Willem Klaas Breman; they married a few months later, in early 1923, after getting permission from her parents. What drove her to tie herself to this man for life at such a young age? In old age, my mother confessed that it wasn't love at first sight but the desire for protection, to escape the life of being a maid.

Getting Married

How did their relationship start? With an 'accidental' meeting on a bridge and presumably talking about what they had in common: their early life on the barges that sailed the country's waterways. Willem Klaas Breman was born in 1895 as the last child of a large family. He was preceded by fourteen brothers and sisters, but nine of them had died at birth or shortly after; this included three sets of twins. Such a high level of infant mortality reduced life expectancy and among bargees' families, this was of course due to their footloose life. Infants did not receive enough breast milk, the hygiene was bad and medical care was difficult to obtain. Willem's father had also been a self-employed barge owner but he opted for waged employment when he was older, shuttling between Amsterdam and Utrecht carrying cargo for a shipping company. He was in charge of a much bigger boat than the one my mother grew up on, made of sheet metal rather than wood and driven by steam. The Breman family originally came from the northwestern corner of a province which bordered Friesland and also abounded in water.

Their different backgrounds and accompanying lifestyles were a source of heated disputes between my parents. The milieu in which Willem was raised – marked by constant work and security of income, at least enough for the household to make do, together with the routine of a regular existence – caused him to be patronizing about the footloose and irregular life that had marked Lolkje's childhood. His memories were of a more balanced and relaxed life than the drifting existence of self-employed boatmen. It meant, among other things, that Willem attended primary school – two at the same time, in fact. The cargo was loaded and unloaded mainly during the day and the vessel went back and forth at night. When they arrived in Utrecht, my father would go to school in the morning and afternoon, and the next day he would do the same in Amsterdam. Lolkje couldn't deny the disadvantages of missing school; she was never more than semi-literate. In the retirement home where my parents spent many happy years until they reached a very old age, she would not play any games that involved reading or spelling, and correspondence of any kind or filling forms remained a real ordeal for her. To my father, she would emphasize the aspects of her childhood that were better than his. Her main argument was that her father was his own boss, had to earn his own living and was not suited to being subordinate to an employer. He would refuse to carry a load if the price, destination or the cargo itself didn't please him. And then there was the freedom to go one's own way, become acquainted with people and places that were different

My parents dressed in formal attire, provided by the photo studio.
As a child I had never seen them in such garments, a far cry from
their working-class outfits: my father in a postal services uniform,
and my mother with an apron tied around her waist when at work.

from those one was familiar with. While my mother had been sailing all over the country, not knowing in advance when and where to go, my father had been forced to shuttle between Amsterdam and Utrecht – that too at night, so he wouldn't even know what he saw along the way. My mother said she couldn't imagine anything duller. But she would remain silent if the burden of bitter poverty that had scarred her youth was mentioned.

After finishing school, Willem had to look for a job himself because the shipping company where his father worked did not need any new employees. He started out as a trainee deck-hand for an independent bargee owner, but after a few years, decreasing demand for labour on the inland water trade led him to seek work ashore where there were more jobs. His two brothers had gone before him and had already settled down and married, and he arranged board and lodging with one of them in Amsterdam. He was taken on as an apprentice electrician, but the technical skills he learned were not enough for him to become a fully skilled craftsman. The outbreak of the First World War in 1914 put an end to any further on-the-job training. Young men of his age, eighteen or nineteen years old, were called up to serve in the army. He spent the war years as a soldier, and even though the Netherlands remained neutral, it was four years before he returned to civilian life. He had gone no further in his trade and was now too old to start again as an apprentice. This explains why he became a postman, doing this work for most of the remainder of his working life. Tired of living with his brother in a working-class neighbourhood of Amsterdam, his marriage to Lolkje was also a form of liberation for Willem.

Bargees or their children who went ashore for good ended up in the lowest echelons of the changing economy. Their unfamiliarity with the urban labour market made them fall behind. They lacked the knowledge and experience to qualify for better-paid factory work. My aunts remained maids or became shop assistants at best. My uncles practised a range of unskilled professions in the services sector. At the time my parents grew up, like elsewhere in northwestern Europe, the Netherlands transformed from a rural agrarian and craft-based economy to an urban industrial one. A broad class of self-employed or waged workers, equipped with very little and no adequate means of production, left the countryside to join the steadily expanding urban workforce. The process of proletarianization they experienced undeniably meant that most of them were downwardly mobile. Awareness of this deterioration in their social standing soon faded because in economic terms at least, they became somewhat better off. Their incomes slowly increased and with that their purchasing power, a leap forward driven by the fact that in the new economy, demand for both skilled and unskilled workers still exceeded supply. The divide between present and past did not, however, lead to a complete break with life on the water. Willem and Lolkje – who was now called Lena by her husband, a name considered more appropriate to civil life – stayed in touch with family members who had not come ashore.

Years of Crisis and War

On getting married, my parents set up house in a multistoreyed apartment block near the beginning of one of the canals in the city centre. The location sounds much grander now than it was in reality. They lived on the top floor at the back in two rooms, one of which included a kitchen unit. There was a tap for running water and gas lighting, but no toilet. They had to use a chamber pot or a bucket which had to be carried downstairs a few times a week and emptied into the municipal cleaning cart. Quite soon my mother had her first daughter; the second child, another daughter, did not follow until more than ten years later; and my arrival in 1936 completed our nuclear family. I was an 'afterthought' and the only son; the one before me was still-born. The limited number of children my parents brought into the world, while they themselves had eleven and fourteen brothers and sisters each, bore witness to the demographic transition that had come about due to social change to an urban industrial order.

My father was ten years older than my mother, a significant difference in age but not unusual. He worked at the main post office in the city centre, and would leave early in the morning to sort the mail, which he would then deliver. The working day was long as, after the first delivery, which started at 7 in the morning, there was a second and even a third round, which he would not finish until the evening. Mother stayed at home, first for child care but also in later years when she had more spare time on her hands. Father didn't really like his wife working outside the house, a reluctance that was not uncommon. In the first half of the twentieth century, the Netherlands became a society where working-class women, once married, would no longer engage in paid work as they had in the earlier agrarian and craft-based economy. Becoming and remaining a housewife was seen as a step forward among the lower-income classes.

My parents were bound to their household and their social life did not extend much further than a family visit in the little spare time they had. They spoke Friesian to each other, giving them the opportunity to keep alive the identity they had to abandon in their wider public interaction. Their modest way of life, with their social interaction limited to close family members, was exacerbated by the fact of neither of them having had a religious upbringing. They had been secularized even before they went to the city. If Lolkje and Willem had any hopes of moving up a step on the social ladder, this ambition would have been nipped in the bud by the outbreak of the economic depression at the end of the 1920s. In these years of cutbacks and recession, Willem remained stuck as ordinary postman, the lowest rank in the mail service. But he was lucky in that he kept his job and did not become unemployed like so many others. On being asked later about this time of crisis, he did not seem impressed when I said it could have been a lot worse. Yes, he had kept his steady job, but the price he had to pay was ongoing poverty. His livelihood did not improve much until the second half of the twentieth century. Willem spoke with gratitude about the upturn in the autumn of his life when the welfare state came about, in the late 1950s.

The Breman–Bergsma household had already moved to the eastern side of the city when the crisis broke out. This was where I was born, in a ground-floor apartment. The nearby open market where our daily provisions were bought dated back to the beginning of the century and fitted in with the congested character of our working-class neighbourhood. Apartments with three upper floors stood in long rows on either side of the narrow streets. These new suburbs were put up by low-grade contractors who sold or rented out these houses. To meet the great demand for cheap workers' homes, eager buyers would acquire a number of such buildings when they were released for sale by the contractors, and rent them out floor-wise. One or two decades later, the better educated sections of the working population, organized in trade unions and political parties, became eligible to rent cheap tenements owned by housing cooperatives in which they were registered as members. During the crisis, people were regularly evicted from their homes. Workers who had been fired could no longer pay the rent and if they were running more than a few months behind, they would leave, either voluntarily or by force. Landlords reduced their rents and, to keep their investments profitable, lured tenants with various promises: to cover removal expenses, new wallpaper, an assurance that the place was free of vermin (bugs, mice and rats mainly), a few rent-free months and a contribution to running maintenance costs. My mother and father also surrendered to such temptations in those years. We moved house several times, finally settling down where I grew up; we stayed there for the next twenty years, throughout my adolescence. Our landlord lived across the street and owned the grocery shop in the four-storeyed house where my parents rented the first floor.

The *mise-en-scène* will now shift to my own experiences and increasing awareness as a young boy growing up. I shall return to our neighbourhood and household, but first discuss how our frugal life fared during the Second World War from 1940 to 1945.

LIFE UNDER SIEGE

The German invasion of our country restricted the freedom to which people in all layers of the Dutch society had become accustomed during the process of advancing democratization, dating back to 1919 when adult suffrage for men and women was introduced. The petty existence in which the lower classes were still trapped left them little room for choice. Free will nonetheless had gained much ground in the preceding decades and played a leading role in making decisions also when they extended beyond day-to-day matters. After the capitulation, the awareness of being left at the mercy of the Nazi power that could dictate what was and was not allowed did not mean that orders were obeyed instantly or without question. The enemy did not show its worst side at the beginning and was also unable to manage without the mediation of the Dutch bureaucracy. Too much attention has been devoted to the underground resistance and too little to recalcitrant obedience or attempts to stay beyond the reach of the occupying force: to ignore rather than to confront, and to avoid the consequences of half-hearted compliance by remaining as much below the official radar as possible. Such forms of covert resistance were not driven by patriotism or royalist sympathies, and appeals to these sentiments were met with incomprehension. When the war broke out, my oldest sister was seeing a butcher's son, but ended the relationship because his family supported the Dutch National Socialist Movement. The difference between good and bad was crystal clear, and defined the distinction between collaboration and resistance. Choosing one side or the other too explicitly was risky, and stating your opinion was not a self-evident virtue but required cautious manoeuvring, especially outside your own trusted circle. To suggest that the lives of the masses in the working-class neighbourhoods of Amsterdam were a continuation of the regime of adversity, deficiency and insecurity that had characterized the pre-war crisis years does no justice to the widely shared view that rejected alien domination. A wide gap separated 'us' and 'them'. While the latter meant the German occupiers, the 'us' feeling did not necessarily extend to the Dutch population as a whole. It had more the sound of 'our kind of people', a collective assertion founded on how work and life were shaped. The militancy that accompanied this sentiment was socially bounded and did not build up to form a huge front in a jointed Dutch citizenship.

The class divide became overshadowed by several other barriers that merited precedence. The prosecution and deportation of Jews was definitely the most far-reaching of these and took place quite early on. Every adult got an identity card showing their personal details. Jews were obliged to wear a yellow star when going outside and their freedom of movement was restricted. They were fired from public services and their children were no longer allowed to attend school. My father came home shocked from his morning shift in the neighbourhood on the day the Jews were rounded up and deported. Their doors were open, he told us, and he had seen with his own eyes how neighbours had taken away their clothes and furniture. When he asked how they could do such a thing, their pat reply was that the Jews would not be coming back, although nobody knew what was going to happen to them.

Another source of grave concern was the shortage of food. Whatever our home economy produced went to Germany as first priority. A distribution system had been introduced to ease the suffering. Flour, cooking oil, sugar, dairy products and meat were rationed, but the monthly quota was far less than a household needed. The municipality opened soup kitchens in working-class neighbourhoods. I used to be sent there with a pan to stand in the long queue and return with soup or cabbage hodgepodge. Fuel was even harder to come by than food. When the stoves were no longer lit at school, we were allowed to wear our coats in class. And when it got too cold for that too, the school was closed. An uncle who worked at the slaughterhouse occasionally gave us meat, bacon and fat, partly for our own use and partly to barter for other necessary supplies. Shopkeepers illegally disposed of parts of their regular stock at higher prices, and members of the occupying force were also prepared to surreptitiously deliver seized goods. The formal economy acquired an underground equivalent and blackmarketeers made a killing on deals between the two. During razzias, the Germans would close off the neighbourhood and send patrols through the streets to search houses at random, to track down Jews, men drafted for labour, members of the resistance and other illegal riff-raff. There was the lurking danger of being betrayed from all sides. You had to be watchful of people who were known to be friendly towards the Germans, but you could not anticipate jealousy or envy from those around you – a neighbour, relative or friend who could not resist the temptation of a reward for turning you in.

As the war continued and German victories changed into defeats, the occupying regime became increasingly malevolent. Life in the city became more and more dire. People were starving and the weaker among them died prematurely, sometimes on the street. In our household, too, there was a great shortage of everything. The daily rations were by no means enough for us all, and during meals we would closely watch each other's plates as we sat around the table to make sure we got our fair share. What we ate was not only too little but also not meant for human consumption, like boiled sugarbeet or stewed flower bulbs. My parents decided to send me to the country, to live with a family they trusted who would take care for me. It must have been one of the addresses my father had visited during his long and far excursions in desperate search of food. He took me there on his bike, a rough and fearful trip, in the autumn of 1944. The understanding was that I would stay there until the war was over, and that is what happened.

Barely eight years old, I was fostered by a Christian family in a small village. The father was a cattle farmer and dealer. While staying there during the last year of the war, I was put to work in the garden and cattle-sheds. A street-wise city boy, I had to get used to a completely different lifestyle: one in which children kept their mouths shut and did as they were told. The man of the house was introduced to me as 'granddad', although he was in fact the father. He was often not at home because the Germans suspected him of being a member of the underground movement and were looking for him. Family life was different to what I was used to – not only because of differences between city and countryside, but also because I came from a different class. But I was young enough to adapt and did, off and on, what was expected of me. I went to the village school wearing clogs like all the other children and experienced things that were completely new to me – like the master who taught two different classes in the same room, or saying prayers at the beginning and at the end of the school day. The feeling of loneliness that crept over me was made even worse by the tensions brought by the war. At night bombers flew overhead on the way to Germany and you could hear anti-aircraft fire.

And then suddenly, at the beginning of May 1945, the war was over and my father came to pick me up – on his bike because the trains were not yet running. Life soon went back to 'normal'. Back home, the looming uncertainty and insecurity began to dissipate.

Growing Up in a Working-Class Neighbourhood

Our country's infrastructure and economy had to be rebuilt and a speedy return to a decent standard of living was out of the question. How did we cope in those initial years after the war? Our apartment on the first floor was of a modest size, 42 square metres. At the front, on the street side, was a common room where we ate and sat together. At the back was my parents' bedroom and in between, a small room or alcove without windows or ventilation, where my younger sister and I slept. A normal bed for her but mine was folded up against the wall during the day so we could pass through freely. Only my oldest sister had the luxury of her own space, a tiny side room to which she could withdraw. From the apartment's outer door on the landing a short corridor led to the kitchen, where it was always busy with my mother at the hub of all the activity. The kitchen had the only water tap in the house, which was in frequent use to prepare food, do the dishes and wash ourselves. In the corridor there was a storage cupboard for shoes and cleaning materials, and next to it a toilet, the only place in the house where you could be alone. Still unfamiliar with rolls of toilet paper, we used old newspapers cut into pieces.

On the second floor lived a man and his wife with their grown-up daughter. He was a waiter, which meant that he worked from spring to autumn and in the winter lived on welfare benefits, most of which seemed to us to go on strong liquor. In this slack season, the household survived on what the daughter earned as a shop assistant. Our third-floor neighbour was an elderly couple. The man had retired from the railways, where he had worked in the shunting yards. Their daughter, a single woman who lived with them, was a teacher and enjoyed our respect for this level of education, which was quite exceptional on our street.

The other neighbours on our street were similar to the cross-section that shared our stairway. A large number of retail shops contributed to the liveliness of the street. Every few houses, there was a small business selling daily commodities. The shops were interspersed with service providers and small workshops. All of these self-employed businesses were within a few hundred metres of my house. The already extensive range on offer was supplemented by ambulant vendors selling from barrows or delivery bikes. Their proceeds were small as their customers had little purchasing power, an indication that a low standard of living persisted. Most of these neighbourhood shops and street vendors disappeared in the course of the 1950s. For groceries, we could now go to a supermarket, a new type of store with, at first, a limited assortment. The shopkeeper no longer weighed our purchase – half a pound or a pound of flour, green soap, sugar, salt, tea or coffee – by scooping it out of round or square tins and wrapping it in a paper bag while chatting to his customers.

Our neighbourhood was dominated by a Roman Catholic enclave. At its centre was a complex of adjoining institutions: the parish church stood on a square – which was our usual playground – and was flanked by two schools, one for boys and one for girls, with separate entrances for poor and well-off children. A boarding school, a convent and a home for the elderly also formed part of this block. A short distance away was the hospital, where Catholic patients were treated and nursed. As non-believers, we kept ourselves far removed from everything to do with this faith. Around the middle of the twentieth century, the Netherlands was still a pillarized society, with all social interaction divided along religious lines. The aura that Catholicism radiated – rosaries, incense, acolytes, religious names with even boys called Maria, nuns' habits – it was all very odd to us. They were 'the other', and as non-believers you couldn't be friends with them. Boys would fight each other during accidental encounters on the way to school, or teaming up in gangs and arrange to meet on the street or in the park to give each other a beating. When sent out to buy something, you knew to avoid Catholic shopkeepers; they were as little to be trusted as their offspring. You had to know their whereabouts because you couldn't tell by looking at them.

This did not apply to another divide based on social class that cut through our quarters. The determining factor in this schism was one's place in the occupational scale, which was also reflected in the layout and the borders of the neighbourhood. Our block of apartments was situated on a street which ended in a main road, along which ran a tramline. You could take the tram to the city centre while in the opposite direction, the line terminated at the old Ajax football stadium. Along the section of the main road bordering our neighbourhood, there were shops that sold a wide variety of durable consumer goods, a photo studio, a pharmacy, a bank branch and a local cinema. On

The house blocks on the street where I was born in 1936 had four storeys on both sides with narrow and steep flights leading up to the higher floors. The neighbourhood dates back to the beginning of the twentieth century when migrants from the countryside flocked to the city in large numbers. The photo is from the early 1930s when motorcars, certainly in working-class districts, were hardly to be seen. Early in the morning the milkman would come on his bicycle, and vegetables were sold from a hand-cart which also went from door to door. Every few years, my parents would decide to move house to find an apartment at a somewhat lower rent. In the 1960s and 1970s, newcomers from the Mediterranean countries came to replace the original population in these neighbourhoods.

the other side of the main street stood a public hospital and a short distance away, a synagogue. Walking around here, you realized that you had entered a middle-class domain. Also close by was a public park, flanked by spacious houses of well-to-do owners. They had lower and upper floors, which meant that the children of these families had their own rooms. Both the low-rise buildings and the large gardens with a wrought iron gate at the front or the back emphasized the higher status of the inhabitants. Our general practitioner lived in one of these houses and saw his patients in the basement of his ample residence. Typical of the neighbourhood as a whole, however, were four-storeyed apartments like ours, which housed members of the working class with few skills and not much schooling but who were not part of the industrial proletariat. These were the deserving poor, who lived modestly and kept a low profile. No doubt, they had great difficulty making ends meet, but found it important to keep up appearances, both among themselves and outside. On the lower side, our neighbourhood was bordered by a railway embankment which separated our apartment block from the adjacent district.

Towards the other end of our street and the ones running parallel to it, there was a gradual transition from a working-class neighbourhood to a slum, a slide-down to a more desolate habitat. The metamorphosis was visible in the increasing inferiority of the apartments. The outsides looked shabby, the doors of the multistoreyed houses were often open, the stairs to the upper floors were narrower, more worn out and not covered with a stair-carpet. The windows were covered with frayed curtains or none at all, the rooms had no wallpaper, vermin abounded and the pavement was covered with garbage. The farther you walked, the poorer it looked. There were hardly any shops, and those that were there sold cheap and second-hand goods. In this part of our street, there was also a branch of the Salvation Army where the homeless could get free food. The Salvationists did missionary work at street corners and their uniformed appearance, singing hymns and preaching the gospel to bystanders, always attracted an audience. Pubs were in abundance and were well frequented during the evening hours. The first instances of public intoxication would occur not too late in the day, which were always a dismal sight. Males and females would hang out of their windows, curious to see what was going on outside. They would keenly watch or take part in arguments, which started indoors and spill out on to the street, and sometimes ended in fisticuffs that were broken up before they became really vicious. Many households consisted of 'broken families', where one of the parents was missing, and unwed couples living together was a common occurrence.

The residents of the more decent parts of our neighbourhood disapproved of the lowly life of these slum-dwellers, not least because of the slang they spoke. The carefree and rough-and-ready style of interaction in these quarters fascinated me. I befriended schoolboys of my age living in our neighbourhood and would walk home with them, but we rarely went indoors, staying out to play in the street instead. The residents here were more uncouth folk than where I came from. The males were day labourers in casual jobs, like navvies, roadmen, heavers, dock workers or sailors in the merchant navy; the females were mostly in cleaning jobs. The womenfolk talked loudly and used coarse language, but were affable and indulgent towards children. Political radicalism was rife and the Dutch Communist Party had strong support in this milieu. Strikes for better pay and better working conditions were accompanied by demonstrations and red flags. In contrast to this tendency to assertive unruliness, in the decent apartment blocks of the labouring poor only a short distance away, the mood was one of acquiescence and obedience to the Christian Democratic or Social Democratic parties in the wide political centre. At election time, these varying preferences were expressed through posters for the different parties pasted to windows and walls, while vehicles with loudspeakers drove through the street to mobilize voters.

These divisions into different working-class clusters show how misleading it is to see homogeneity as a characteristic factor in understanding the concept of neighbourhood. Portraying it as a spatial unit of community, a territory with well-defined borders, is equally problematic. I got to know working-class districts elsewhere in the city with a more uniform character and larger in size than mine when visiting family members who lived there. Just how far the communal feeling went depended on the site where people lived, and that radius also increased as I was growing up. Children spent a lot of time outdoors, with the youngest among them staying within shouting distance and close to home so mothers or neighbours could call them to order if they misbehaved. Playing on the street was possible because there were as yet few motorized vehicles. Indoors there was not only too little space, but also not many toys. Friends never came up into my house but rang the doorbell to ask if I was coming down. I seldom went to visit other boys' homes either. That could have been possible in the small belt where the bourgeois class lived, because they had larger houses and preferred to keep their offspring at home. But that was a setting that closed itself off from interaction with both the old and the young of working-class stock, just as our parents didn't want us to be friends with mates of my age from the sprawling, disreputable side of the neighbourhood.

As girls grew up, they usually stayed indoors because it wasn't decent

On summer days physical instruction took place in the open. We did not have sports gear but simply took off our shirts (we used to call them blouses and this is certainly what girls wore), the girls not even that. The teacher here is explaining the rules of baseball, but football was of course our favourite game. We needed no coach for that but without an adult around, we had to watch out for policemen who did not allow us to play on the grass – or even in public squares – and chased us away.

for them to be seen hanging around the streets. I hardly noticed their marginality because, after a shared infanthood, a sharp gender division had developed with my siblings before we reached puberty. My youngest sister – the older one was now married and far beyond my daily horizon – kept meeting her girlfriends, but how and where that happened I had no idea. I knew my neighbourhood like the back of my hand and slowly ventured further afield. My friends joined me beyond our bounded territory. Our favourite pastime was to play football in the public park. We also went on sorties to neighbourhoods close by, and swam in lakes and canals on the city outskirts on summer days.

Our Household

Mother took care of the day-to-day business of the household, helping father to leave the house early in the morning and making sure we went to school and to bed in the evening on time. The housework took up most of her day: preparing meals, keeping the house clean when there were as yet no household appliances, washing as well as mending clothes, and making sure she had bought everything we needed. Father helped out in the household work and took care of the major purchases. As we grew up, we too were given chores to do – my sister especially; I got off lightly because boys did not do housework. One of the few responsibilities I was given was to bring the coal down from the chest in the attic in winter for the stove, which heated only the living room. We washed ourselves in the morning with cold water at the kitchen tap, just our hands and face. Once a week we were given a hot bath in a tub; my sister first, and then I would follow in the still tepid water. When we were older, our weekly all-over wash took place at the municipal bath house. We would sit in the waiting room with many others, waiting our turn for a shower (twenty cents) or a bath (five cents more expensive). I was given clean underwear twice a week, upper garments less often.

Our living conditions were cramped, of which we were well aware. On the other hand, we stayed in good health and the costs of medical care were covered by national health insurance. My father was in charge of the finances. He gave my mother housekeeping money of 15 guilders a week, which she was expected to manage with. Willem took care of all the other expenses: rent and other overheads like gas, water and light, the radio licence, national health contributions, and funeral and burglary insurance. In 1950, his weekly income was a little over 50 guilders and it was not easy to make that stretch to meet the needs of a family with growing children. It meant skimping on all expenses other than food, and even that called for moderation. At the baker's, bread from the day before was available at half price before 10 in the morning. We didn't eat meat every day, but it had to be bought twice a week so that we had enough gravy for the staple, potatoes and vegetables. Every now and then I was sent to buy something from the greengrocer's or the milkman. I was given no money but had to tell the shopkeeper to put it on the tab. Buying on tick was very common and lack of compliance with late payment meant that customers would go elsewhere. At the table, our manner of eating was as simple as the food. I was not familiar with proper use of cutlery, like the middle classes did, until much later. Despite the meagre housekeeping my mother managed to save a little from her weekly allowance to cover unforeseen expenses or spend on a treat for all of us. Clothes were not a high priority and we wore them until they were threadbare. Father always dressed in his postman's uniform, much to the annoyance of my mother, who hated him wearing his working clothes during his off hours. Like most men, father didn't shave daily. He kept his shaving set at the barber and would go there twice a week for a shave. When my sister grew out of her clothes, they would be altered for me. Since this had been taken into account when they were bought, there was no point protesting.

To bring in more income, when my youngest sister and I were able to take care of ourselves, my mother decided to go out to work as a house cleaner two days a week. I got pocket money only much later, not a lot but enough for the small pleasures I learned to enjoy – like going to the local cinema to see a Western cowboy film for half price on a Wednesday afternoon. We had to pass our spare time without spending much money, visiting relatives who lived ashore or the still footloose ones plying the waterways, when they were in harbour. Once in a while, I would go out somewhere alone with my father: in good weather, to a football match at the Ajax stadium, and if it rained, to the nearby Colonial Museum. There was no money to join a football club or the Scouts. In the holidays, I was allowed to stay with relatives who lived elsewhere in the country and didn't mind an extra mouth to feed for a week or so.

My parents' social contacts were mainly limited to the family circle. They were not members of any clubs and would not have known how to meet the costs this might entail. Their life revolved around caring for their children. Both my sisters, first the older one and then the younger one, attended primary school and then went to the domestic science school for two years. It was considered more than enough for girls to be taught to keep the house clean, cook, sew, do the washing and ironing, and other household jobs that awaited them when they were married. It was not time for them to marry yet, and they first went to work to earn their own living. They handed over part of their income at home for bed and board. With what was left, they were allowed to buy clothes and save for their 'bottom drawer'. My oldest sister worked as a shop assistant until she was married, immediately after the war. The youngest started off as a seamstress in a workshop; she then took a course and got a job as a typist at a municipal office, a clear step forward. As the younger brother, I was now the only child still dependent on my parents, and that would not change for many years.

I have painted quite a positive picture of our daily life, but this does not do justice to the inevitable tensions of living in poverty. The children were scolded for wanting more than was possible, and our parents would quarrel when they didn't have enough to make life pleasant for their offspring or themselves. These were sources of disagreement that had a depressing impact on the happiness of all of us.

FATHER'S JOB AND SOCIAL STANDING

The post office where Willem spent most of his working life was a public institution and was open all day. People came here to buy stamps, send registered letters or parcels, transfer money or put it in their savings account, and fill in and submit a wide variety of official forms. All these transactions took place at windows manned by white-collar employees who had been properly trained for these administrative services. There was a world of difference between the clerks and the postmen. The former were civil servants who were more educated and of course better paid. The latter occupied the lowest rank in the public sector, which also included doormen, messengers, refuse collectors and street sweepers. At the post office, there was a strict divide between these two segments, which went much further than class-wise separation. The counter clerks were neatly dressed in an office suit with a tie, and used a different part of the building and an entrance to it than the postmen. Both used the same canteen but at different times. Each stayed within their own circle, avoiding contact with higher or lower-ranking staff.

I used to visit Willem regularly at his workplace. This was because of the overtime at night for which he volunteered because of the extra pay. When he had no time to come home after the last afternoon shift, my mother would send his evening meal with me, and I woud wait till he had finished to take the tiffin carrier back home. This was how I got to see how things went at my father's place of work. The mail received from the head-office in sacks had to be sorted out for distribution. Seated behind a big table or standing around with colleagues, their talk would concentrate on daily goings-on in the neighbourhood, politics, football and the wiles of women. There was enough time to take a break in between to smoke a cigarette, drink tea or play cards. Willem joined in all this but kept a low profile. He spoke rarely, laughed when it was appropriate, responded when addressed, but was not one of the ringleaders. He did not possess the canny ease of give-and-take associated with working-class culture in the big city. He could play cards, but lacked the ability that distinguishes winners from losers. Instead of making himself popular by cracking jokes, he was more often the butt of others' wisecracks. The atmosphere seemed to be more defined by getting the better of each other than by camaraderie. Father managed to hold his own by being who he was and doing what he did, but he was certainly not a model of assertiveness. At home, he was a quiet man who had taken his place at the foot of the urban economy, but not in a way that made him happy. It is difficult to say whether he adopted this muted style because of the modest position he occupied in the labour hierarchy or the noisy environment in which he felt ill at ease.

Father did not display strong political commitment. After the war, the workforce in the lower echelons of public service, especially in Amsterdam, joined a trade union with distinctly left-wing leanings. This choice was not based on any radical beliefs but was mainly inspired by the broad backing that the union had managed to acquire at the post office, the municipal sanitation department and local transport company, the railways and other public sector institutions – and in response to the many demands for higher pay, better working conditions and social security. The trade union had been set up because of dissatisfaction about the compliant and soft-pedalling course adopted by the Christian Democratic and Social Democratic associations. The new union stood for a kind of activism that was rejected by the established political order. Its alliance with the Dutch Communist Party implied a condemnation of the decision by the ruling parties after the Second World War to grant independence to Indonesia. The communist movement was the only one to unconditionally reject the continuation of colonial rule. My father agreed with this view and occasionally went to meetings held to protest against the conservative 'Indies lost, all lost' lobby. Its demands for labour rights as well as its political agenda excluded this union from regular consultations with the government and employers' organizations. The government, anxious to consolidate the capitalist frame of the economy and society, threatened to dismiss workers from their tenured employment in the public sector if they did not give up their membership of the union. Like most of his workmates, my father too succumbed to this ultimate sanction. It did not reinforce his confidence in the middle-of the-road course of national politics and he also avoided joining another trade union. Some colleagues who did apply for membership, believing that collective action was the only way to improve their lot, were rejected on suspicion of being agitators. The radical union was eventually wound up. Willem took early retirement, rendered invalid for work due to a bent back and worn-out knees as a result of having carried around a heavy post-bag on his rounds for close to forty years.

There was an observable emancipatory trend in wider society, which also benefited Lolkje. The young girl who had come to Amsterdam to work as a live-in maid had acquired dignity as a married woman by raising her children and running her own household. But the sharp class differences that had existed before the war were still in place and meant that even when she was older, my mother was addressed as 'miss' rather than 'madam', like women of the middle class. There was now increased commonality between the social classes and a process of embourgeoisement meant that status distinctions made way for some levelling down of differences in rank. Mother went to work again and was no longer called a maid but a cleaning lady. Later this would be upgraded to management of housekeeping. It was of course a facade that disguised the difference between high and low, between more and less, but even the appearance of equal standing gave a degree of social leverage.

This was the start of better times for my parents, made possible by the intrusion of the welfare state. Collectors no longer came to your doorstep every week to demand the compulsory contribution that grown-up children had to pay for their elderly parents. The older generation felt redeemed from dependence on not always grateful offspring and the embarrassment associated with it, when the state started providing support. That also meant shifting to a home for the elderly when incapacitated and unable to run their own household. Arranging accommodation, daily care and, when needed, nursing was seen as the government's duty, paid for from the public coffers. These measures guaranteed the preservation of dignity at an advanced age. Without a doubt, the services that became available signified an improvement in the lives of the low-income classes. Housed in a spacious apartment with its own bathroom, Willem and Lolkje were surrounded by gadgets which, if they existed before, had been far above their budget: a refrigerator, a washing machine and dryer, warm and cold water all day long, central heating, a television and the convenience of a telephone, which both of them used as if they had been doing it all their lives.

My School Life

When I turned six, I was admitted to the first standard of the primary school, which was only a few streets away from home. In the early 1960s, it was one of the largest schools in Amsterdam filled only with children of the working class.[1] Interrupted by the break in the last year of the Second World War, I studied there till 1948, and picked up the basics of reading, writing and arithmetic. At first, I learned to write on a slate. Only when it was going reasonably well were we allowed to use pen and paper. We were not only being taught what we didn't know, but also had to unlearn certain other things, such as lack of discipline and unruly behaviour – uncouth language in particular. I passed through primary school as an unremarkable pupil. In fact, throughout my time at school, I came across boys and girls cleverer than me, who knew more and were deservedly praised for their understanding and knowledge of the subjects. My classmates came from the whole of our neighbourhood, including the less well-off quarters. This mixture didn't cause any problems, but the teacher checked us regularly for cleanliness. When the school reopened after the war several of the pupils, including me, proved to be infected with scabies. But even when this affliction had been eradicated,

---

[1] As described in the weekly *De Groene Amsterdammer*, 15 October 2020.

a teacher would often stand at the front door of the school to inspect our hands and neck and check our hair for lice. If you were not clean enough you would be sent home to wash, while the self-care of girls was taken for granted. Though once in a while I played truant, it had little appeal for me unless it was in the company of others and with a clear goal in mind. I went to school willingly, as we had plenty of spare time outside school and were not yet bothered with homework that had to be handed in. We learned what the teacher told us and self-study did not become important until much later.

What was in store for us after primary school? For most of the children the choice was already made. Boys went to the elementary technical school and the girls to the household school. There was a seventh class for those who did not go on to further education. They were mostly classmates from the slum areas of our neighbourhood, where there was insufficient social capital to spark the need for further education. The school-leaving age was twelve, and for these boys and girls there was nothing else to do than wait until they could go out to work. It was the teacher of the final class who decided who was suitable for what. Only in very exceptional cases would he advise parents to send their son or daughter for the highest level of schooling, which was both geographically and academically way beyond the reach of children in our neighbourhood.

The teacher considered me a borderline case and suggested to my parents that I do a test at the municipal agency which provided occupational counselling. The results showed that due to a clear lack of technical ability, I was unsuitable for training in a craft. Becoming a gardener, for example, in the city parks department seemed a better job prospect for me. Or a form of low-grade education which offered access to the bottom ranks of the service sector. This type of school offered courses for either three or four years. Because my capacity to achieve was not rated very highly, my parents decided that a year longer at school would raise my chances of passing successfully. It was an unintended but fortunate choice since the school which took four years offered more opportunity to climb up the occupational ladder.

The school that I attended from 1948 to 1952 was in a lower middle-class neighbourhood, where the majority of the pupils lived. I soon acquired a better insight into what they and their families were like. They proved to be ordinary people who had larger houses, were a little better off, and had fathers engaged in higher qualified jobs than males from my working-class background. My parents felt I should have a bicycle to cover the long distance from home, and my father bought me a second-hand one. I passed the lower classes uneventfully, doing my homework at the kitchen table. I now had

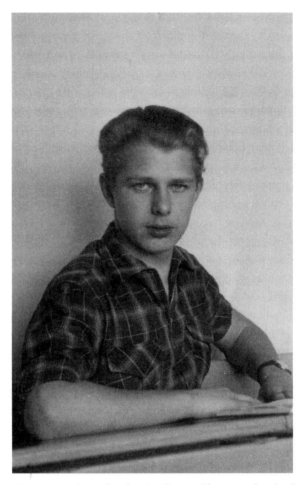

Once a year, the studio photographer would come to the school to make a portrait. This one, taken in 1951, marks the end of my studies in the lower secondary school. I am proudly showing off my wristwatch, the first one I ever had. It was a present from my two sisters who had already earned their keep for many years. The elder one worked as a shop assistant and the younger one, after a stint in a garment atelier, had joined the typing pool of the municipal tax office. Both contributed to the household budget but were allowed to keep a part of their weekly wage packets, saving up for their trousseaus.

the middle bedroom to myself, as my younger sister got the side room when our older sister got married and moved out. In the higher classes I started to distinguish myself with my school achievements. I liked to learn and got good grades, doing so well that some of my teachers told my parents to send me to a higher secondary school. That was very unusual as most friends of my age had by now started their working lives, taking night courses in typing, shorthand, book-keeping, business correspondence, etc. With these qualifications they were eligible for administrative jobs. A more realistic option to move upwards socially was via the teachers' training college, which would have been a considerable step forward. But my aspirations extended farther than this, and the prospect of attending higher secondary school appealed to me.

I didn't have a lot of choice because the only school in Amsterdam willing to take pupils from the lower secondary level was far from home. Moreover, I had to sit for an entrance examination and successful applicants had to agree to start in the third year. That meant going down two years for the privilege of being selected to the five-year course. I prepared myself by taking coaching lessons in mathematics, which I had been badly taught. In early autumn of 1952, a large group that had passed the low-grade secondary school from all over the city took the test; a week later, the results were out. We all gathered in a hall and the school janitor loudly read out four names, one of which was mine. He asked us to go with him and I expected to hear that our results were not good enough. But no, the four of us had passed and the remaining more than thirty boys and girls had been rejected. This incident is worth recounting because it illustrates the strict divisions between social classes. It was not entirely unthinkable to break through the ceiling of the working class milieu, but it was forcefully resisted by means of an educational policy of discouragement.

To earn money for coaching lessons, I got a temporary job in a large brewery as a sixteen-year-old. The working day was from 8 in the morning till 5 in the evening, with half an hour for lunch. That seemed enough but proved a little tight in practice. From the third floor, where I worked in the bottling section, I had to run back and forth to the canteen, and the foreman kept a close eye on the time. It was noisy in the workplace and I could only make myself audible to the man next to me by shouting. He was already getting old and had spent all of his working life in this factory. 'Make sure you get out,' he confided to me, 'because you will not achieve anything here. Just look at me.' My weekly pay was seven guilders, but two guilders were docked from my first wage for late arrival. I had clocked in at the gate in the morning, but then walked upstairs in a leisurely manner while chatting with my workmates, not knowing there was a second time-check there. I couldn't keep the rest of the money either, as father told me that my first wage packet should be a present for my mother. It was a time-honoured custom which I gladly owned up to.

Back at school in the autumn, I was two years older than my classmates and studying lessons that did not contain much that was new. I continued to do well, to the extent that when the final examination came up, a few of my teachers urged me to go to university. This was a path that lay far beyond the horizons of my upbringing and it met with little approval. On the contrary, both my sisters accused me of being selfish, saying that our mother was a victim of my persistent refusal to stop studying and start earning a living. After all, she still went to work and did that partly to pay for my upkeep. I accepted their reasoning, felt guilty about it and promised that whatever happened, I would pay my own way. My father objected for completely different reasons, and he went to the school to talk to the headmaster about it. Willem preferred to have me attending the cost-free and professional college of the postal service, to be trained as a manager. Then I might even work my way up to become the director of a district post office. The idea came to him without doubt spiralled by the disrespectful way he had been treated as a postman. Not only seeing his son going through the other office entrance but, who knows, even being in charge of all the staff – there could not be a better way, from his perspective, of demonstrating how we had gone up in the world.

I refused to do as my father wished, but did apply to the postal corporation for a scholarship. The stipends were intended to enable children of post office employees to train for jobs that required a university education. It was exactly what I wanted. If awarded a grant, I would no longer be a burden on my parents. I was summoned to the head office in The Hague in the summer of 1955 to undergo a psychological test followed by an interview by a panel of board officials. It had never happened before, I was told, that the son of a postman had applied for a scholarship. The results came a couple of weeks later: my application had been denied. Not because of any doubt about my ability to complete my studies, but because such a radical move upwards in the social scale would lead to a break with my family. So it was for my own good and that of my parents that I was turned down. There was nothing else I could do now than look for a side job to be able to pay my enrolment fees at the University of Amsterdam and for maintenance cost at home. I started working in the evenings as a sorter at the postal distribution office next to Amsterdam Central Station, but soon found out that it was hard to combine work and study because the former occurred at the expense of the latter. Studying comprised more than going to lectures. The periodical exams required a great deal of self-study. The evening hours were the perfect time to do that, but I had to spend them earning money.

The solution came at the start of my second year of study when the government announced that it would provide interest-free loans to make it easier for students from low-income social classes to go to university. I fulfilled the criteria and received this allowance which covered all my expenses. This new facility was even more appealing since you didn't have to pay back the debt after graduation, if you committed yourself to enter the teaching profession and stay on for at least five years. Joining a profession which had paved my way upwards was a prospect that I didn't find at all daunting. Besides, the social class I grew up in anxiously tried to avoid accumulated indebtedness because of the problem of repaying loans on a low income. What kind of study did I choose? Several disciplines were beyond access, such as law and medicine. These were not only class-related to a large degree, but also tended to be strongly family-related, being practised from generation to generation. My first choice would have been to study history, which was impossible because I had not learned Greek and Latin at secondary school. Knowledge of the classical languages, only taught at the gymnasium for children of the higher bourgeoisie, was a precondition for admittance. I opted for the faculty of the social sciences. What exactly this new field of study entailed and what you would be trained for was as yet unclear. The staff and students were recruited from a wider social pool than most other disciplines. The pioneers of this department in Amsterdam were renowned scholars to the left of the political spectrum. Their progressive leanings paralleled those of the Amsterdam city council, under which the university fell as a municipal institution.

The way my study proceeded and later my career are beyond the scope of this account. The choice I made early on was focused on societies and civilizations different from the one in which I myself had grown up. The milieu I came from did not care much about the Dutch rule in the East Indies. Interest in colonialism was the domain of the higher and middle classes in Holland, the labouring classes lacked any direct ties with it. At best, they signed up to serve in the colonial army, which put them at a distance from the colonized population. What drove me to develop that peculiar interest? It was a curiosity I acquired young and which had its roots in the neighbourhood I was brought up in. On the other side of the nearby public park was the Colonial Museum, where I would go at a tender age with my father during the weekend, and watch *wayang* dancing and listen to *gamelan* music. I became acquainted with the tropical landscape, pressing my eyes to small holes in the peep-boxes to see how rice was grown on *sawah*s or what a Javanese bazar looked like. Or clicking buttons on the large-scale model of a plantation to light up storehouses, workplaces and coolie lines. I stepped into a different world and could even smell it by standing above the netting of an aromatic cabinet in which cloves, cinnamon and other spices were laid out.

Certainly, the exhibition laid emphasis on all the wonderful achievements of the Dutch colonists over the centuries – such as the promotion of health care, education and economic development. When I was a little older, I frequented the children's library at the museum to leaf through magazines and read books about life in the tropics. These images were imprinted on my mind when I embarked on my academic study with growing interest now in the landscape beyond Europe. Of unique value to me for deepening my interest in the theme of my choice was Professor W.F. Wertheim, a famed scholar of Southeast Asia, who became my guru. In 1960, I was assigned to him as a research assistant and enjoyed the pleasure of working in the building which, after decolonization, had been renamed the Royal Tropical Institute.

LOOKING BACK AND AHEAD

The idea of using my family history to examine how Dutch society changed during the course of the twentieth century – or, conversely and more modestly, to look at how this process of transformation had manifested itself in the ups and downs of the lives of my parents and my own life – occurred to me many years ago. It was during my first stay in India in the early 1960s, where I was confronted with a degree of poverty that I had never experienced before. Shocked by what I saw, I wrote home about it and received a letter back from my mother, one of the few she ever sent in her life. As a young girl in her bargee's family, Lolkje had seen backward regions in my own country, where they cut peat for sale as fuel. In a few sentences, she described her memories of that depressing time, adding that people everywhere have to fight to escape such misery. My mother was convinced that a better future also awaited the landless labourers in the village where I was doing my research. Her hopeful assumption was that what came to be known as the developing countries would follow the same path to progress as that taken in the western hemisphere a century earlier. This has not been confirmed by what I have observed at the bottom of the economy in the countries of my anthropological fieldwork over more than five decades. What obstacles to catching up prevented them from following suit? Were such dismal features missing in the west in its trajectory leading up to what was called development? Or, if such barriers did shape up, how were they overcome? The answers to these questions lie beyond the scope of this prologue, but are of crucial significance to what caused me to write it.

Amsterdam, January 2023

Dispossession as the Roadmap to Labour Bondage

Freedom has often been hailed as owing its origin to the transformation of the economic and political fabric of society to capitalism. It is a perspective which maintains that the slow march to domination of the new mode of production in the West European/North American up-and-coming nation state eventually allowed for the spread of democratic rights from the top down to the bottom ranks of citizenship. Redemption from feudal servitude was heralded by all adversaries of the *ancien régime* as paving the route to progress. Although critical of the exploitation and repression to which the dispossessed working masses fell prey, classical Marxism welcomed capitalism as the ultimate harbinger of proletarian emancipation. Phrased as a double bind, the rationale was that freedom from means of production would enable the dispossessed proletariat to freely sell its labour power. It was a time-bound and Eurocentric assumption which took for granted that the ongoing switch in some regions of the Northern hemisphere from an agrarian-rural to an industrial-urban way of life would figure as the evolutionary passage eventually followed by humankind worldwide. But the wisdom of hindsight has clarified that capitalism and unfree labour are not inimical at all. Eric Williams put forward this proposition in the title of his seminal treatise. His claim was that the high profits made from slavery in the agro-industry of the colonized Caribbean economy had fuelled the capital required for the Industrial Revolution in its metropole (Williams [1944] 2014, p. 45). As a matter of fact, the abolition of slavery, enacted first in Great Britain in 1834 and in subsequent decades also in other territories under European colonial rule, immediately gave rise to new forms of serfdom in these colonized domains. The substitutes found for the workforce redeemed from enslavement were debt-contracted as coolies for employment on plantations, in mines, or engaged to build roads, railways, canals, ports and other public works. There is ample documentation of these vast armies being recruited and locked up at work sites far away from where they were corralled in debt-dependency by middlemen acting as agents for employers. Hugh Tinker was the author of a classical study on coolies from India sent abroad (see Tinker 1974; also Breman 2022).

My study zooms in on the origin of labour bondage in the peasant economies which have dominated the subcontinent of South Asia from an unrecorded pre-colonial past until the post-colonial present. This remote past was of no immediate concern when I started my investigations. I had come to India as a young PhD student in 1962 with only a faint idea of the topic of my research. It would have to be fieldwork-based, which was the prescribed method of investigation in the discipline of my choice. It meant locating myself in the arena of data collection for a full annual cycle to monitor what went on. In rhyme with the fashion of the moment, the village setting would have to be the focal point. I desisted, however, from producing a community study in which all inhabitants and their interconnections get duly registered (Breman, Kloos and Saith, eds 1997, pp. 15–75). Feeling uneasy with such a broad range, my template singled out the polar ends of the agrarian hierarchy as the main stakeholders of the peasant economy: the set of major landowners at the top end and the landless residuum at the bottom. Bondage cemented their inter-relationship, which meant that most members of the tribal caste of agricultural labourers were attached to households of the dominant caste. It became a relationship structured and cultured in a capitalist mode of interaction. My findings clearly indicated that the serfdom instituted was on the verge of collapse. Both masters and servants, for completely opposite reasons, were unwilling to continue their inter-relationship on the same footing. This conclusion of my first round of fieldwork triggered my interest to query why, when and how this system of bondage had become standard practice.

While writing up the information gathered, I simultaneously shifted to archival research to trace the heritage of unfree labour in south Gujarat, the state along the west coast of India where I had located my fieldwork. It meant postponing submission of my thesis until I had added the historical background. The origin of servitude dates back to the peasant–tribal frontier in the pre-colonial past, an era which did not leave behind any written documentation. Its existence could be substantiated on the basis of early colonial accounts. My dissertation, 'Meester en Knecht' ('Master and Servant'; Breman 1970), tells the story why and how shifting cultivators of tribal stock became attached to Hindu caste landowners to till the soil and, under the direction of their masters, to cultivate crops. The dependency that bonded the tribal family to the landowner was pre-capitalist in nature. The exploitation and repression imposed was not meant to maximize the landowner's income but to set the master free from work considered unclean. Avoidance of peasant toil, handling of the plough in particular, allowed him and his family to claim the status of twice-born superiority. To separate purity from impurity was the foundation and organizing principle of the ordained inequality underlying the caste system. This perception was made manifest by fixing the line of pollution, downgrading the segments beyond the pale and stigmatizing them in ritualized inferiority.

Responding to a parliamentary questionnaire on slavery in the early 1830s, in preparation of its abolition a few years later on, officials of the East India Company emphatically identified labour bondage in south Gujarat as a form of enslavement. However, its practice continued to exist because the early-colonial authorities were careful not to antagonize the major landowners by depriving them of their servile workforce. This decision was justified by arguing that the landless tribals, for lack of any other livelihood, were eager to engage themselves in bondage – which was now explained as a contractual arrangement agreed to by both sides. The formation of the colonial state established in the second half of the nineteenth century brought no change to the servitude of the peasant class, deprived from owning land and other means of production. But the intrusion of capitalism into the agrarian economy during the second half of the nineteenth century resulted in commodification of their attachment. The cultivation of cash crops, cotton above all, speeded up the increasing use of money in exchange relationships. The commercialization which boosted market production changed the structure and culture of the peasant economy. Bonded labourers were now treated by their employers as means of production to raise higher incomes. It was a lens that still insisted on their inferiority, but now without the features of patronage. This side of the bargain had in the past pledged to guarantee their subsistence, although then too it was often more honoured in the breach than the observance.

While the contrast between the better off and the worse off was a feature of the peasantry from the very beginning, the divide became more polarized in the course of time. Squeezing landless labour to mere survival levels and sometimes not even that, as for instance during the outbreak of the plague at the beginning of the twentieth century, did not result in shedding light on the downside of the economic fabric. In the fight against colonial rule, the nationalist movement promised to deliver redemption from poverty and redistribution of agricultural holdings, which had been cornered by the well-endowed ranks of the peasantry. While Mahatma Gandhi drew attention to the pauperized state of the landless community in south Gujarat, he did not speak out against the caste system but merely asked the better off to care for the people left behind in the struggle for Independence. Sardar Patel was more adamant in backing the interests of his own privileged caste and class, roundly blaming the bonded labourers for their defective way of life.

In the aftermath of Independence, the Congress leadership did not change its political stance. Large-scale landlordism was wiped out but the appropriated land was added to the agrarian property held by the dominant castes throughout the country. On the pretext that small holdings would not be sufficiently viable, the land reforms carried through left the landless workforce completely untouched. In most states they were not even provided a small plot for shelter. Sardar Patel advised the agrarian proletariat in south Gujarat, already by then lacking regular work and income, to leave the countryside and search for jobs in the industries which were going to come up in the urban economy. Meanwhile many of them were still stuck, like the generations before them, in a beck-and-call relationship that fell short of the income needed to adequately maintain themselves and their dependants. From long-standing practice, the farmers knew how to deal with individualized protest against maltreatment. Sometimes, resistance against bondage flared up in spurts of collective action. Whenever and wherever this occurred, such revolts were treated as a law and order problem, and quelled by the strong arm of the state machinery.

A decade after my first round of fieldwork, I came back to the by-now familiar locales to further investigate the pace and direction of change in rural labour relations. My village-based research in 1962–63 had concluded that the system of agrarian bondage which used to attach the landless proletariat to landowning households was in a state of disintegration. Although many labourers were still permanently working for high-caste farmers, they considered themselves not any longer to be at the unrestricted disposal of their employers. The younger age set also tried to avoid the bind of permanency, and looked around for other opportunities to earn their living through more casual arrangements. Likewise, many landowners also preferred to deal with at least a part of the workforce they needed in a hire–fire rotation. This trend accelerated a decade later. A clear indication of the increased gap that separated the top and bottom of the agrarian hierarchy was the removal of many proletarian households from the precincts of the farmers for whom they worked. I now found a major portion of them relocated on the village outskirts in colonies inhabited by only members of their community. But it was not a togetherness that coagulated into taking a stand in joint action.

My new round of fieldwork in 1971–72 was meant to find out whether the rural proletariat had managed to qualify for jobs other than the ones in which they had been stuck from the remote past, and in which a high percentage had become redundant to demand. I had become engaged in a new research project based in a town along the south–north railway line crossing south Gujarat which was the district headquarters. The economic diversification of this urban centre attracted many migrants from the nearby countryside to settle down there, but not more than a tiny fraction among them belonged to the rural proletariat. Although situated close to the villages in this district where I did my fieldwork, I found that none of the agricultural labourers here had been able to relocate their households to this rapidly growing town. Of course, upon marriage, the females went to the village where their husbands lived and worked. Or sons-in-law joined their wives' habitat if that happened to have more employment opportunities. A few members of the landless community had left for good, but nobody knew where they had gone and what they were doing. A handful of them, only males, commuted on a daily basis to the district town to sell their unskilled labour power in one of the early morning markets. My urban-based investigations were framed in the conceptualization of the informal economy, which in the subsequent decades cascaded into a prominent research topic (Breman 1977, Part 1; republished as Breman 1994, pp. 3–130).

The rural economy had remained firmly rooted in agricultural production and when the crops schedule did not offer sufficient employment throughout the year, as was the case in one of my fieldwork villages, many households of the landless proletariat became dependent on what I have called hunting and gathering wages elsewhere. Outmigration for the duration of the dry season helped to solve the problem of lack of employment at home. In the winter and early summer months, many members of the landless households considered of working age – adults as well as minors – would go away, to come back again before the onset of the monsoon. Labour migration had taken the shape of circulation and, in the course of time, this form of labour mobility appeared to have increased greatly. The growing magnitude was due to the spread of seasonal migration to land-poor households with marginal holdings that were too small to yield an income adequate at least to cover the annual cost of living. Even more alarming was another aspect of the same phenomenon. This concerned my finding that the growing seasonal exodus of low-paid and unskilled labour coincided with a massive influx of labour into the village habitat from elsewhere, which deprived the local workforce of the niches of waged work for which they used to be hired.

This observation became the point of departure for my next round of fieldwork in 1986–87, conducted in the two villages I had investigated earlier and to which a third one was added in another district of south Gujarat. The autochthonous workers, members of the main tribal caste, were now replaced by swarms of migrants brought in from elsewhere at the high tide of the agrarian cycle. In my assessment, this new phase of labour mobility, the substitution of local workers by outside workers, was how the dominant caste-class of landowners reacted to the growing frustration and agitation of the agrarian proletariat against the widening divide between the polar ends of the caste-cum-class hierarchy. Reducing dependence on the local workforce was a strategy to which the better-off farmers resorted in order to cheapen the cost of labour by weakening their bargaining power. The mood of mutual antagonism that I encountered while engaged in these investigations encouraged the stakeholders on both sides to detach themselves from each other to the extent possible. For the landless community, it meant finding a way out of the village economy by contracting themselves out for seasonal employment away from their habitat.

Attempts to escape from remaining bogged down in underpaid and irregular agrarian work at home encouraged the rural proletariat to loosen the shackles which kept them tied down. Yearning for waged labour which did not imply a lasting attachment to the local landowners made their craving for freedom manifest. During the rainy season, when the agrarian proletariat sat unemployed in their hutment colonies, jobbers went around acting as agents for faraway employers to contract labour gangs for brick kilns, stone quarries, salt pans or road construction. Recruitment for such seasonal activity had also taken place in the preceding decades but became much more voluminous with the passing of time. Better connectivity due to infrastructural development which opened up the countryside to the outside world reduced the time spent and cost involved in mobility. More importantly, going away to find employment elsewhere was not an option any more for the landless but a necessity, because of the growing scarcity of waged work at home.

Switching my field view from sedentary to footloose labour, either coming in or going out at the sites of my local-level research in south Gujarat, I described and analysed how such labour gangs were put to work away from home. Their daily performance was usually supervised by the jobber who had contracted them with the payment of some earnest money which they badly needed to tide over the lack of income when there was no call for their labour power in the village. This middleman, for the duration of their stay away from home, was in charge of all dealings with them, took care of their maintenance and shelter, and also settled accounts with members of his gang when the contract ran out. Receipt of earnest money bound the migrants to the stipulations of the contract and settlement of accounts postponed till the very end prevented the labourers from leaving the worksite in between. The combination of advance and postponed wage payment meant that the labour migrants sold their freedom for the full duration of their contract. Depriving migrants of control over their labour power is a mode of engagement under duress, which I have labelled as neo-bondage to mark its dissimilarity from the pre-capitalist form of attachment.

Circular labour migration has remained a major subject of my writings from the late 1980s onwards but it was later contextualized within the wider setting of the informal economy. Spatial mobility is not a new phenomenon; it went on in the past as well, in close accordance with the annual cycle of agricultural production. However, the swelling supply of land-poor or fully dispossessed labour, for which there was no longer viable demand in what had been from generation to generation the prime sector of the economy, led to driving out the land-poor and landless classes from their rural abodes more frequently and to destinations far away from home. With the transition to neoliberal capitalism in the last decades of the twentieth century, segments of the workforce were increasingly made redundant at home and became mobile for longer bouts of absence, not seldom for the duration of their working life. The households of the rural proletariat are today split up between members who hive off to find work elsewhere and dependants who stay back because, being too old, too young or of ill health, they are unable to even earn their own upkeep. Multi-locality instead of joint cohabitation of adults with minors has contributed to the fragility facing this primary unit of social life at the bottom of the village economy. The disruption resulting from a neoliberal code of conduct not only erodes solidarity from shaping up at the class level but, to no lesser degree, affects ties of sharing within households of the labouring poor.

In a last round of investigations on the changing social fabric in the countryside of south Gujarat, I added another village situated in the shadow of an industrial estate to the earlier sites of my fieldwork. I conducted a survey in these four locations spread across south Gujarat to draw the profile of the rural proletariat in the early twenty-first century. Summing up my findings which were collected in recurrent local-level research (Breman 2007b), I concluded that the portrayed workforce remained stuck in the trajectory from which they came, agricultural labourers, rather than what they were supposed to become – millhands. The design of transformation to an industrial-urban way of life has failed to materialize. The factory jobs that would offer regular employment and freedom from want and dependency did not absorb more than a tiny fraction of the working classes (Breman 2021). Dispossession has been the roadmap of labour bondage in both the past and the present. Debt bondage in kind bedevilled the livelihoods of households which were disowned from agrarian property in the pre-colonial past. Reshaped in capitalist exploitation and oppression to neo-bondage – either advance payment for future employment or loans taken from moneylenders at usurious interest rates – lasting indenture is still, for many of them, a major dimension of their defective existence. I have held neoliberal capitalism culpable for the failure to realize freedom from want and abysmal treatment of the labouring poor. But the halting pace of emancipation towards decent work and a dignified life for the proletarianized masses in post-colonial India should also be attributed to the doublespeak of the ruling elite, which enacts labour legislation promising a fair deal but does not implement these ordinances. In similar fashion, social security provisions are arbitrarily provided by the government but they seldom reach more than a handful of the targeted beneficiaries. Having observed at close quarters the process of decision-making in the villages of my recurrent research stretching over nearly five decades and three landless generations, the non-participation of ancestral tillers of the soil stands out in a country boasting to be the largest democracy in the world.

A civilizational heritage of ingrained inequality has aggravated the plight of people at the lower end of the economy and society. The supremo in charge of the authoritarian brand of Hindutva politics which holds sway at the national level announced in 2020 that self-reliance is an essential clause of its ideological frame. Having failed in its political economy to generate jobs for the classes dependent for income on the sale of their labour power, the workforce is sternly commanded to engage in self-employment and self-provisioning to make ends meet. The substantial segment that is unable to do so is castigated for falling short of the *aatmanirbhar* dictate. This verdict marks the animus which in the erstwhile fabric used to be expressed against human species considered beyond the pale of inclusion. In its modernized gestalt it resembles the contingent identified as the 'undeserving poor', stigmatized in social Darwinist rhetoric, which did not qualify for relief from adversity. It is a mindset that needs to be countered by the building up of a common front to insist on rights of citizenship, and inclusion within instead of fractured exclusion from mainstream society.

CHAPTER ONE

Servitude in the Pre-colonial and Colonial Past

THE ONSET OF SERFDOM

The Dublas in south Gujarat were one of the tribal communities which, in the ancient past, had been domesticated as bonded servants to Hindu landowners. The confinement of Dublas to the bottom of the Hindu order can be traced to the settlement of peasant castes familiar with sedentary cultivation on the plain of south Gujarat. Anavil brahmans played a prominent role in the development of the agricultural economy, but there are no written sources about when and how this process came about in pre-colonial times. Did they already outrank other segments of the peasantry before the transition from shifting cultivation to regular tillage had taken place? Or was their elevation as landlords due to the introduction of more advanced agricultural techniques? A moot question also is whether the Anavils originated from the region inhabited by them, or did they move into these until then unsettled lands from elsewhere? Colonial accounts have put on record how, in a process of agrarian colonization, Hindu civilization gradually spread over a still predominantly tribal landscape.

> Where agriculture is practised with crude implements and without the aid of domestic animals, where the working population is scarce, where the land must be reclaimed from the wilds and marshes, and where soil and climate act as limiting factors for the employment of imported labour – it is not capital that is wanted, but native labour to reclaim the land and cultivate it under difficult environmental conditions. Under these circumstances bond-labour of the native population is introduced and is pinned to the soil in conditions akin to slavery. (Lorenzo 1947, pp. 57–69; see also Baines 1912, Kosambi 1956, Khela 2012)

In line with brahmanical lore, the Anavils were wont to attribute their rank at the top of the caste hierarchy to divine intervention. In one version of this origin myth, brahman colonists from the Gangetic plain came to settle in the villages and cultivate the wild country to which they had been brought between the rivers Vapi and Tapi in south Gujarat. The colonists were granted domination over the local people by subjecting them to do the polluting work of tilling the soil, from which the brahmans sought to exempt themselves. Interestingly, another version of the same myth narrates how Rama or Krishna raised a segment of the hill tribes above the dark-skinned inhabitants of the region. In a purifying ritual, the Anavils articulated their elevation to *ujli paraj* (the twice-born or high castes) status. Anaval, the venue at which this baptism took place, is situated in the interior of Surat district, the historical heartland of the *kali paraj* (tribals registered as Scheduled Tribes) people and culture. This locality is venerated as their place of origin by the community at the apex of the caste hierarchy. It is a heritage that has persuaded me to lean towards the thesis that the caste hierarchy is an outcome of internal differentiation.

Rather than ascribing the origin of the caste order to interference from outside, I am inclined to relate its gradual and long-winded emergence in the pre-colonial era to the peasant–tribal frontier which started the cycle of dispossession versus accumulation of landed property. As Alexis de Tocqueville wrote in his *Memoir on Pauperism*: 'from the moment that landed property was recognized and men had converted the vast forests into fertile cropland and rich pasture . . . individuals arose who accumulated more land than they required to feed themselves and so perpetuated property in the hands of their progeny'(Breman 2019, p. 3). Under subsequent colonial rule, the caste order became more ranked in hierarchical stratification than it had been before (Dirks 2001). This interpretation signals a dynamic interdependence between upgrading and downgrading in ritual rank, social class and political power. How they managed to rise up to domination and occupy most of the arable land by depriving other communities of ownership has remained covered up in an unrecorded past. However, this dark heritage of impurity was imprinted in a customary way of life that continued to oblige the lower section of the Bhathelas to till the soil themselves until late in the colonial era while the whole Anavil caste is known as *khatho-pitho* brahman, i.e. meat-eating and alcohol-drinking.

The Dublas were locked at the base of the agrarian economy and its social order in the area which has been the domicile of this tribal community from time immemorial. In addition to hunting and gathering in their unsettled habitat, their ancestry may have taken to rudimentary agriculture as shifting cultivators. No recollection has survived of that predial existence. Subjugation under servitude prevented these forebears from laying claim to ownership rights of the lands on which they lived. Dispossessed from independent livelihoods, they were forced to cultivate the fields of the peasantry, which gained ascendancy as *ujli paraj*. Acknowledgement of their assertion of a twice-born heritage was founded on their engagement of contingents stuck at the bottom of the pile as bondsmen. All over the Gangetic plain and the river deltas in the south, these tribes got incorporated as Scheduled Castes at the 'untouchable' foot of the Hinduized order. In south Gujarat and many other regions where sedentary agriculture and caste-ranking along the purity–impurity axis came about at a later date, the tribal frontier continued to hold sway. In those districts, in the early colonial era, the *kali paraj* communities despite their degradation to a landless existence had still retained their ancestral identity. Together with other tribal communities, the Dublas inhabited the hilly and sparsely cultivated tracks between Vapi and Dahanu bordering on what is today Maharashtra. In these thinly populated subdistricts, which were never settled by the Anavils or other peasant predators, the Dublas managed to retain ownership of the land they had used as shifting cultivators in the past.

The Anavils and the Dublas came to occupy polar ends in the agrarian economy and also in the ritual ranking, since the servitude of the latter paved the way to the brahmanization of the former. When the Mughal reign expanded over the coastal and inland tracks of west India, the Anavil elite was nominated as tax farmers in the imposed system of governance. It both expressed as well as promoted their political dominance. At the end of the eighteenth century, the East India Company started to make inroads into this feudalistic domain. In the next few decades, its officials took charge of large parts of south Gujarat while the remaining territory was established as the Baroda principality, ruled by the Gaekwad dynasty which had split away from the Maratha confederacy. The first batch of British administrators had adopted the collection of land revenue which they found upon arrival, but then replaced it with the *ryotwari* settlement which eliminated all intermediaries between the landowner and the colonial state. The tax farmers were dismissed, but were compensated for their loss of influence and income. They were also allowed to keep the land they had appropriated and managed to consolidate their domination over dependent ranks of the peasantry.

Subsistence production was the mainstay of the village economy with various foodgrains heading the list of crops. The agrarian yield served primarily to satisfy the consumption needs of households belonging to the local community. Most inhabitants were members of higher- to lower-ranking peasant castes, with non-agrarian activities represented by a sample of artisanal and service castes. They were all interconnected with each other in a network of barter known as the *jajmani* system. Goods and services were exchanged in a hierarchical flow with the households of the dominant landowning caste in distributional control. As the founders of the settlement, such Anavil families were in supreme command.

> These people, with their servants and 'Halis', fixed the village site, dug the well and tank, planted the groves, built the village temple, and thus exercised the right of possession. They then induced artisans to settle in their village, who were the servants of the community, and to whom they gave houses, bits of land rent-free, grain cesses, etc. Other cultivators, mostly of inferior castes, were in process of time attracted to the village, and the proprietary body permitted them to cultivate such land as they did not want themselves, but gave them no proprietary rights. (Prescott 1865, p. 29; see also Mukhtyar 1930, pp. 44–45)

The revenue was procured in cash but monetization played little or no role at the local level since, within the community, exchange relations were predominantly, if not only, dealt with in kind. There was little need to engage with what went on outside the locality. The harvest surplus was bartered at intermittently held market spots throughout the district, but more often, tradesmen toured the countryside to buy what the people could do without or held in stock for future disposal. In the rationale of the subsistence economy, there was little impetus for raising growth and productivity.

Bondage: A Relationship of Patronage and Exploitation

'Meester en Knecht' ('Master and Servant') was the Dutch title of my dissertation submitted to the University of Amsterdam in 1970 (Breman 1970). For the English translation published in 1974, the title was rephrased as 'Patronage and Exploitation' to express the relationship between landlords and landless labourers in the past. Deprived of means to provide for their own livelihood, members of the Dubla tribe were attached to Anavil households in life-long servitude which used to be passed on to the next generation. When a Dubla boy wanted to get married, he found the master of his father, who had already employed him to tend cattle, willing to provide what was needed for this rite of passage. Early in the nineteenth century the advance he received would range from Rs 10 to Rs 50. However, it was not handed in cash but in kind: a quantity of grain enough for the wedding meal, some copper ornaments and a set of clothes gifted to the bride. The debt he now started to run up made the young Dubla a *hali* who, in compensation for his cost of maintenance, assigned himself to serve his master. The relationship was on both sides a household arrangement. The *hali's* wife or *harekwali* got employed as a maid, washing clothes and dishes, grinding the grain, fetching water from the well, cleaning out the cattle-shed, tidying the master's house and working in the fields whenever required to do so. Already at a very young age the couple's daughters helped their mother; the sons grazed the cattle during the day and gave company to the animals in the owner's shed at night. In addition to a meal late in the morning, the *hali* would receive as his wage in the evening, a daily grain ration of millet (*bhata*) to meet his own needs and that of his dependants. Hours of work were not fixed and all the members of the Dubla's household could be summoned day or night. To facilitate instant availability, their shelter was a hut built on the master's land at shouting distance from his courtyard.

The master was obliged to ensure that his servants could gratify their minimal requirements, which in addition to daily food consisted of various perquisites also allotted in kind: clothing once a year, a cloak at the start of the cold season to cover the body, sandals to wear on special occasions and once in a while, if in a good mood, a little tobacco or a few low-value coins (*paisas*) to buy a drink or two. Their show of docile behaviour would include permission to cultivate a small plot of land (*vavla*), the yield of which was deducted from what the master spent on the upkeep of his *halis*. Keeping them alive was of course also in the best interests of the landlord, but his maintenance care seldom went beyond food provisioning, the most elementary pieces of cloth and stalks for thatching the roof of his servant's hut. All that came over and above the outlay in kind at survival level – such as absence due to illness and the cost of recovery, expenses of events marking the passage through life and the celebration of festivals – were added to the liability that featured bondage.

The social reproduction of the servile underclass among the tribals had all the symptoms of exploitation. Confined within an agrarian existence which relegated them to dispossession from the means of production, the Dublas had no option but to put themselves at the disposal of the higher-ranking peasantry eager to engage them. At the end of his working life, the *hali* would be even poorer than when he had indentured himself. Moreover, his sons would be held accountable for the staggered income deficit their father would have left behind on his demise. What were the benefits Anavil landowners derived from attaching landless Dublas to their households? No doubt, the opportunity to make use of low-cost labour readily available among the tribal stock in the midst of whom they had settled. This prime objective aimed to set them and their families free from strenuous and unclean labour tasks, tilling the soil in particular. Although the extraction of labour power was a major dimension of the *hali pratha* (institution), the bond between master and servant cannot be narrowed down to merely an employer–employee relationship.

Early colonial accounts spoke of 'a rude kind of kindness' as typical of the treatment that the peasant elite meted out to the tribals they held captive. As already mentioned, in legal terms the Dublas did not attach themselves under duress to Anavil masters. In their landless existence, they were tempted to do so in the hope to achieve a modicum of security and protection. However, the wage due to them fell short of all that they needed beyond their precarious livelihood. On top of the initial engagement bonus, an endless round of tedious bargaining took place for ever-more and haltingly supplied 'advances' which could never be worked off to the satisfaction of the master. Clearance of the steadily growing debt or a net balance tilted in favour of the servant was out of the question. At the same time, it would be incorrect to imply that both parties endeavoured to break their bond. While landowners tried to keep the outstanding 'debt' within reasonable limits, their servants manoeuvred to persuade the landowner to allow the inevitable deficit to last and even grow. The latter, not wanting to risk their investment, would dally and refuse to offer more than the customary standard.

The first batch of colonial officials conveyed that the *halis* were better off than members of this tribe who remained unattached. Their reports did not specify the magnitude of this minority or how the unbonded landless made a living. To assume that this masterless segment chose to live and work in freedom is less plausible than that, for a variety of reasons, they had not managed to find a landowner prepared to cater to their minimal needs. This might simply have been because the supply of labour exceeded demand, or because this rejected lot lacked the required qualities of the *hali*: willingness to be at the beck and call of his benefactor in a sustained display of servility. The perception that bonded labourers must be envied rather than pitied is evident in the obsequious praise for the master or *dhaniyamo*, he who bestows wealth. The evincing of such excessive flattery is difficult to rhyme with the deprivations and improprieties to which the *halis* were standardly exposed. But it was a show of submissiveness that had to be demonstrated to qualify for the landlord's compliance to keep his servant's household alive on idle days and weeks, when there was no call for his labour power. In the heat of the summer months and for long spells during the monsoon season, there was little or no work to be done in the fields, apart from cutting a headload of grass for the cattle. The servant still came to the master's abode in the evening to collect his usual ration supplied to him as *khavathi*, allowance for eating. On such days without meaningful employment, it would be added to his outstanding debt. This was also the case when the *hali* fell ill or did not turn up in the morning for any other reason. However, his master was obliged to take regular care of him even beyond working age, when he had grown too old to be of any further use.

Bondage has been discussed so far for its merits and demerits as a labour relationship, weighing the benefits of permanent engagement against the costs of servants maintained also when unemployed. In the early colonial era, the amount of waste land far exceeded the acreage under cultivation and the crop schedule was not a very busy one, leaving the fields untended in slack parts of the year. Officials in the late-colonial machinery exerted the main landowners in vain to replace their permanent workforce with daily-wage earners. Hiring the latter whenever needed, i.e. occasionally rather than permanently as their detailed calculations indicated, employers could significantly reduce their wage bill. Such advice fell on deaf ears since much more was at stake than figuring out the economic rationale of *hali pratha*. The appropriation of surplus value included other gains than just the advantageous disposal of cheap labour power.

Patronage was an important dimension of the system of bondage. From this perspective, the Anavil elite engaged servants not only to cultivate their land but also to retain clients in their aspiration for a leisurely lifestyle. The attachment of the *hali*s served their ambition to raise their political power and social status. When the colonial administration decided to no longer operate through tax farmers for collecting the land revenue, the dislocated upper crust among the Anavils resisted this attempt to drive them back into the ranks of the peasantry. Behind the scenes, they managed to remain influential, not infrequently holding crucial posts in the bureaucratic apparatus, which, after the introduction of the *ryotwari* system, extended from the Collector in the district headquarters to nominated village officials. Colonial records were critical of the extravagant claims of these landowning families, habituated to act in their domain as petty *raja*s. Despite their loss of official status, this elite section of the Anavils was allowed to keep the land property it had amassed, a disproportionately large share of the total area in south Gujarat under tillage. Emulating the behaviour of their caste members higher up the political, economic and social scales, the lower Anavil segments also now began to prosper. It was an improvement in well-being attributed to the meagre wages they were apt to hand out to their *halis*. As an additional benefit, for being tilled by the downgraded and improvident Dublas of *kali paraj* stock, the fields they owned were also fixed at a much lower rate than at which other peasant castes within the Hindu fold were taxed.

The size of the retinue an Anavil had under his tutelage expressed his standing. The ambit which drove him was not how many *halis* he needed but how many he could afford. Appropriate clientelist behaviour prescribed that the Dublas display deference and obedient allegiance to their lord and master in profuse acknowledgement of his domination and their subordination. The seigneurial style that the Anavil aspired to obliged him to treat his underlings with generosity and affection. The *hali* was in effect the property of the master, an extension of his household. Remaining dispossessed from all means of production as well as consumption, the servant was a recipient of his patron's gifts and benevolence, 'riches' which entailed no more than a bare livelihood. The divide in well-being was however mitigated by a way of life marked not only by their contrasts but also by how much they had in common. The master would eat the same food as his *hali*, allowed him into the intimacy of his household and addressed his dependants in familial terms. This frame of paternalistic affiliation, presented in this way, concurs with the ideology of patronage which is bound to stress the idealized behaviour of both parties and their mutual affection. On the basis of her local-level research in Karnataka, Scarlett Epstein evaluated the patronage dimension of the employer–employee relationship in the pre-capitalist past in economic terms.

> In a system in which employers are obliged to provide for the subsistence of their hereditary servants and the latter have no other income earning opportunities, masters will employ labourers as long as the total product does not decrease through the employment of an additional worker. Since the employer would only have to give in charity what he saved in wages, he incurs no net loss by engaging labourers whose employment does not add to the total product. The number of workers employed in India's non-market peasant societies is thus determined by the maximization of total product, rather than by the interaction of marginal productivity and wage rates. (Epstein 1967, p. 9)

HALI PRATHA IN THE EARLY COLONIAL ERA

Most colonial accounts made light of the coercion that servitude incurred, and suggested that *halis* had internalized the subjugation in which they lived and worked. It was a biased view which suggested that a Dubla was proud of being associated with a prominent Anavil master and seemed to have no problem with his subservience. Such testimonies ignored the abuse of power, the vile treatment meted out to the landlord's dependants, his wilful discretion to grant or withhold allowances. The patron could decide whether or not to provide a loan needed for an emergency, or to distribute the daily grain rations when according to him the *hali* had failed in his duties. As Max Weber noted in his seminal study on the plight of agricultural labourers in eastern Germany at the end of the nineteenth century, such capriciousness is rooted in the prerogatives that come with domination. For the landless serfs, engaging in joint action to lodge their protest against such high-handed behaviour was out of the question.

> Except in times of extreme political toil, a class consciousness among the rural proletariat directed against the masters could only develop purely individually with relation to one master alone insofar as he failed to show the average combination of naive brutishness and personal kindness. That, on the other hand, the agricultural labourers were not normally exposed to the pressure of a purely commercial exploitation was in complete accordance with this. For the man opposite them was not an 'entrepreneur' but a territorial lord in miniature. (Weber 1924, p. 474)

How did the *hali*s in south Gujarat react when they remained bereft of due support and protection? Their vulnerability did not prevent them from resorting to obstruction, sabotage, a display of ignorance, lethargy, evasion and other weapons from the subaltern arsenal, and in the last resort desertion, if all that failed. These acts of resistance added, of course, to their being denounced as wayward good-for-nothings. But this dark underside tended to remain veiled by a colonial administration meant to report optimistically on having come to terms with the dominating landowners as the main stakeholders in the terrain of operation. Such accounts of compliance were required to suggest that the risk of antagonizing the landed interests on which the exercise of authority rested had been adroitly avoided. It explains why *hali pratha* was put on the colonial record as expressive of a customary code of conduct that should not be tampered with. 'From close enquiries I have made, I can say with certainty that those poor people are treated with kindness and consideration, and are looked upon as humble dependants who have great claims on their masters and their families' (Prescott 1865, p. 5).

Such acclamations of care and compassion should not be taken at face value. Of course, actual practice fell short of this imagery. Given their lack of language proficiency, the British officials would only rarely, if at all, be in direct touch with the agrarian underclass. Verbal information about them probably came from intermediaries familiar with English. It would be hearsay evidence, quite likely channelled through the very elite holding a watchful eye over their tribal attendants. One issue that never came up in official correspondence was how licentious male adults or adolescents of the landlord's family were apt to consider the females attached as dependants to their households as sexual prey.

Hali pratha was, of course, a gendered relationship, but in the ample documentation of bondage, sexual abuse of the servant's wife and daughter has been reluctantly if at all discussed. It was dealt with as a taboo, swept under the colonial carpet of propriety then and not less so in the wake of Independence.

One of the first Collectors of Surat did not mince words when he responded in 1815 to queries from the headquarters.

> The Dessaees Buttela Brahmins [the higher and lower segments of Anavils which entertained a hypergamous relationship] in Parchole Soopa, and some other pergunnahs, possess as large a portion of slaves as may be found perhaps in any part of India. Those who are frequently attached to the soil, as well as bond-servants who voluntarily engage to labour in payment of loans to them for their marriages, or the like occasion. . . . I believe the slaves to be more comfortable than the free portion of their respective castes. (W.J. Lumsden, Collector and Magistrate of Surat, dated 8 August 1825)[1]

His despatch was in reply to a circular letter in which the board of the East India Company solicited information on unfree labour in preparation of a parliamentary debate on how to deal with slavery in the colonial territories.[2] The correspondence went on for several decades because the issue remained on the political agenda of the British empire for a long time. Subsequent reports sent from Surat further discussed the plight of *hali*s, so called because they handled the plough (*hal*) when tilling the land. Slavery was now recorded as a labour relationship which enabled high-caste landowners to act as managers of their agrarian property. In this revised assessment, the Dublas were described as hereditary bondsmen who voluntarily entered into servitude for the security and protection such engagement offered.

What should have been addressed as a liaison revolving around domination and subordination, made manifest in how top and bottom ranks in the agrarian hierarchy were connected, became in colonial parlance reduced to an economic transaction and classified as debt bondage. In legal terms, it meant that the *hali* lost his freedom on acceptance of an advance which deprived him of the latitude to decide when, where and to whom to sell his labour power for the duration of his liability. It was an interpretation which also required portraying the Dublas as slothful, indolent, drunkards, unreliable, deceitful, etc. This stigmatization would endure and implied that officials were apt to settle disputes in favour of the landlord. The argument that confining the Dublas in bondage was the only way to overcome their work shyness seemed to find more and more ground. In 1837, the Political Commissioner for Gujarat signalled the recurrent problem created by fugitives absconding from the bond in which they were engaged. He wanted, 'except when decided ill-treatment appears to have taken place, to be authorized to interfere to cause the restoration of run-away slaves, or compensation and satisfaction to their owners from the parties obtaining them' (Breman 2007a, p. 45). My added comment to this official notification is that the *halis* apparently ran away not to regain freedom, but to find another and more lenient master than they had deserted. Such instances might also be surmised as illustration of the rivalry between the Anavils in their mutual bidding for power and status, with the *halis* being pawns in their build-up of a clientele.

The colonial state, eager to recover the cost of governance, set out to raise crop production and productivity to broaden its revenue base and increase the tax rate. With the introduction of the *ryotwari* settlement the initially low man–land ratio gradually grew denser. On the central plain, most of the land suitable for tillage had come under cultivation by the end of the nineteenth century. The promotion of irrigation resulted in a lengthening of the agricultural schedule and higher crop yields. Even on the village waste which was left open for common purpose – grazing of cattle, collection of firewood and edible plants, defecation though at separated sites for the inhabitants – taxes were now levied. The area of south Gujarat under advanced development with villages every few miles from each other had become readily accessible due to the construction of country as well as all-weather roads. It was the imprint of a landscape in stark contrast with the hillier and wood-covered eastern zone of the district, populated by tribal communities which were still at the stage of shifting cultivation. The colonial authorities forced these unsettled people to get sedentarized in dispersed hamlets in order to bring them within the fold of administrative control, and by doing so, submit them to tax payment.

In the course of time, peasant colonizers from elsewhere came and settled in their midst. These intruding outsiders, mainly Kanbi Patels and Parsis, slowly appropriated the land that the original inhabitants had inherited from their ancestors. I have investigated and documented this massive transfer of ownership rights which took place when colonial authority was already firmly established (Breman 1985b). It shows that, from the very beginning of the colonial rule, agrarian policies were tilted in favour of landowners belonging to upwardly mobile peasant castes. Moreover, sourcing this history recorded in the colonial archives would seem to confirm my assumption about the origin of *hali pratha*. I tend to see the arrival of Kanbi Patels in south Gujarat as a repeat story of how already in the pre-colonial era the Dublas were downgraded to landlessness, while the Anavils had managed to upgrade themselves in the caste hierarchy to dominate over the tribals they had dispossessed and tied to servile subalternity. Before discussing, next, the major changes which came about in the countryside of south Gujarat, I want to reaffirm that in my opinion, the bond between the Anavils and the Dublas at the polar ends of the agrarian hierarchy remained, above all, driven by economic motives. For the master, it was the need for additional labour to exhibit conspicuous leisure and consumption; for the labourer, it meant presumed attainment of livelihood security and protection. Were those ambitions equally gratified on both sides?

Labour in the Process of Commercialization and Monetization

Although I have, in various publications, criticized the notion of the peasant village as a closed and self-reliant community, I concur with the view that economic activity under the ancient regime was limited in scope – with exchange of goods and services largely restricted to the locality, and a limited spare quantity exchanged for other wares and needs available in periodically held markets or in other settlements in the vicinity. The links of the main landowners with 'the market' remained confined to ambulant traders from nearby towns who visited the surrounding villages at harvest time to buy up whatever surplus was available, either on their own account or as commission agents for merchants outside the region. The amount and value of currency used in these localized conduits of trade tended to be quite restricted, mainly for tax payment, for buying land and cattle, and as dowry paid by the bride's family to the husband's family at marriage. The currency, coinage mainly, would have been predominantly owned and spent by the better-off segments of the peasantry. To assess the emerging enlargement in scale of the agrarian landscape as a sudden turnaround from a closed, subsistence-oriented village economy to an open, market-driven commercialized economy is an unwarranted simplification. Indicative for an early stage of the slowly evolving integration in a widening canvas of monetized exchange relationships is a report dating back to only a few decades after British officials employed by the East India Company had taken charge of the district administration.

Nowsaree, Gundevee, Chikhlee, Balda, Pardi, and Damaun, and Surat, are all places at which the agricultural produce of these purgunnas is largely consumed, and such surplus produce which is not consumed at these market towns is readily bought up for exportation, the facility of water-carriage to other parts being great. Besides these market towns, much business is carried out at the *Atwaras*, or weekly fairs, held in different villages of the Bhugwara and Parnera purgunnas, Banians from Bulsar, Gundevee, Chiklee, Balda, Pardi, and Damaun regularly frequent these fairs, with a variety of price goods, cloths, cutlery, cooking utensils, beads, bangles, Native ornaments, pepper, ginger, tobacco, and such articles of general consumption and luxury. The neighbouring villagers attend, bringing with them garden produce, wood, salt, and grain. The mode of transacting business is generally by barter, and little money is used. (Bellasis 1854, p. 6)

From the middle of the nineteenth century onwards, the sale of agricultural commodities expanded to more distant markets. Infrastructural development, the construction of railway lines in particular, facilitated as well as promoted the emergence of commercial agriculture. The cultivation schedule changed in response to growing demand for merchandise from elsewhere. Sugarcane and cotton became major cash crops, and both needed more labour than had been employed before. Commodities and facilities for which there had been little or no previous demand entered the region from outside. This much-increased flow of traffic in both directions boosted new but now monetized forms of distribution and consumption. Its strongly differentiated impact threw the already existing gross divide between rich and poor into still sharper relief. A letter in 1896 written by the Collector of Surat described the lifestyle of the well-to-do: 'A more luxurious generation seeks after *pan-supari*, chiroots, hired servants, sweetmeats, and American watches, and will borrow money to get them' (Breman 2007a, p. 62).

How did the surge of commercialization and monetization which marked the intrusion of agrarian capitalism affect *hali pratha*? To cut a longer story short, not by a progressive change of their employment modality. Apart from what may have been the beginning in some tracks of seasonal migration to brickyards and saltpans on the outskirts of Bombay, due to improved connectivity, the already huge class of landless labour stayed put in their familiar habitat. Urbanization and diversification of the economy were slow to take hold in south Gujarat. The major part of the waged workforce, the Dublas, shunned from outside contacts in particular, continued as before to work in agriculture and live in the countryside.

The middle-caste/class peasantry also took to market production, the cultivation of cotton in particular, on the land they owned or held in tenancy, and the income gained raised their economic standing. The demand for labour went up both due to a longer and more diverse crop schedule, and also, duplicating the lifestyle of the landlords, the avoidance of manual and demeaning work. To set themselves free from hard physical toil, these lower-ranking landowners, Kanbi Patels above all, followed suit and engaged the Dublas as *halis* with their wives and children for domestic help in the household (Keatinge 1921; J.M. Mehta, 1930; Shukla 1937). The maintenance cost of farm servants by the end of the nineteenth century had increased to about Rs 100, double the amount calculated fifty years earlier. However, to conclude from this that the labour price had doubled in this period would be misconceived. What the *hali* together with his dependants went on to receive was the same as before, only its money value increased over time. The daily grain ration and usual perquisites did not rise above the quantity required for bare survival. Wages continued to be paid in kind and did not come out of the cash income the landowner generated. *Hali pratha* continued to exist but became more commodified. Landowners looked at the landless in a different light: they wanted to live a more comfortable life, with better houses, better food and better clothing, and to allow their children to reach out to the outside world by investing in their education.

In this changing social climate, farm servants were no longer the object of the landowner's ambition to achieve power and prestige in the traditional way. They remained bonded to their employer, but the dimension of patronage which had been a crucial feature of their past relationship faded away. Little was left of the protection and security they could assume to be provided, guaranteeing bare survival in case of adversity. In his monograph based on local-level investigations in Surat district at the beginning of the 1930s, Shukla wrote: 'If the master's work does not suffer in the event of the *hali's* sickness he may be allowed to rot in his cottage' (Shukla 1937, p. 123). The Dublas responded to this change by no longer displaying the kind of conduct that had characterized their show of clientelism: loyalty, deference and docility, to entice their master to greater 'generosity'. Once the *dhaniyamo* no longer complied with the code of patronage, the farm servant considered himself released from the obligation to express rank subalternity.

For their part, the landowners saw such disloyalty as proof of bad faith. The refusal of *hali*s to perform the beck-and-call duties to which they had committed themselves on becoming bonded was experienced as tantamount to a breach of contract which had been sealed with 'loans' that had to be worked off. The investment already made for attachment of the farm servant might get lost in case of his desertion. With this eventuality in mind, the better-off peasantry now became even less generous and forthcoming than they had been before.

The redrawn scenario of the agrarian economy not only affected the relationship between master and servant, but also eroded the closing of ranks among the landowners which used to imply that they did not engage a *hali* who had deserted his *dhaniyamo*. It made little sense to hold runaway servants accountable for their staggered debt as they had nothing that could be retrieved from them. The new employer now rejected claims from the former master to return these deserters or settle their arrears in cash. The government had also become wary to accept such demands. The belief, held in the past, that colonial rule should adapt to 'the customs of the land' made way for awareness that paying agricultural labourers a wage insufficient to live on forced them to bargain for unavoidable advances needed beyond their daily ration. Yet the authorities in south Gujarat under direct British rule never went as far as introducing a ban on *hali pratha*. On the other hand, they also did not give in to suggestions made to enact special legislation which would make absconding a criminal offence.

In an official memorandum presented in the 1920s to the Royal Commission on Agriculture, the Deputy Director of Agriculture of Bombay Presidency – a spokesman for landowners' interests in Gujarat – had in vain called for the introduction of an identity card detailing the worker's track record, to show to a new employer that he was not indebted to a former one. Despite some reports at the beginning of the twentieth century that the system of agrarian bondage was on the point of disappearing, or had already collapsed as a consequence of the dissatisfaction of both the landless and landowners, this was not confirmed by observers monitoring what went on at the local level in south Gujarat during the late-colonial era. As Shukla wrote: 'We have failed to observe any signs of disappearance of the system, at least in the near future' (Shukla 1937). Mukhtyar (1930) had come to the same conclusion in his village monograph.

A Commodified Workforce

The majority of colonial subjects on the subcontinent of South Asia worked in agriculture and lived in rural areas. Since India was a peasant society, probably more so than before because of the policy of agrarianization followed under the British rule, the Congress movement for Independence had to mobilize massive support in its myriad villages. It was M.K. Gandhi on his return from South Africa who set out this political course ideologically and strategically, evidently with success, given his resolute statement at the annual meeting held in 1931 that the Indian National Congress was a peasant organization. But of which peasants? For a movement aiming at unity which tended to see the agrarian order as a homogeneous mass of *kisans*, this was a tricky issue. The social debate that arose show how the leadership dealt with the agrarian question that ranked high on the political agenda in the late-colonial period. Inadequate attention was paid to differentiation within the peasantry, a divide which aggravated and also became more explicit in the transition to capitalist production. From the very beginning, the Indian National Congress favoured the interests of the dominant caste-class of landowners, comprising at best 10 to 15 per cent of the village population, but owning two-thirds to three-quarters of the cultivated land. Gujarat became an important platform for the agrarian agitation that was launched. The no-tax campaign which Gandhi had pushed for in 1918 in Kheda district of central Gujarat turned out to be a dismal failure. In his study of this first round of anti-colonial peasant militancy, David Hardiman (1981) argued that the struggle broke down because the land-poor cultivators and landless labourers refused to join a fracas which would only benefit the better-off. In striking contrast, the Bardoli *satyagraha* of 1928, organized for the same purpose and this time in south Gujarat, ended in marked success. Forced to a compromise and to reduce the land tax to a much lower rate, it meant a major defeat for the colonial authorities.

Praise was showered on Vallabhbhai Patel, who had, in a resolute and shrewd style of operation lasting more than one year, managed to mobilize 'the people of Bardoli' to victory. The fame he acquired earned him the title of 'Sardar', which Gandhi awarded him in public. Had he managed to overcome the rank divisions which existed within the agrarian hierarchy consisting of owners, tenants, sharecroppers and landless peasants? Not at all. The Kanbi Patels, who in their upward mobility had managed to style themselves as Patidars, had urged him to lead the campaign rather than Gandhi whom they distrusted as biased towards 'the least, the last and the lost'. He had agreed to do so by keeping this caste of main landowners at the forefront of the agitation, steamrolling the large majority of the tribal peasantry. The medium to small cultivators, and often not any longer owners of their holdings, were lukewarm towards joining the agitation. The Dublas, the largest peasant community in Bardoli which the Kanbi Patels had browbeaten and dispossessed from holding land, were downgraded by Sardar Patel as too uncivilized to take part in a civil disobedience movement. Gandhi did not oppose Patel's high-handed running of the *satyagraha*, but neither did he back him in his hand-in-glove collaboration with the rich peasantry, acknowledged now to be of the same caste status as Patel himself. Gandhi never visited Bardoli while the campaign was on, but obliquely gave to understand his commitment for all the downtrodden and his anguish for the Dublas held in bondage in particular. He had seen them in their hutment colonies at the village margins during his tour in 1920 around Bardoli. In *Young India*, he published a column headlined 'Face to Face with the Pauper', and wrote in this issue that he himself edited a few months later: 'There is no hope for this land so long as the upper and well-to-do classes do not realize their duty by their unfortunate and ignorant brothers who after all are the backbone of this country' (Gandhi 1927a).

In his recurrent tours around the region, the Father of the Nation repeatedly berated his audiences that the struggle against colonial oppression was justified only if it put an end to the lack of freedom within the country's own ranks, such as was suffered by the *hali*s throughout south Gujarat. However, eschewing all class-based struggles and the concomitant articulation of class consciousness, Gandhian activists who had established *ashram*s in the area for the upliftment of the tribal communities were prone to indict the Dublas themselves for their lack of progress. Their bias boiled down to arguing that this tribe remained stuck in servility because of their own defects. This is the well-worn argument that slaves become slaves because they lack the resolve to work and live in freedom. The landless class was asked to join the fight for Independence but, as it turned out, it would be freedom of a kind that did not want to end but to retain labour bondage.

The story of Bardoli was propagated far and wide to highlight the vigour with which the agrarian population resisted foreign domination. This also applies to the claim that landowners and the landless were united in vertical *kisan* solidarity against colonial rule, branded as the common enemy. The problem is of course that the manner in which the *satyagraha* was recorded did not allow the notion of a very different social consciousness, antagonistic or not, for the Dublas to exist. Even sceptical observers were too far removed from the worldview of the agrarian underclass to realize that the campaign of civil disobedience opened some scope for 'the weapons of the weak' to come to the fore. The political setting that unfolded could have been used to increase their resilience, and express frustration and anger about their oppression. Living and working in the shadow of their masters as most of them did, made it very difficult for them to develop a collective identity and a sense of horizontal solidarity. But for the Gandhian activists, the question of how to deal with *hali pratha* was a tricky one. They decided to adopt a strategy of non-intervention in order to not antagonize the dominant peasant caste. The leading disciple of Gandhi in south Gujarat explained later why the reform movement remained silent on the issue of bondage.

> We could recognize that to serve the Halpatis was not so simple a task, as it appeared to be. It involved an age-long economic tradition. We should first patiently secure the confidence of the farmers' community. Only by a long service of years together we should be in a position to awaken in them the feeling of human sympathy and justice for Halpatis. So from 1924 to 1938 we, as volunteers, never raised this issue. (Dave 1946, p. 35; my translation from Gujarati)

However, reading between the lines of the campaign chronicles and reports, a different picture emerges that refutes the coalition between the peasant elite and the Congress stalwarts. It was clear that in the gradual transition to a capitalist mode of production, the agrarian regime had undergone far-reaching changes. The Gandhian social workers held tightly to the notion of the 'good master' and his 'loyal servant' as a construction of a past harmony that should and could be restored. During the *swaraj* agitation of 1921–22, Gandhi had flatly told his Patidar hosts in Bardoli that they could only consider themselves fighters for independence if they put a stop to the exclusion and repression in their own society. The message fell on deaf ears among the *ujli paraj*, but it must have penetrated the milieu of the landless to some extent. The Dublas had begun to develop their own agenda of resistance which, only a few years later, became more organized as well as more public.

Notes

[1] 'Correspondence Between the Directors of the East India Company and the Company's Government in India on the Subject of Slavery', *Accounts and Papers*, vol. 16, sections 15–10–1837 to 16–8–1838, part LI.

[2] Ibid., p. 433.

CHAPTER TWO

Silencing the Voice of Labour in the Call for Nationalism

THE RISING AND FALLING TIDE OF RADICAL AGITATION

Two young social workers, Dinkar Mehta and Indulal Yagnik, who had joined Gandhi's entourage broke away from him in protest against the victimization of the land-poor and landless masses in south Gujarat. As advocates of a more radical policy, both of them joined a socialist wing which had been set up in 1934 within the Congress movement. As a member of the staff Sardar Patel had brought with him from Ahmedabad to Bardoli, Mehta criticized his boss for his indifference to the bondage imposed on the Dublas and called for abolition of debt bondage in a pamphlet he wrote on agrarian class composition in Gujarat. For similar reasons as Mehta, Yagnik revolted against the lack of support when he asked for funds for schooling Dalit and Adivasi children. Having been denied the subsidy, he offered to step down as secretary of the Gujarat Pradesh Congress Committee and saw his resignation letter accepted by both Patel and Gandhi.

Yagnik's break with Congress turned out to be irreparable, and after his break with Gandhi as well, he went to Great Britain in 1930 for a few years. During his stay there, he read a census report about the *hali pratha* system in Surat district. Shortly after his return to India in 1935, Yagnik got in touch with Swami Sahajanand Saraswati in Bihar and helped him set up the All India Kisan Sabha (AIKS) in 1936. On top of the agenda of the AIKS stood the abolition of landlordism. The only item addressing the problem of agricultural labour was that all wastelands still available should be set aside for them. Although the Congress had not objected to the first meeting of the AIKS, its conservative stalwarts soon started to question its critical stance on the agrarian question. During the late 1930s, the AIKS leadership split when Saraswati, probably pressurized by Yagnik, started to give more attention to the agrarian underclass, which implied a shift in a more radical direction. Pursuing agrarian agitation with greater vigour now, the Congress high command rejected the union's demands for radical reforms such as redistribution of land and higher wages for agricultural labourers. A head-on clash between the divergent policy courses of the Congress and the peasant union was immanent, and it materialized in late 1937.

An excellent opportunity to draw public attention to the existence of widespread labour bondage in south Gujarat was the February 1938 convention of the All India Congress Committee (AICC) held in Haripura, a village close to Bardoli town. Dinkar Mehta published a short brochure in which he explained that the masters of the *halis* were capitalist farmers, and that even many petty landowners from the middle-ranking castes in Surat district held landless labourers of the main tribal caste in debt bondage. He estimated their number at a hundred thousand, and urged for a ban on this form of serfdom and a penalty for employers who refused to pay heed to its abolition. Swami Sahajanand toured the district with great success and addressed a wide range of tribal peasants clamouring to give sharecroppers a bigger part of the crop they had cultivated. In processions and demonstrations, participants were roused to carry banners, wave the red flag and shout slogans: *Inquilab zindabad* (long live the revolution), *Adh Bhagni Pratha Nabud Karo* (abolish the system of half share), *Hali pratha murdabad* (death to the *hali* system) and *Kisan Sabha zindabad* (long live the peasant union). More than ten thousand participants joined a rally and marched into the camp where Congress delegates were sitting together in a meeting chaired by Sardar Patel, to hand over the list of demands.

The protests continued for some time but by the end of the year, the euphoric mood had tempered. The dominating peasantry did not budge and neither were the Gandhian social workers anxious to step in and lend a shoulder to the outburst of militancy. The Congress high command, afraid that the agitation might resurge again, was obliged to reconsider its earlier abstinence from interference. In December 1937, Sardar Patel addressed a gathering of Dublas drummed up for the occasion. He told them that conditional to their promise to stop drinking alcohol, they would be set free. In an earlier meeting held in Bardoli's Swaraj *ashram*, he reprimanded a delegation of main landowners, a few leading ones from each village in the vicinity, for their obtuse unwillingness to get rid of *hali pratha*. In his speech, he indicated that the forthcoming liberation of the country from colonial rule made it intolerable that persistent slavery in the countryside around, which according to him did not exist anywhere else in India, should be permitted to continue. In plain peasant language, he blamed his audience for looking after their cattle better than caring for their servants.

Swami Sahajanand could not have expressed it better. The difference was that the latter was not only more familiar with the lives of the landless but also, like Yagnik and Mehta, approached them as equals. This was evidently not the case with Sardar Patel. The Congress supremo continued his harangue against the agricultural labourers in a subsequent series of lectures. In reply to admonitions and pleas from the Dublas to be redeemed from bondage, he coolly reacted that they must no longer borrow from the landlords to get married. The amount spent on their daily needs and life events had to go down, and they had to earn and not borrow whatever they wanted. After all, he summarized, 'if you get enough food to eat, open space to live, and clothes to cover your body, all your needs are fulfilled' (Varod village, mid-December 1937).

A Fake Attempt to End *Hali Pratha* in the Gandhian Way

A long round of consultations with the stakeholders followed – in separate meetings with a delegation of the main landowners on one side and Gandhian social workers as spokesmen for the landless labourers on the other side. The crux of the agreement reached was that the Dublas would henceforth live in freedom, released from the attachment in which the landowners held them captive. The payment for the labour power rendered remained the same as they used to get, and was far too low to live on. The daily wage for men was set at four to five *annas*, for women at three *annas*. Their outstanding debts were cancelled, but only for those *halis* who had been with the same master longer than twelve years. Those who had worked for him for a shorter time had to repay a twelfth part of the debt for each year less than twelve. It meant that their wage would be cut by one *anna* a day.

The Gandhian workers insisted on changing the wage payment from kind to cash. They argued that the farm servant had to be encouraged to become self-reliant, to provide for his own food, to share the yield of his labour, and to stay with wife and children in his own shelter. Rather than behaving as an extension of the master's household, the homely atmosphere at the end of the day would inculcate a sense of responsibility and care for his dependants which was missing now. In the presence of Gandhi, Sardar Patel announced a formal end to *hali pratha* on 26 January 1939. He chose to do this on what was celebrated in Bombay already as Independence Day, in the hope that in the collective memory of the nation, this day would also come to be known as 'bonded labourers' liberation day'. Ironically enough, the ceremony was held at the headquarters of Patidar Gin, an agro-industrial cooperative that was the bulwark of the dominant landowners. Here, too, Patel entreated the Dublas to do what they blatantly refused to do: work hard and live within their modest means. He also warned them that the supply of labour in agriculture was much greater than the demand, and that the landless multitude would have to search for a livelihood away from agriculture and possibly also away from the countryside.

The Father of the Nation gave the agreement his blessing at the meeting in Bardoli, a festive occasion also attended by Nehru and five ministers from Bombay Province. Gandhi was remarkably blunt early in his speech, stating that the wage settled was unjust. In his view, the farmers had proved themselves hard businessmen by fixing the wage rates for both men and women far too low. Both were entitled to at least eight *anna*s (half a rupee) for an eight-hour working day. But he qualified his criticism by rhetorically asking why he should veto a compromise that landowners and labourers had entered into on their own accord. His comments were actually shockingly naive since they implied that he was unaware that the landless had no bargaining power at all and were not a party to the deal faked in their name. Gandhi also suggested, as did Sardar Patel before him, that an eight-hour working day would leave the labourers plenty of time to arduously supplement their meagre income by spinning and weaving. He blessed the Dublas by giving them a new identity on this auspicious day. To erase the derogation attached to their menial status – Dubla means 'weaklings' – he baptised them as *hal patis*, lords of the plough, to dignify their work and wipe out the abuse they had suffered in the past. The new name got stuck and was also accepted by them, but not by their employers. The celebration ended with a song and all the guests joined the chorus at the top of their voices: '*Chhuta thaya re, chhuta thaya, Halpati chhuta thay re*' (the Halpatis will be free).

The joyful mood was short-lived, however, and conflict soon regained the upper hand. To begin with, in many villages, the main landowners did not concur with the deal saying that their delegation lacked the authority to represent them. On their part, the Halpatis now refused to continue working under the old regime. As the unrest escalated, the next step came from the weakest stakeholder, the *harekwalis* – the wives of the *halis* refused the tasks they used to perform in the master's household: domestic chores such as fetching water, washing clothes, cleaning the house and the stable, etc. This enraged their employers, who were not accustomed any more to doing such demeaning and polluting work themselves. The Gandhian reformers rushed to the site of conflict to persuade the Halpatis to end their strike. Some of them tried to arrange for public works that would provide some income to the landless which they badly needed for sheer survival. Soon, for lack of alternative employment, they were obliged to give up their resistance and forced to return to their master's bidding.

Why did Sardar Patel not insist on a government order or legislation to ban labour bondage? His trust on the free interplay of social forces, with the losing side bereft of all bargaining power and without proper representation to voice their interests, was bound to end in failure. In his speech on Independence Day, he pointed out that bondage had no legal basis, but that did not motivate him to enforce compliance with a legal ban. The Congress leaders, wont to back the power of the dominant landowners, did not want to antagonize them by introducing reforms adverse to their interests and were not overly concerned about improving the fate of the landless proletariat. They were more considerate to the tribal cultivators who had become tenants and sharecroppers on their ancestral land in the more recent past, and agitated to secure ownership rights to their former holdings. The government did not deny that the class of agricultural labourers had also become restive; but to deal with that problem meant just ignoring it for the time being.

Agrarian Trade Unionism Prohibited

But the end of the radical trade union movement was now in sight (Vishwanath 1985). Swami Sahajanand was arrested on charges of disturbing the peace. The *kisan* conference in April 1940 was the last one of the Gujarat branch which Indulal Yagnik organized and led. In late 1940, he was arrested and sentenced to eighteen months in prison. Only a few months earlier the District Magistrate of Surat reported that 'the agitation had already resulted in a number of minor clashes and in the growth of a spirit of lawlessness'. There was great disappointment among the peasant activists at the refusal of the Congress to implement the 'land to the tiller' promise of yesteryears. The agrarian programme approved at the Faizpur session of the AICC in 1937 did not even include abolition of the zamindari system. Politicians from the nationalist movement who came to power in several provinces, including Bombay the next year, did introduce reforms to the lopsided tenancy contract but stopped short of a radical redistribution of land ownership. The thoroughly dispossessed class of agricultural labour did not qualify for getting a share from the meagre surplus of cultivable land below the fixed ceiling which was sequestered.

During his detention, Swami Sahajanand came to the conclusion that the All India Kisan Sabha had consistently and grossly understated and under-represented the interests of landless labour, the largest agrarian class. While in prison, he wrote in 1941 an essay, 'Who Cares for the Poor?', in which he examined the origin of landlessness and the social identity of this vast mass at the bottom of the rural economy (Hauser 1994). The Congress ministry that had come to power in Bombay Province took the side of the landlords in Surat district and declared that, given the organized and random violence going on, it was forced to counteract the class hatred preached by radical agitators and their followers. It was the same argument that colonial authorities had always practised in case of agrarian revolt, to justify sending in armed police to preserve law and order.

Considering all the obstacles and restrictions, it is not surprising that the agrarian agitation was short-lived, localized and fragmented due to lack of organization and careful coordination. Its political impact was neither wide nor lasting. Yagnik's claim in 1940 that victory was immanent illustrated wishful thinking among the leaders of the agrarian movement. Or was it a case of whistling in the dark? However, it should not temper our admiration for the thousands of activists throughout the country who were brave enough to help launch campaigns in the years leading up to Independence. They gave voice to the rural underclasses which showed signs of increasing assertiveness but were not heeded by the nationalist movement. It was Yagnik and his Kisan Sabha cadre who were mobilized by the landless Halpatis to help them in their struggle to end bondage. In response to the same pressure from below Sardar Patel had felt obliged to abolish *hali pratha,* even though he did it in a way that was doomed to fail. The main landowning class had long experience in repressing demands from below for a decent and more dignified existence.

The refusal to grant the agrarian poor their human right would have been challenged more critically if the rural elite had not capitalized on their privileged rank within the nationalist movement. The radical vanguard which aimed to represent the landless peasants in the turbulent 1930s stood no chance against the alliance forged a decade earlier in Bardoli between the dominant caste of landowners and Congress politicians. Had the main landless community in south Gujarat twenty years after the start of the wave of radical agitation indeed remained, to use one of Gandhi's expressions, 'untouched like a lotus in the water' (I.I. Desai 1971)? Not in my opinion. Little scope was left for manoeuvre, but to suggest that the situation stayed the same as it had always been ignores the fact that the landlords had lost some of their legitimacy and the landless mass had started to express their unwillingness to abide in debt bondage. When I began my first round of anthropological fieldwork in south Gujarat in the early 1960s, it was hardly conceivable that on the eve of Independence this area had been the scene of a fierce political struggle for releasing the landless from bondage. As Sumit Sarkar wrote:

'History from below' has to face the problem of the ultimate *relative* failure of mass initiative in colonial India, if the justly abandoned stereotype of the eternally passive peasant is not to be replaced by an opposite romantic stereotype of perennial rural rebelliousness. For an essential fact surely is that the 'subaltern' classes have remained subaltern, often surprisingly dormant despite abject poverty and ample provocation, and subordinate to their social 'betters' even when they become politically active. (Sarkar 1983)

Is this despondent conclusion about the persistent passivity at the foot of colonial society justified? The eminent historian quoted above did well to moderate his pessimistic assessment. The literature which discusses the slow intrusion of Hinduism in the tribal tracks is replete with tales of how the Adivasis resisted their integration at the bottom of the caste hierarchy. What we also come across in colonial records is that political activists often did not have to mobilize the tribal land-poor and landless to join a protest campaign. What needs to be signalled is that these peasants themselves came to seek support to redress the injustices to which they were subjected, be it a reduction in the share of the harvested crop, to gain freedom or to get higher wages. There is ample archival evidence to show that this was certainly the case of the *hali*s and sharecroppers in Surat district.

In 1938, a National Planning Committee was set up, chaired by Jawaharlal Nehru, to draft the main outlines of the economic policy to be followed after decolonization was completed. A subcommittee charged to write the report on land policy drafted proposals to abolish landlordism and to transfer ownership rights to actual cultivators. Farming should remain private business and the property held should be large enough to qualify as an economic holding. Also, the maximum size was specified: 'a family . . . should not occupy a holding of a size that may under normal conditions require permanent outside labour'. This design for the post-colonial era envisaged an agrarian order composed of self-cultivating owners. The planners called for the state to impose an immediate ban on labour bondage as prevalent in various parts of the country. This tied-down workforce should be released from debts that were more than five years old. They also should be allocated uncultivated land to help them to attain self-reliance. But the Halpatis did not benefit at all from the land reforms carried through. Swami Sahajanand had figured out that only half of the landless would become landowners if the uncultivated land under the control of the village panchayat were to be allocated to them. Although the National Planning Committee had proposed to do so, that promise was not effectuated. Everyone had free access to this common property, which was extremely important to the landless who used it to graze cattle leased out to them, to cut grass, collect firewood and, not least, for defecation.

In the subsequent decades village land lying waste was privatized, which invariably meant that it became the property of the dominant landowners. A last chance for the Halpatis to join the class of owner-cultivators came with the launch of the *Bhoodan* (land gift) movement of Acharya Vinoba Bhave. This social reformer, a staunch follower of Gandhian principles, called upon landowners to donate land in excess of their requirements to land-poor farmers, voluntarily and without any compensation. The Gandhian workers whom I came across in south Gujarat during my fieldwork in 1962–63 were keen to adopt this idea but so far had failed to find it accepted. As one of them told me, Halpatis in particular were not considered eligible for being allotted surplus land under this scheme. According to the dominant castes of landowners, they lacked the acumen to become self-owned cultivators. I concluded that the land reforms in post-colonial India were designed and implemented such that the labouring classes were denied access to land ownership. The usual argument for their exclusion was the lack of cultivable land above the fixed ceiling that became available for redistribution. The explanation given was that an uneconomic holding would be more of a burden than a benefit to them, as it would prevent them from exiting the rural economy. Sardar Patel had already told the landless to escape from bondage by turning away from agriculture and the village. His opponent, Swami Sahajanand, made it equally clear that the agrarian economy did not provide sufficient employment for the surplus labour stagnating in the countryside. His solution was for at least half of the landless multitude to go and work in the urban industries which were going to be set up after Independence – in accordance with the scenario that the National Planning Committee had laid out.

The *Hali* System as Before?

By now, *hali pratha* had been reduced to a labour relationship, pure and simple. The vertical pattern of relationships that had been held to be characteristic of the traditional situation was replaced by mutual animosity.

Landowners on the one hand, and agricultural labourers on the other, had become stakeholders with conflicting interests. With the further penetration of capitalism in the agrarian economy, the former features of patronage, which conditioned the manner in which pre-capitalist bondage was instituted, were no longer practised. The *halis* had become commodified, but were still attached to their employer in a bond of indenture which threw their exploitation into sharper relief. The terms of employment and the wage rate for it remained the same. As a result of the rapid rise in food prices during the Second World War, they themselves opted for payment in kind rather than in cash. At the end of the day they would receive the traditional *bhata,* supplied in a mixture of millet and paddy. Since many employers cheated when measuring the ration, it was not enough to feed the labouring household. To take full advantage of the high price paid for grain, farmers started to claim back the *vavla,* the small plot of land for self-cultivation which the *halis* badly needed to make up their daily food deficit.

In the same year that national freedom was declared, the Bombay government set up a panel to investigate the plight of the *halis* in south Gujarat. Two experts, M.L. Dantwala and M.B. Desai, were instructed to make recommendations to collect the data required for 'suggesting measures necessary for rehabilitating the class of agricultural labourers and for enabling them to live a life consistent with human dignity and self-respect'. The Commissioners drew up a questionnaire to obtain information in twenty selected villages, invited 92 respondents to make statements, interviewed another 104 persons and constructed the profiles of fifteen *hali* households in each of the surveyed villages. The report of the Hali Labour Enquiry Committee (HLEC) was submitted in 1948 and remained unpublished.

Although meant for official use and eyes only, I managed to get hold of a copy many years later. The investigators conservatively estimated that one-fifth of the rural population in Surat district were debt-bonded labourers, the overwhelming majority of them (90 per cent) being Halpatis. Their very first recommendation was to abolish *hali pratha* by issuing a ban on the practice of bondage. Eradication was required forthwith to defuse a rising class conflict and to prevent the political radicalism that had begun to gain ground from spreading, the authors warned. Wages had to be fixed at not less than one rupee a day, and paid in cash unless the labourer himself preferred to receive a grain ration. If the farmer paid the labourer anything extra, he could no longer deduct it from the daily wage. It would now be seen as what it was – extra pay for extra work. Debts older than three years had to be cancelled. The farmers who were questioned agreed that the *hali* system belonged to the past but insisted that any other arrangement should include the obligation to provide labour power at the high tide of the annual cycle. During slack periods in the monsoon season and the cold winter months, farmers were supposed to give the servants their usual grain ration. But as in the past, this was seen as credit, an advance on future work, and added to the *hali's* debt.

In order to allow for independent shelter for the *halis* after their release from servitude, the government would have to help them to build huts on their own land, and hopefully better than the ones they inhabited.

> The huts of the Halis are in an indescribably bad condition. Almost invariably they are improvised out of inadequate and inferior material, with the consequence that they do not provide adequate protection against rain and the sun. The thatching material decomposes after contacting rain water for some time and water percolates into the hut from many spots. There is no arrangement for proper ventilation. Practically none of the huts inspected by us were divided or partitioned in some sort of apartments to ensure privacy. . . . The inside of the hut, therefore, is in perpetual darkness, lit up occasionally by the fire place during the day and by a crude kerosene lamp for some time at night. The provision of the kitchen inside a hut made of highly ignitable material leads to frequent fires, reducing the huts to ashes and destroying the small belongings of the Halis. . . . For the size of the Hali family the space inside the hut is inadequate. Investigations into this aspect indicated 20 square feet of living space on an average per individual. This space is further reduced when animals share the hut in common with the Hali. (HLEC report 1948, p. 18)

Specifying the near to total lack of property of their household, the average value of clothes, eating utensils and other commodities owned was Rs 11 and 6 *annas*, hardly more the the *hali's* monthly income. It was impossible to gather information on indebtedness since the illiterate Halpatis had no clue when, what and how much they had 'borrowed'. Also, the masters rarely kept meticulous accounts and on being asked how much they had advanced, were apt to mention a fictitious amount, arrived at by inflating and converting into cash what they had given in kind. The report concluded that

> the *hali's* requirements and purchases are few and that he subsists at a sub-human standard of living. But all reforms would turn out to be ineffective as long as agricultural labour remained stuck in a mindset that prevented progress. Custom and tradition have stultified not only their living but also

their aspirations. Their tallest prayer is to be blessed with a *dhaniyamo* who is kind and considerate. No wonder, there are many Halis who in their heart of hearts dread the abolition of the system. (Ibid., p. 36)

This assessment put the onus for ending labour bondage on its victims, blamed for their pauperized mindset, rather than on the master who forced the farm servant and his dependants to live in his shadow.

Knowing that the outcome of the investigations had reached the authorities, some press media wondered why no official steps were taken to prohibit the pernicious system. The official reaction formulated in a press release by two ministers, Morarji Desai and Gulzarilal Nanda, stated that the government saw no reason to enforce the ban proposed by legislation. '[T]here was no legal sanction to the system and, therefore, the question of its abolition by a special law did not arise at all.' The Congress Agrarian Reforms Committee in 1951 reported that labour bondage continued to be practised in Gujarat, and strongly criticized the party's leadership for not having addressed the problem of landless labour in the agrarian reforms after Independence. When the Scheduled Areas and Scheduled Tribes Commission expressed the same blame in its report ten years later, the party leadership insisted as before, that this was because the victims did not want to see their bondage terminated. Acknowledging the massive number and significance of the workforce at the bottom of the country's prime economic sector, the Indian government arranged for a large-scale Agricultural Labour Enquiry (ALE) in 1950–51. Average waged employment amounted to about 200 days a year for male workers. This figure was much lower for daily-wage earners, while farm servants classified as attached had the highest number of workdays. West India had the largest proportion of landless households and of their annual income with Rs 91 per capita, the lowest in the country, of which 85 per cent had to be spent on foodgrains, leaving next to nothing for other bare necessities. It explains why nearly half of these families were indebted.

Daniel Thorner questioned the most important distinction between attached labour and casual labour, arguing that the first category had not been defined properly and was thus highly underestimated (A. Thorner and D. Thorner 1962, pp. 173–89). A second enquiry conducted only a five years later reported that one of four landless households were listed as attached, a much higher figure than found in the first round. The percentage of agricultural labour households in debt had increased from 45 per cent in 1950–51 to 64 per cent in 1956–57, while the average amount of debt had nearly doubled. The finding that a quarter of all agricultural labourers were not free to decide for whom to work must have been quite embarrassing politically. After all, social justice and the commitment to a welfare state for all and sundry was codified in India's Constitution.

Phasing out Labour Bondage in South Gujarat

The government of Gujarat, which became a separate state in 1960, appointed a Minimum Wages Advisory Committee (MWAC) two years later to propose a minimum wage rate for employment in agriculture. The initiative was prompted by recurrent clashes between the main landowners and agricultural labourers. The chairman of the MWAC was one of the two panelists who had conducted the investigation into *hali* labour in 1947–48. He had then added a minute of dissent that the recommended daily pay of one rupee, scorned by Gandhi as much too low, was in his opinion unduly high. Respected for his expertise on Gujarat's rural-agrarian economy and hailing from the class of landlords himself, Professor M.B. Desai was once more the main author of the drafted report and remained as biased as before. In the fifteen years that had passed, he decided that a modest rise – from one rupee to one-and-half rupees or maximally two rupees for men, and for women much less than that – was good enough.

The *hali*'s accumulated debt was a mixture of cash payment and a wide variety of allowances in kind. Many of these perks did not involve an extra outlay but were in the character of leftovers, as in the case of hand-me-down clothes given a new lease of life after having been worn by the master's wife and children. On days of unemployment, which amounted to more than 100 a year, the provision of a grain ration was of crucial importance for feeding the labouring family. The report mentioned that when all these wage items were computed in monetary terms, the total amount would add up to a cash payment much above the rate the committee was willing to fix. It had to be settled in cash, since allowances in kind were considered to be degrading; whimsically given or withheld, they undermined the dignity of the labourer. The report signalled loud and clear that attachment in debt was obsolete and had to be wiped out.

> The detestable *hali* system seems to have been considerably loosened. There are now no restrictions on the Dubla *hali*s to change their employers. Even then the methods of wage payment under the old system sticks. It is not only exploitative but soul killing. The employer under the system is deprived of

his emotional upsurge. He is not moved by the misery of the labourer. The compassion that he shows towards his Dubla worker is discretionary and *ad hoc*. The labourer under the system has lost all initiative and is an embodiment of frustration. (GoG 1966, p. 64)

Although over time the number of the tribal landless in casual employment had increased, farm servants working throughout the year were still a very sizeable contingent. Supervisory cultivation had spread to a middle tier of landowners. Growing cash crops, cotton mainly, these upwardly mobile cultivators had also replaced their own labour power for that of regular servants attached to their households. As the HLEC had done before, the report of the MWAC was prone to attribute the tenacious hold of labour bondage one-sidedly to the defective behaviour of the landless. The Halpatis were singled out among the Adivasis for their lack of efficiency, accused of being work-shy and too apathic to search for other employment. They were similarly criticized for their addiction to energy-sapping vices, drinking self-concocted and prohibited country liquor. The report, published in 1966, urged the authorities to act quickly in view of the spreading radical agitation. Indicative of the alarm signalled is the following passage.

The implication of a lack of policy for agrarian labour to the political and social stability would be easily appreciated. The developments in Asia and Africa are an eye-opener. The working class in general and the agrarian labour in particular has retained their moorings to our basic philosophy of life and living. They might have grown restless and frustrated now and again, but by and large they have shown great patience in the otherwise discouraging situation around them. . . . The forces of extremism are waiting to take over the situation once these indications intensify a little. (Ibid., pp. 78–79)

Despite the concern expressed, the Gujarat government took six more years to prescribe a minimum wage. When finally enacted in 1972, it was set at such a low level that the employed landless had to incur debts to cover their budgetary deficit. Even at that rate it remained unenforced. On a tour around his constituency, which happened to be the subdistrict of my fieldwork locale in 1962–63, the minister in charge of minimum wage enactment was heckled by angry farmers for having acted against their interests. He pacified them with the curt comment that some laws, like the one they disputed, were not meant to be implemented. By now the former mood of acquiescence had made way for a disgruntled demeanour among the landless. Their obstinacy and assertion in the face of stark oppression and exploitation made farmers wary to engage new *halis*, since many in the younger generation resisted the abominable treatment and were not shy to desert their master without working off their debt.

While the wave of radical agitation in south Gujarat dissipated towards the end of the 1930s, it kept going in the bordering Thane district of Maharashtra with great vigour. The tribal Varlis, who had become bonded as labourers-cum-sharecroppers to high-caste landowners, rose in revolt against their servitude in the mid-1940s. Kisan Sabha activists came to know about their resistance and joined them in their confrontation with the landlords. The struggle which aimed to restore tribal land ownership and abolition of bonded labour lasted until 1947, when state repression ended it (Calman 1987). The Congress ministers in the Bombay government put an end to the rebellion in the proclaimed interest of law and order. The radical activists who insisted on drastic land and labour reforms were once again portrayed as rebels who only provoked unrest and caused harm to those they claimed to defend. The decision to adopt harsh measures to end the conflict was partly out of fear that the tribal resistance would spread to neighbouring districts, including Surat. The ban on membership of the Communist Party of India introduced in 1948 applied also to the Kisan Sabha, and the offices of this militant organization were closed down across the country. Its leaders were accused of subversive activities and jailed. The Hali Labour Enquiry report candidly admitted that these left-wing radicals had managed to mobilize the Halpatis, but warned that an escalation of the unrest would have a disruptive impact on the economy and society.

> . . . the workers of the Kisan Sabha, a Communist dominated organization, are active among the Halis, of Olpad, Chikhli and Bulsar talukas. They have succeeded in enlightening the Halis of these places who were hitherto unconscious of their conditions and rights and privileges. A few unpleasant aspects of their activities should, however, be noted with regret. In their zeal to improve the lots of the Halis, they are unmindful of the economic conditions in the district in particular and the country in general. With their record in the Thana district, grave apprehension will be felt about their method of approach and the end in view. If things proceed along the lines pursued today in which poisonous propaganda is dinned into the ears of the Halis without putting the entire question in its proper perspective before them, the conclusion is irresistible that a violent class conflict leading to considerable destruction might be in store. (HLEC report 1948, p. 25)

Henceforth, the tribals would act under the mandate and coaching of Gandhian reformers. No other politically motivated form of activism wanting to represent the interests of these land-poor and landless segments was able to intrude into the exclusive domain of the Gandhian *sevaks*. In 1942, an association called Halpati Mahajan was set up to uplift the members of this tribal community. Most likely, it was a network through which the social reformers, operating from *ashrams* established in and around Bardoli, maintained contact with each other. The participants registered the network as a formal organization in 1946, and pledged to base their activities on the Gandhian principles of 'truth, non-violence and arbitration'.

The name Mahajan was a direct reference to the Majoor Mahajan Sangh, the union Gandhi had founded in Ahmedabad in 1920 for textile workers. His initiative was not only meant to achieve improvements in their economic condition, but also to imbue morality and discipline in a workforce bereft of the capability to develop traits of civility on its own initiative. In 1961, the Halpati Seva Sangh (HSS) was established, with the Gandhian veteran Jugatram Dave as its president and Arvind Desai, scion of a family of landlords, as its secretary. The organization initially restricted its activities to Surat district, but, from 1967 on, was active throughout south Gujarat. The HSS explicitly avoided becoming a trade union, calling itself an agency for the promotion of welfare and liaising between the (Congress) government and the target group. Charged with the programme of constructive work, the Gandhian *sevaks* considered it their core task to coach the Halpatis towards a better, a more civilized way of life.

> In pre-prohibition period, a Dubla hamlet at night was a battleground, crowded with drunkards. Heavily drunk men and women were found making rows, using abusive language and sometimes lying unconscious in a most hideous state. But now the fears of punishment and loss of prestige has considerably disciplined their behaviour. In the same way, the drunken brawls at marriage and such other religious and social occasions caused by excessive drinking are certainly less common. The money spent extravagantly in drinks has also been saved to a great extent. (P.G. Shah 1958, p. 128)

The mission entrusted to the Gandhian workers aimed at detribalizing their code of conduct and substituting it with Hindu mores and customs. This concern of what to do and how to do it is why I have used tribal caste as a label for the community. Raising the issue of class conflict and class struggle is anathema to Gandhian doctrine, and where conflicts flared up, the disciples of the Mahatma rushed to restore 'harmony' (Breman 1974b). The association has acted as a loyal instrument for the Congress. The landless mass in south

Gujarat became an important vote bank for the party that determined the course of Indian politics in the decades following Independence. Its cadre called on the Halpatis to follow these political leaders who promised to end their deprivation. No doubt, the introduction of democracy without restrictions founded on gender, creed, wealth and literacy has had a profound emancipatory impact. If, as was often the case, I had difficulty finding concrete and lasting evidence of this sea change, I needed only to think of the frustration and powerless rage it invoked among the high-caste landowners with whom I broached this issue. Since 1947, the interests and powers that be have had resounding success in capitalizing on the added value they claim for themselves. Yet the vote of every 'Dubla', a term loaded with contempt, counts for just as much as that of an Anavil or Patidar.

Looking at the current political theatre and scenario, that principle of universal equality which was preached but never practised, is in jeopardy of collapse. At the end of my treatise, I shall come back to this conclusion. In my discussion of labour bondage, we have passed through a landscape of change, from the pre-colonial to early-colonial rule, and from the politics of the late-colonial state to the formation of India as a sovereign nation in the early years of its freedom from foreign rule. Having reached the early 1960s, I shall sum up next, and still at the midway stage of my historicizing narrative, the situation of the class of landless labour I documented in my first round of fieldwork in south Gujarat between 1962 and 1963.

CHAPTER THREE

Fieldwork Findings, 1962–63

THE DOMINANT AND DOMINATED CASTE-CLASS IN CHIKHLIGAM

When I started my research in India as a young PhD student in the early 1960s, it was taken for granted that I would locate myself in the countryside. India used to be written up in the social sciences as a peasant society, as it had been already long before the beginning of colonial occupation. Finding out about its institutions, its shape and direction after Independence, the village stood out as a focal point for informing myself about its changing structure and culture. To get familiar with this landscape required staying on in anthropological fashion, 'doing fieldwork'. Hailing from a working-class background myself, I had decided that my study would concentrate on people at the bottom of the economy and society, and trace their relationship to those higher up in the local fabric. When I conducted my investigations, the village was portrayed as 'a community'. The ethos of sharing and the inclusive participation it was supposed to be equipped with should, for the sake of national unity, be retained and promoted. Labelled policy-wise as community development, the targets set were rather nebulous. The imagery of joint interests and objectives of its inhabitants was certainly not what I found.

In my dissertation, I sketched the course and intents of my fieldwork practice, and discussed briefly how I dealt with the inevitable dilemma of taking sides while engaged in so-called participant observation. In a much later published essay, I elaborated on this anthropological method of data collection in a setting of antagonism and confrontation between stakeholders (Breman 1994, pp. 370–407). The two villages I selected in south Gujarat for comparative purposes are situated in the subdistricts of Gandevi and Chikhli.

They differ from each other in terms of land fertility and crop schedule (more or less labour-intensive), infrastructure (connectivity with urban locations) and social history (British rule or princely authority). However, they have a similar caste-class hierarchy with, respectively, Anavil brahmins at the top as the main landowners and Halpatis down below as landless agricultural labourers. All those in the first contingent were the main and often exclusive employers, and in that role demonstrated their status and rank as members of the dominant caste, as Srinivas (1959, 1987) had categorized this segment in his writings – dominant in the sense of being in command of local power, property and prestige. While numerically a minority of between 10 per cent to, at most, 20 per cent of the village inhabitants, as farmers they lay claim to a large and the best part of arable land in the locality. Halpatis are placed on the opposite end of the scale as a tribal caste dispossessed in all respects from ownership rights. Demographically, they dominate as the largest community in the central plain of south Gujarat, where they outnumber the Anavil Brahmins in a ratio of about four to one, although in my fieldwork villages this proportion is lower than that: about one Anavil unit of residence and cohabitation as against two to three Halpati households.

In both villages, which I identified as Chikhligam and Gandevigam, *hali pratha* had disintegrated in the preceding decades. However, features of the past had clearly lingered on, as could be observed from the very sizeable segment of farm servants who the Anavils as the main landowners still engaged to cultivate the crops grown. In my initial understanding, I tried to explain the changed nature of their relationship in terms of the disappearance of ongoing attachment, a shift from unfreedom to freedom. This would have implied that although many Halpatis remained employed as farm servants, they were no longer tied down in bondage. However, I was soon compelled to abandon this idea. The suggestion of a straightforward, abrupt transition of redemption from attachment was definitely a misconceived appraisal of the changes that had taken place. A more nuanced interpretation of what had gone from and what remained in their relationship was required. The plight of indebtedness which prevailed among nearly all of them had not withered away. The state of destitution in which I found them entrapped went together with a lack of manoeuvrability in their arduous search for waged work that would at least provide a bearable livelihood. Although in both villages, more than half of all male Halpatis working as agricultural labourers were still engaged as farm servants, the contingent among them of daily-wage earners was higher than in the past. Also, the percentage of the male workforce in this community which was neither employed in agriculture nor in the village had gone up, in a process indicating casualization of employment as well as diversification of the economy. In this respect, Chikhligam and Gandevigam had quite different profiles. I shall first specify my findings of the contrasting evidence I came across in both localities and then point out the features they have in common.

In Chikhligam, I collected data on 51 families belonging to the Halpati community, of which 26 resided in the village nucleus while 25 inhabited self-built huts in a hamlet belonging to an adjacent locality. Altogether, these shelters had on average 6.4 occupants, adding up to 327 household members. Of its male working population (older than sixteen years) – 95 in total – 38 were employed in agriculture, 21 as farm servants and 17 as day-labourers, of which 11 were hired as full-time and 6 as part-time labourers; 5 Halpati men were locally engaged but outside agriculture, and 52 had, at the time of my fieldwork, gone as seasonal migrants to brickyards or salt pans on the outskirts of Bombay. The seasonal employment of more than half of all working males of the landless community outside agriculture and away from the village was the consequence of a shift towards a less diverse and labour-intensive crop schedule. The oldest farm servants in the village had entered service as *hali*s thirty or more years ago; that is, they were married at the expense of their fathers' masters after having already worked for them as cowherds. They were exceptions, however, and most of today's farm servants became engaged at a later age. When younger, nearly all of them had worked in faraway brickyards for a number of years. Some found the toil in these industries too strenuous, but others said that they might go again in future. In other words, the attachment now was seen as a temporary one and the servant status did not automatically pass from father to son. The Anavil employer was keen to give his farm servant as little credit as possible in order to limit eventual monetary loss extended as advances; neither did he put trust in the other's goodwill because the personal tie between them had eroded. Servitude, in fact, had been reduced to a contractual arrangement between partners who distrusted each other. The servant did not want to be at his master's beck and call and tried to restrict his duties to agricultural labour, nor did he take it for granted that his wife should be available for work in his employer's household. The fourteen Halpati women engaged as domestic servants were by no means all married to farm servants.

Labour engagement was no longer a tie which bound landowning and landless households together from generation to generation. But members of working age in the servant's household were still expected to place themselves at the master's disposal as extra hands during peak periods in the annual cycle. The wage rate for farm servants had gone up to 8 *anna*s (half a rupee) a day plus some allowances in kind off and on. Employers manipulated perquisites as means of pressure to make a reluctant or unwilling servant see reason. Maids still received a mid-day meal, which they usually took home to share with children, and one or two rupees a month in addition. Remuneration was inadequate to afford livelihood for the servant's household. This explained why the amount of debt incurred at the beginning of the relationship was bound to go up. The grain allowance which the farm servant received for the days he did not work – because of heavy rains during the monsoon, for instance – was debited to his account. Expected to give the usual food ration as *khavathi* (literally: in order to eat), the master added its value in cash to the outstanding debt. The Anavils admitted that a Halpati would be unable to discharge the debt so long as he worked as a servant. But when he ran away to the brickyards, as often happened, the employer tried to recover what the seasonal absconder had saved from his earnings. Male labourers casually at work in agriculture were paid 12 *anna*s a day during my stay in the village, but did not qualify for allowances in kind. The prospect of a day labourer's life was hardly inviting. Facing this predicament, most Halpatis regarded it as an in-between phase in their search for more than off-and-on employment. Also, their freedom was rather debatable. On days without work – and there were many – they would approach a large landowner for *khavathi*, promising to work on days the employer selected, and then earning 8 *anna*s which was the same amount that farm servants used to get.

Going off for seasonal employment to the brickyards or salt pans was for them a better option than carrying on as unattached labour. Considering all this, it was not surprising that the majority of male Halpatis were and remained involved in this annual trek. There was virtually no hut in the new hamlet beyond the village habitat from which one or more occupants were not recruited into the brickyards or salt pans. Usually the whole family went, so as to utilize the labour power of all adults and children above five years of age. Only males went to the salt pans because the toil was considered too harsh for females. Very old men and women with very young children also did not join the gangs going to the brickyards but remained behind, forced to provide for themselves somehow. Weekly grain allowances in the brickyards were low and strictly for those at work there, so that little to nothing was left to support those at home.

One Anavil told me that he was convinced that the majority of migrants would prefer to work for him if he guaranteed them a daily wage of a little over one rupee all the year round. But in my view, he underestimated the desire of Halpatis to escape, if only temporarily, the yoke imposed by the landlords. At the same time, the Anavil's claim confirmed my opinion that seasonal migration did not offer a much better option. The work regime was as debilitating and improvident as their existence in the village was; their shelter or rather the lack of it in the brick kilns or salt pans was even worse. Back in the village, they could not recuperate from their toil in the brick kilns. On their return shortly before the breaking of the monsoon, they were compelled to join agricultural labour again. Half the male migrants – 25 out of the 52 who had been away – were attached to the landowner to work off their earlier debts. I have described them as monsoon servants. In the morning, they had to cut a headload of green grass for their employer's cattle, transplant the paddy plants, do occasional weeding in the fields and participate in the rice harvest at the end of the monsoon. Were the Anavils not annoyed by the constant coming and going of a large part of the landless workforce? They expressed their indifference with a proverb: 'Like a hare, a Dubla does not stay long in the same place.' The yearly trek to the brickyards actually fits neatly into the agricultural calendar. Their presence in Chikhligam coincides with the period of peak activity in agriculture. As one of the landlords succinctly put it, the Halpatis continue to work for us 'under obligation of debt and for future credit'.

Cultivation in Chikhligam mainly depended on rainfall and half of the arable land (about 800 acres) was quite infertile and stony, currently only used for growing grass. From a total of twenty-one Anavil households, all with their domicile in the village centre, sixteen adult males in the productive age-set derived their income from agricultural yield. They owned four-fifths of the most fertile land, which they had turned into fruit (mango) orchards. Another thirteen males in the productive age-set of this dominant caste were in non-agrarian jobs; all but one of them lived outside the village. The biggest landlord families, the Desais, had left the village to settle abroad and sold off their agrarian property to other members of the dominant caste before departure. The urban Anavils were mostly professional men, managers or clerks with government agencies and in private business. Most of them were in white-collar jobs, for which advanced education was required. A lifestyle of 'conspicuous leisure' had become possible for nearly all the Anavils who had stayed on in the village. To facilitate this gentrified behaviour, half of them engaged one or two farm servants and one or more Halpati women as domestic maids, to lighten the burden of their work in the master's household and courtyard.

The village panchayat was the lowest link in the bureaucracy and its main functionaries of village headman and police *patel* had always been and still were Anavils. Connections with higher seats of power and authority – with the government apparatus and political parties at and above district level – were still a sovereign means of commanding respect and prestige at the local level. More than half of all farm servants worked for the most active members of the dominant caste – three separate households of a joint family – who cultivated fruit trees and also grew mango trees, which required greater, and more frequently applied, labour power. Only eight Anavil households had one or more farm servants at their disposal and were able to abstain from all agricultural operations. Wearing white *topis* and carrying long sticks, they would walk around their property in a leisurely manner to inspect labourers at work, shouting instructions or abuse. Two Anavil households no longer possessed much land – they had sold off fields to invest in children's education and/or urban real estate – and were not as comfortably housed as their well-to-do caste members. Yet they conformed as much as possible to the way of life considered fitting for an Anavil. For ploughing, an activity despised by brahmans, they engaged a lower-caste tribal small farmer with a pair of bullocks. Other work in the fields was done by day labourers. Four Anavil households had leased out their land on a crop-sharing basis. The produce of their orchards was usually sold in advance to a trader who brought his own labour gang for picking the mangoes. Their income would have been higher if they exerted themselves, but they supplemented it with the earnings of a son who had an urban job. Their simple daily routine was as follows: morning tea – breakfast – bath – noon meal – afternoon nap – walk to and around the orchard – tea – evening meal. In the evening as in the daytime, they could be found on their porch swings in front of their houses. Evidently, they were landlords but not farmers.

As the relations between the master and servant households became contractual, the additional chores that the Halpatis were asked to perform off and on received more emphasis. It was a source of mutual irritation which applied to both the farm servants and the maids. These women were often on bad terms with their mistresses, who left the most unpleasant work in and around the master's house to them and had also adapted to a fashionable lifestyle of leisure. No Halpati girl liked to marry an agricultural labourer and most certainly not one who was a farm servant, afraid that she might be called upon to serve in the master's household. The Halpatis felt that the big landowners no longer cared for them and were embittered that the Anavils only needed their labour power, exploiting them mercilessly when they did. They tended to paint the past in rosy colours, but the stereotypical image of the generous and honest master of bygone days was more a projection of their dismay about the treatment to which they were now exposed.

The changeover to money wages contributed to the deterioration of their condition. The misery and poverty in which the Halpatis lived were visible in their decrepit shelter – a mud hut with a thatched roof, an opening but no door and no windows. Inside, when my eyes could see again in the dark, there was nothing to see apart from a few spare clothes and some utensils for cooking and eating – no other items of any value to speak of. Against this lasting improvidence stood the wealth of the leading members of the dominant caste in sharp contrast. Nearly all the Anavils lived in brick houses; only a few still had old-style dwellings of mud-brick. Their multiple rooms spread over two floors were furnished more expensively than in former times with a sofa, cupboards, a wall clock, tables with chairs, kitchen utensils of coveted stainless steel. The well-to-do owners were eager to show off a wide array of 'novelties'. Men, women and children were well dressed, the food and snacks were of better quality. Wheat instead of millet, refined sugar instead of *gur*, cigarettes instead of *bidis* and milk tea flavoured with condiments had found general acceptance among them.

A gap between the standards of living between landlords and labourers had, of course, always existed, but the difference in the past used to be more one of quantity than of quality. As main features of the transformation to capitalist production and consumption, accumulation versus dispossession was indicative of the growing divergence between the top and the bottom of the socio-economic spectrum. For the employing landowners, maximization of income had become an end in itself. The utility of labour in a cost–benefit calculation had become a chief criterion for the Anavils to engage another farm servant or to refuse to do so. They were driven in their choice by the profitability argument. The kind of life they were expected to lead required a high income. Admitting that the wages of agricultural labourers were low, they would add that the Halpatis had few needs and were prone to spend unwisely whatever they were given. Defective behaviour remained the standard explanation in the mindset of the leisure class for the deficiency and vagaries of the landless class.

THE DOMINANT AND DOMINATED CASTE-CLASS IN GANDEVIGAM

Gandevigam is situated along the bank of the Ambika river and was already, at the time of my first round of fieldwork, well connected by an asphalt road to neighbouring towns. Further on, the more sizeable urban localities of

Bilimora or Navsari were also easy to access. Both towns are stations on the main railway line traversing south Gujarat, leading northward to Surat and southward to Mumbai. The subdistrict of Gandevi, the name that I adopted for the other village of my research, is an old and densely populated area, well known for its crop-rich agrarian economy. It owes this reputation to the high soil fertility along the river, a tract of garden land that was well-irrigated and highly productive. Surrounded by five other villages, Gandevigam had in 1962 a little over 1,000 inhabitants, out of which 225 were Anavil Brahmins and 429 Halpatis. Together, though in a ratio of 1:2, they made up two-thirds of the village population under the panchayat administration. The household survey I conducted gave slightly different figures: 185 Anavils in 26 houses and 381 Halpatis in 61 huts.

In the two Anavil streets of the village nucleus, many abodes were empty for the greater part of the year. To stay in the shaded garden covered with orchards, their pride and pleasure, was far more agreeable. During the rainy season the narrow footpaths in the gardens became all but impassable, and the dominant-caste dwellers here were wont to return to their houses in the village centre. Increasingly, however, many of them replaced their garden cottages with large two-storeyed mansions, which had spacious front and back yards and separate outhouses. This more comfortable accomodation expressed the affluence the owners enjoyed and their eagerness to demonstrate this.

The Halpatis lived along the asphalt road at the village fringe. Their small, low mud huts with overhanging thatched roofs and consisting of one room only, were built on rough and low-lying terrain that was waterlogged during the monsoon. A handful were a little better accommodated in dwellings partly of wood or brick and with tiled roofs. Although this Halpati quarter was of fairly recent date and was the largest hamlet in the village, its inhabitants had to make do with only one well among them. Until the early 1950s, their huts had been scattered in the gardens of the Anavils who engaged them. In my wanderings around the habitat, I happened to come across one such cluster of five huts which were hidden away on the outskirts of the village. Concentration of the landless in their separated colonies on the one side and a tendency towards habitual dispersal of the landowners on the other side were marked changes in the residential pattern, which meant that the two communities had spatially distanced themselves from each other.

For most inhabitants of Gandevigam, agriculture was the mainstay of work and life, based on 360 acres of arable land. The dominant caste which accounted for 22 per cent of the village population owned 260 acres or 70 per cent of the cultivated land, and more than 90 per cent of the most fertile part. They owned almost all the *bagayat* or garden land, which added up to 145 acres or 40 per cent of the soil under crops. Nearly all Halpatis, the largest caste-class comprising 43 per cent of the inhabitants, were landless. The only exception was a man who had received a quarter-acre of land from his master whom he had faithfully served as a *hali* from a young to an old age. He was still alive and I found him in a hut on this small plot of land he cultivated with his two sons. The remaining part of arable land was divided between Kolis – a caste of petty cultivators who comprised 35 per cent of the village population and owned 17 per cent of the arable land – and outsiders who lived in adjacent villages and were also Anavils.

In the course of time, the agricultural economy underwent drastic changes. At the beginning of the twentieth century, sugarcane was the main marketed crop in the whole subdistrict. In Gandevigam, the cultivation of income-yielding garden crops such as ginger, tuberous plants and condiments was then mixed with crops grown for home consumption – mainly paddy, pulses, vegetables, oilseeds and tobacco. The steadily increasing production of cash crops was accompanied by more specialized cultivation and extension of the irrigated acreage. A pump station had been constructed in a neighbouring village, and the water lifted from the Ambika river was distributed through canals which also reached Gandevigam. In fields beyond this network, 56 borewells were dug. From the 1940s onwards mango cultivation became widespread, followed in the late 1950s by the planting of *chiku* (sapodilla) trees. As mentioned before, the garden land was completely covered by orchards when I went to stay in the village. Rice was grown during the monsoon on well-irrigated *kyari* land (105 acres), followed by vegetables (potatoes, onions and cabbage) and pulses but in rotation with sugarcane and bananas. The non-irrigated *jarayat* land (110 acres) served as grassland which provided feed for the cattle in the village. The soil conditions here were noticeably different from that in Chikhligam, where much of the slightly undulating land was considered uncultivable. In contrast to that arid and barren landscape in summer and winter months, the much more intensive cultivation in garden land gave the area in and around Gandevigam a lively and pleasing appearance. Mango orchards, the greenery of sugarcane fields, rice fields, beds of vegetables and banana plantations made for an attractively diversified picture, as compared to the colourless and monotonous rural scenery in my other fieldwork locality.

Collection of data on Anavil brahmins and Halpatis was the main purpose also of my stay in Gandevigam. While in Chikhligam a very substantial part of the total income is earned by its inhabitants outside agriculture and the village, it might be expected that in Gandevigam this would even be higher. After all, this village is situated closer to various urban localities with which it is much better connected as well as in frequent interaction with. But this plausible supposition was not confirmed. Census data showed that in 1961, 88 per cent of the workforce in Gandevigam was engaged in agriculture, a much higher proportion than in Chikhligam. For both landowners and landless labourers, livelihood was firmly based on earnings from agriculture. Until a few decades earlier, the relationships between Anavils and Halpatis were embedded in *hali pratha*. There was no contingent of casual labourers in those days and, if only for that reason, almost all Halpatis had a master. Most of them worked throughout the year for their employers. If an Anavil was not able to maintain his *hali* continuously, the latter was allowed to work for someone else occasionally and make do with what he received. The Anavils in the garden region were from ordinary peasant stock and had for many generations been actively involved in agricultural work. They knew about the seigneurial way of life of their more illustrious caste members. A Desai family in Gandevi town was considered the most eminent among this higher segment of Anavil brahmins in south Gujarat.

The Anavil community I found in Gandevigam certainly aspired to an existence in grand style. On their main street in the village centre the ruins can be seen of a large, three-storeyed brick house. The mansion bore witness to the wealth of its family, of which the last son had left for a better future somewhere in East Africa. His forebears had lived extravagantly, like maharajas, I was told, in a mixture of admiration and derision. In the end, they lost all they had – land, cattle and also the many *hali*s who had served them. Another Anavil told me with glee how his grandfather had prospered. He owned 100 acres of land, had twenty oxen and twelve *hali*s in his employ. The grandson, the owner of the empty house in which I had been installed for the duration of my stay, still took pride in the fact that his father had taken an oath never to eat without guests. Certainly, not all dominant caste members had sizeable property on which conspicuous leisure and consumption were founded. The current generation still had vivid memories of the economic crisis in the 1930s when they were forced to dismiss their farm servants temporarily or even permanently.

Having been dependent for long on urban traders who squeezed prices to the lowest possible level, some Anavils from Gandevigam and other garden villages in the neighbourhood took the initiative in 1944 to set up an agrarian cooperative for marketing the main crops that its members produced. Mango cultivation freed them from manual work and enabled them to opt out of active participation in agriculture. This was their most important incentive for changing the cultivation schedule to the new crop, which is much less labour-intensive. By sinking new wells, the bigger landowners reclaimed also the higher-lying *kyari* land for horticulture. To offset their temporary loss of income, many different crops used to be grown between the not-yet fruit-bearing, young trees. They did not bother to do this themselves any more but leased out the new orchards for the time being to small Koli farmers on a sharecropping basis.

The change in the agrarian calendar of Gandevigam was fuelled by the yearning of the main landowning caste to reduce their participation in agricultural work to supervisory management, and to contract cultivation to a few cash crops. Aiming to set themselves up as landlords instead of self-cultivating farmers had major consequences for the landless Halpatis in the village. For the landowners, this implied a more cost-effective and business-like handling of their agrarian property. Payment made to their workforce in kind was replaced by cash wages. At the same time, because of the reduced cultivation pattern of foodgrain in particular, it was no longer possible to set aside a substantial part of the total produce for redistribution within the village. The growing trend towards a fully monetized economy further depressed the already very low standard of life of landless labour. The more general use of money moreover widened the divergence in lifestyle between landowners and agricultural labourers. The former were the only inhabitants of the village who could afford to buy a great many previously unknown items – new foodstuffs and other consumer goods. It would be incorrect to suggest that, earlier, the contrast in housing, clothing, food and health care between the top and the bottom castes–classes was small. But the gap had widened enormously and this was realized on both ends of the scale. The Anavils conceded that their preference for the new crop schedule was also inspired by their urge to not be obliged to provide security and welfare for the agricultural labourers they employed, and refused to be held accountable for their livelihood. The mindset based on which the former master–servant relationship had operated – though more as a promise than a practice – no longer obtained. *Hali pratha* in the two villages of my fieldwork had dissolved because in the domination–subjugation axis on which it was founded, the patronage dimension had disappeared.

Of the 103 male Halpatis (aged above sixteen) who comprised the landless workforce, 73 or nearly 70 per cent were agricultural labourers – a much higher share than the 40 per cent of agricultural labourers still engaged in the primary sector of the economy in Chikhligam. The Halpati contingent thus employed in the garden village was split up into 51 farm servants, 7 sharecroppers and 15 day-labourers. Most adult females in the landless households also worked on the land in case there was a need for their labour power, particularly during paddy cultivation, and served as maids in the houses of the main landowners. Farm servants comprised half the total Halpati workforce, and more than two-thirds of them worked in agriculture. As used to be the case in the past as well, labour engagement started with a debt and was on both sides contracted for an indeterminate time. Of the 51 farm servants, 39 had spent the cash 'advance' they received – about Rs 300 to Rs 400 – to arrange for the cost of their marriage at adolescence. The remaining one-third had entered service at a later age and obtained loans for other purposes, such as to pay for the cost of illness in the household or other adversities. Sometimes the attachment evolved gradually, by an accumulation of small advances. Discussing the implications of tenured employment, my informants insisted that it was not a lifetime relationship. Still, thirty-six of the farm servants had continued to work for the same master since marriage.

Contrary to what I found in Chikhligam, an ongoing relationship for several decades was not exceptional at all in Gandevigam. More than half of all farm servants were actually with an Anavil family who had employed their father before them. It was a finding which I could not match with the complaint of many main landowners about the faithlessness of agricultural labourers. These exaggerated accounts about the fickleness of their regular labourers were undoubtedly inspired by the fear of losing money that had not yet been worked off. But if breach of agreement was the exception rather than the rule, why did the Halpatis themselves think of attachment as an arrangement for the time being, or attempt to deny lasting attachment even if they knew better? As a rule, their monetary obligations to the employer tended to increase in the course of years. The lack of secure employment both within and outside agriculture compelled them to enter attachment, which made their lack of alternatives so apparent. Although the farm servants did not live any longer in the gardens, in the shadow of their employers, most of them were still occupied almost exclusively in agricultural labour.

However, the Halpatis were no longer in regular attendance to do all kinds of chores in the master's house or courtyard. The latter rarely came to the colony in which they congregated. Only two wealthy landowners had male house servants, one of whom a bachelor who lived in his master's house. Some Anavils employed Halpati boys who were charged with various duties and errands formerly done by *halis*. Moreover, the relationship was restricted to the servant alone, and was no longer a household arrangement which also included the *hali*'s wife and children. While many Halpati women still worked as domestic maids, they were often employed by Anavils other than their husbands' employers. As a consequence, the renumeration of the farm servant was based on his own labour power and did not include other members of his household.

The wage for a full workday was 8 *anna*s, a loaf in the morning plus a mid-day meal, and tea twice daily. Some Anavils paid a little more cash but all allowances in kind had stopped. Even if some annual emoluments were still provided, the Halpatis complained that they were given worn clothes and old shoes, sometimes bought for the purpose in the nearby town. The pitiable wage the farm servants were paid was not sufficient for their livelihood, let alone for coping with adversities that were bound to occur, such as bouts of illness and injuries, family affairs costing money, growing old and loss of labour power. The master dallied and skimped, but could not afford not to pay up if he wanted to retain his servant. The drawback, of course, was profound dependence, with the employer manipulating the increasing debt to impose obedience, and off and on not fulfilling his minimal obligations. On days without employment, the servant was permitted or actually obliged to work for somebody else, and then, of course, was not given the maintenance allowance he received from the landowner who retained him. The master knew how to ensure that his authority was acknowledged. Recalcitrant servants were sometimes not given work for days on end to teach them a lesson, nor were they given *khavathi* until after prolonged insistence.

To remain attached was what most of them wanted. Repayment of the debt incurred was above all an attempt to render themselves less dependent. Of the eight Halpatis who had somehow managed to balance accounts, three were still employed as servants and four were freed from debt through no action of their own – they became redundant when the master to whom they were attached sold his land, left the village or died. Severance of the tie was usually due to the sudden flaring up of a conflict which had already been smouldering for long. To break with the master could mean being forced to leave the village without a clear notion about where to go and what to do. This was the background of the sons-in-law (*ghar jamai*) I found in the Halpati quarters. They had settled down in their wives' villages in the hope of striking a better deal, with a new boss, than where they came from. Running away was often an impulsive decision, an act of despair rather than an expression of indifference or unreliability, as the Anavils claimed. The master's reluctance to give more credit was inspired by an abundance of labour supply, not by the servants' dishonesty. Resolute and repeated refusal to give further credit implied, in fact, that the advantages of secured livelihood were lost, overshadowed by the disadvantages of attachment.

Until the recent past, all Halpati men in Gandevigam used to be engaged as *halis*. Still working in agriculture, two other categories had emerged in this landless tribal community with a different labouring profile: seven sharecroppers and twice as many daily-wage earners. Only trustworthy landless labourers were considered for sharecropping. In the young orchards planted with mango seedlings, perennial crops could be grown and such plots used to be cultivated by small farmers who were members of the sizeable Koli caste in the village. Among them, quite a number had been dispossessed during the recession of the 1930s, and become tenants on their own *kyari* and *jarayat* land. Under the Tenancy Act in the late 1940s, many Kolis managed to get reinstalled again on the plots of one to one-and-half acres they had lost to traders–moneylenders who were not residing in the village. Also, Anavils had to give up land in those years of depression, but they had benefited much more from the land reforms on the eve of Independence, laying claim to larger parcels which absentee owners had confiscated. They did not lose property above the ceiling of the Tenancy Act, but in the same way and with much larger gains, had increased the amount of land they already possessed.

Paradoxically enough, the Tenancy Act, which was meant to strengthen the economic position of land-poor cultivators in particular, actually weakened the bargaining power of the Kolis. Afraid that they might try to register themselves under the new law as owners of plots given to them for sharecropping, the Anavils avoided that risk by shifting this arrangement to the landless community which was much more under their control. It was actually an open question whether the Halpati sharecroppers should not be included among the farm servants. In giving a plot of land to seven of them for banana cultivation, the Anavils found a new means to assure themselves of dependable labour. For a part of their time at work they were at the disposal of the landlord, and I found that several of them had sons employed by the same Anavil. The deal was also more profitable for the landowner, since the Halpati sharecroppers were given a smaller share of the yield than the one-half the Kolis used to get. For such a labour-intensive crop as bananas, according to Koli informers, a one-third share was not enough. But a Halpati, who measured his earnings by those of an agricultural labourer, clearly thought otherwise.

Another kind of sharecropping was farming out unproductive cattle to farm servants. A young calf was given in care and kept with the Halpati, who was allowed in addition to cut grass in the landowner's garden. When the animal – a cow or a buffalo – was in milk, it went back to the employer, who rewarded the caretaker with half its estimated value. The added benefit for the employer was that in this way he could recoup part of the cash amount invested in his servant and continue to give credit, while the debt remained within reasonable limits. In Chikhligam, the Anavils told me that they could not practise this arrangement because most Halpatis were absent for the greater part of the year. In Gandevigam also, the sharecropping of cattle to landless Halpatis would probably be phased out in the near future due to mechanization of farm equipment. In early 1963, the agricultural cooperative had bought a tractor which, together with a driver, was hired out to its members for cultivation purposes and transport of commodities. Some Anavils had already bought mechanical hand tillers and oil pumps were installed for well irrigation. Animal traction would thus gradually be replaced by capital. Moreover, the big landowners appeared to have lost interest in keeping buffaloes and cows, tended by their servants, for dairy production, especially ghee. This used to be manufactured for their own home consumption, but was now bought by them.

During my stay in Gandevigam, I counted fifteen male day-labourers among the Halpatis who had a different occupational identity. They kept themselves informed about casual work in adjacent villages and got employed by Anavil as well as, once in a while, Koli farmers, but also applied for paid work outside agriculture, in transport or construction. Their wage was 12 *annas* plus two meals for a full workday, and one rupee but without meals at harvest time. As a matter of fact, several Kolis were willing to pay a little bit more as they hired them only occasionally. The younger ones among these landless workers were still unmarried and for that reason, were able to remain unattached for the time being. Others were former farm servants who had broken ties with the landlord or been dismissed for their lack of performance. Among them, a few were sons-in-law from other villages who had joined at marriage their wives, born and bred in Gandevigam. This group did not live apart but had their huts in the same colony.

I also found farm servants and day labourers in one and the same household. When unattached, they needed to shop around more in search of work, but they did not impress me as more resourceful or better-off than the farm servants. The somewhat higher daily wage was no compensation for the risk of more days of unemployment. I also observed that the divide was not watertight and permanent. Further, day labourers tried to procure advance payment, promising their availability if the landowner needed them and then at a lower pay of 8 *annas*. The abysmally low wage rate also forced them to ask for bigger loans to meet the costs of adverse eventualities which were bound to occur sooner or later. It meant that they became part-time servants, an in-between sort of status which either continued or finally changed into complete attachment if the Anavil agreed.

Thirty Halpatis, less than one-third their total male workforce, had found income outside agriculture and the village. Only five of them were locally engaged – one as a peon in the panchayat office, one in the same capacity in the village school, one as a tractor driver with the agricultural cooperative and two in its warehouse. Of the twenty-five working outside the village, two were itinerant tinkers who ventured around the vicinity to practise their trade, three were timber cutters for a merchant in a nearby village where two other Halpatis also worked in a grain mill; after the monsoon, one went daily to a brickyard at a short distance from Gandevigam. Seventeen were employed in the towns of Gandevi or Bilimora – three as hands in a paper mill, three others as employees in shops or artisanal workshops, four more as transport workers and seven as bricklayers. Most of them walked the three miles to Gandevi town and had not yet been able to buy a second-hand bicycle. Those among them who had regular jobs were envied by other members of their community. Their good luck was relative, however, earning as they did not more than Rs 1.50 a day. Although it was double the amount of a casual labourer in the village, those who worked in Bilimora also went on foot as they could not afford to spend 12 *annas* on a return bus ticket. The worker who was employed in a paper factory and the two engaged by a wood merchant had taken loans from their employers for getting married. This also meant that their manoeuvrability became limited.

How did they manage to qualify for these non-agrarian occupations? It was clear that recommendation by an Anavil landlord, their father or mother's employer, carried a lot of weight. Owing to their familiarity with the urban milieu and how to find work there, those who had already managed to escape subjugation to the regime of domination in the village were connecting points for others to follow in their footsteps, as time would show. The Halpatis were aware of the influential role of the landlords, and complained that the Anavils used their authority to block rather than facilitate the departure of landless labour from the village. When I asked employers why so few of the agrarian workforce searched for livelihood away from Gandevigam, their pat reply was that Halpatis lacked discipline, intelligence and versatility to do work other than what they were accustomed to generation after generation.

The condition of the Halpati caste-class stuck in Gandevigam was strikingly similar to the substance of the Hali Labour Enquiry Committee (HLEC) report of 1948. No major improvement had been made. Their shelter in the hutment colony had so little floor space that not all members of the household could sleep inside. There was hardly any furnishing inside. I found myself counting the nails in the beams on which some garments were hanging – rags to me, but to the owners, the only spare clothes they possessed. Only the men wore shoes, which were indispensable for work in the field. Small children were either not or barely dressed. As for food, cooking oil was scantily used. Salt and spices were bought in the neighbourhood shop or bartered for the eggs of hens that a few of them kept. Only farm servants and maids ate some vegetables as part of the meals they were given in the master's household. On workless days, they were reduced to living on a gruel of foodgrain mixed with undermilk, occasionally supplemented by a species of weed. The only shopkeeper sold many articles in tiny quantities: a pinch of salt, a handful of chillies, a small bag of salt, etc. His customers, when in debt to an extent of Rs 3 to Rs 4, were refused credit beyond this amount. When the wage rate rose at harvest time, accounts got settled. Malnourishment resulted, of course, in bad health. Chronic illness and injuries on the legs, arms and hands were prevalent more or less in nearly every household. Widespread high and daily consumption of home-brewed alcohol completed the picture of pauperism. Indicative of the situation described was the view of the landlords that lethargy and alcoholism were the cause of the improvidence marking the existence of the landless, instead of seeing it as an escape from immense misery.

The Halpatis noted the rising prosperity of most Anavils over the last decades, and compared their own deplorable conditions with the comfort and leisure of the main landowners. Reflecting on their former lives in the gardens attached to their master's household, they commiserated the loss of close interaction with their employer who used to work with them in the field and shared with them the mid-day meal brought from his house. Livelihood was better and more secure then. The daily allowance was paid in kind and the prices of items that had to be purchased were much lower. This was no doubt, an unwarranted picture of a harmonious past, obliterating the compulsion, brow-beating and whimsical arbitrariness which also existed then. But a worse condition than their current plight had become inconceivable. Ageing farm servants who had lost their labour power were curtly dismissed and not provided for any longer. They became dependent on children and other relatives who found it difficult enough to keep their own heads above water. The absence of mutual support even between near relatives accentuated the prevalent mood of hopelessness.

The Halpatis were badly equipped to find release from their subhuman existence. Also, outside agriculture they were only eligible for the meanest and lowest-paid jobs. Only a handful Halpati children attended the village school regularly, and for not longer than a few years. Indifference towards schooling among the older age-set was not the main reason for the sustained illiteracy. Children of six to seven years had to stay home to look after their younger brothers and sisters. Boys and girls from the age of eight to ten were encouraged to join the labour process, at first as unpaid helpers of their parents, but occasionally also sent out separately to gain practice with mean treatment awaiting them. Schooling and skilling as preconditions of a better standard of life were beyond the reach of the landless community.

Awareness of their lasting subordination had certainly grown in their midst, but a way out was not in sight. The settlements of Halpatis in their own and separate quarters at the margin of the village implied that they were more in interaction with each other than before. However, I failed to find clear signs of a growing shared consciousness. Realization of the regime of exploitation and oppression to which they were exposed was given vent to when I met them away from supervised work and beyond the surveillance of their employers. It was a recurrent topic of conversation in their hutment colony and among the younger generation in particular. It rarely shaped up into collective action – except for an occasional wild strike to try and raise the excessively low wage rate, or a joint protest of men and women for not being allowed any longer to collect firewood in the gardens, or an explosion of fury when once again a girl or woman was raped. But these were the weapons of the weak to which they commonly resorted in their vulnerability – that is, personalized forms of resistance.

Loosened Ties of Agrarian Attachment in Both Villages

'Gentlemen farmers' is how I named the Anavils in Gandevigam and Chikhligam in 1962–63. Even more than to the size of their landholdings, the term referred to their leisurely lifestyle and the degree to which they absolved themselves from remaining physically engaged in agriculture. The hardworking peasants of former times had become landlords who managed their property by remote control. However, such a sumptuous life did not apply to all members of the dominant caste in Gandevigam. Of the twenty-six dominant caste households in the village, seventeen employed a total of forty-three farm servants and twenty-nine maids. Nine other households had to get along without labourers in permanent service. Three of them did not work themselves but made do with the low proceeds of their neglected garden, leaving the annual fruit-picking to a trader who brought his own labour gang. The remaining six households did not own enough land to afford the convenience of paid help. Work in the fields and gardens was done by male members of these households. Only when they could not cope did they call in casual labour for the least favoured operations, tilling in particular.

These Anavils were hardworking farmers who still grew traditional garden crops. They did so, partly because they could not afford the investment required for laying out an orchard which would attract a lean income in the initial years. Their dire conditions of living were apparent not only from their own toil, but also from such evidence as a shabby house and making do with one woman shared by two or three brothers of whom one was the registered spouse. They kept a low social profile and lived more or less hidden, deep in the gardens. Though their poor existence was acknowledged by their well-to-do caste members, I came to understand that such a down-to-earth livelihood was quite exceptional and for 'ordinary' Anavils, not acceptable. The much better-off sections among them boasted about their attained prosperity and were not shy to parade it. By avoiding agricultural labour themselves, the dominant caste accentuated the social function of servitude. Light work was allowed, such as sheaving paddy or sorting mangoes, but most Anavils applied themselves to the management of their agrarian property and checking on their workforce. For the majority of them, the cultivation of fruit trees reconciled two divergent aspirations – the highest possible income and the least possible effort. It was a combination seen by them as their prerogative. When a Halpati planted a small mango tree in front of his shelter in the hutment colony, it was regarded as intolerable and some Anavil boys uprooted it.

There was an interesting contrast with members of the same caste in Chikhligam. The latter had distanced themselves much farther from involvement in agriculture, whereas the landlords in Gandevigam were more frequently present in their gardens or fields Their greater commitment to cultivation was apparent in the eagerness with which they had taken to the introduction of *chikus*, a new fruit tree. This crop, though yielding a higher income than mangoes, required much more care (irrigation and labour), which was for their caste fellows in Chikhligam sufficient reason for not introducing it. While the Anavils of Gandevigam laid stress on their role as managers, they attended with greater zeal the business of cultivation, assembling in front of the storage shed and office of the cooperative in the late afternoon with members from other villages to discuss the latest prices, the rising cost of inputs and market conditions. The sharp business acumen which I detected also coloured their mutual relationships. They were prepared to vilify each other and did not shy away from accusing their neighbours of greed or denouncing them as inveterate liars. But in their contention on how to rank the pecking order, the Anavil notables did not refrain from postulating a closed front to articulate their caste and class domination. With 700 members from twelve different castes spread over nine villages in the neighbourhood, the agricultural cooperative established to market the cash crops was entirely an Anavil affair with all of its fifteen board members sharing this identity. They were regarded as preferential members who could obtain credit more rapidly on easier terms and in greater amounts. Another important institution founded by them was the secondary school in a nearby village to which their sons and daughters were sent after having finished elementary education in the village school. This high school was also considered to be an Anavil domain in the vicinity.

For young adolescents, boys in particular but an increasing number of girls as well, college education in nearby towns was the next step. This longer trajectory of education had remained the prerogative of the local elite who prepared their offspring for work and life outside the village. A common lifestyle that gradually evolved among the younger age-set inspired, on the one hand, the typical behaviour of a dominant caste and, on the other hand, an urban and gentrified ambience. Domination was also radiated when, once a year, all Anavils assembled for a festive meal in front of their houses in the main street of Gandevigam, in a notable demonstration of togetherness. Were the Anavil youth in the garden village, like the educated ones in Chikkhligam, inclined to detach themselves from their agrarian livelihood? My assumption was that this eventuality seemed rather unlikely. No doubt, nine members of this caste were already at work outside the village and they all belonged to the younger generation. But for the main landowners, the horticultural crop schedule yielded, even without very active farm management, a lucrative income, higher than most fellow caste members in town were able to earn. Horticulture had turned out to be too profitable to be simply abandoned. Moreover, a rural livelihood in these developed tracks had lost its former stigma of backwardness. Improved road connections had brought the surrounding towns and its amenities within easy reach. Several Anavils already had their own and motorized means of transport. With the installation of electricity and water taps, housing had become quite comfortable. The prospect that I could foresee was that an urban job for at least one son prevented the setback to split up agrarian property in the next generation. Profiting from agrarian business without much bothering about what it entailed seemed to be the future scenario.

In the course of my fieldwork, I was invited to many weddings, lavish affairs of well-to-do landowners celebrated with pomp and circumstance. The marriage ceremonies expressed relations of reciprocity, but for the role assigned to Halpatis, such occasions were loaded with the stigma of their subordinate status of attachment. The contribution of servants and maids of the household consisted of manual and physical chores during these festivities, from which the Anavils abstained in auspicious superiority. Many hundreds of guests queued up to partake in the marriage meal. Members of the landless caste were of course not included. They stood at some distance waiting until the meal was over to vie, together with the stray dogs of the village, for the leftovers. The display of conspicuous prosperity with decrepit improvidence was a shocking sight and marked by near-total absence of patronage. The Halpatis never tired of grumbling about the egotism, greed and viciousness of their employers. Conversely, the Anavils expressed annoyance and anger about how the landless caste had changed from being docile and industrious to recalcitrant, dishonest, indolent good-for-nothings. They accused the agricultural labourers of theft of fruits and vegetables, selling or trading for other commodities what they managed to collect at night from the fields and orchards. A few of the masters were prone to inspect the small bundles Halpatis carried at the end of the workday; others made nocturnal tours of their gardens; and the bigger landowners hired a field watchman from outside at harvest time. Some Anavils were not shy to admit that labourers were treated badly, behaviour they regretted as falling short of the concern that people from a lower caste-class were also entitled to. Yet, the large majority of landlords were thoroughly indifferent to the misery of the landless. They also no longer abided by the unwritten code of allotting waged work to the Halpatis of Gandevigam. At harvest time, at the peak of mango cultivation, they hired labour from outside the village. These migrant gangs who were contracted for the duration of the season made use of improvised shelter in the fields and orchards, and brought their own food. Employing outside labour was a clear demonstration that the main landowners did not want to accept a moral commitment to employ the local landless.

Living together in their own colony on the fringe of the village enabled the Halpatis to strengthen their caste and class bonds. The direct control that the Anavils could exercise when the *halis* used to live in the shadow of their masters, with their huts scattered around the gardens, had weakened. To that extent, relocation did help to generate recognition of a shared identity among the landless. However, it was an awareness that remained fragmented since the social space needed for collective action did not exist. Resistance against domination and exploitation did occur but was individualized, and often ended in failure if it was a joint and mustered protest. Restraining abusive behaviour was primarily inward-directed. A servant who too easily gave in to his master's predilections would be censured by his caste mates for his meekness and inability, for instance, to stop his wife or daughter from having sexual relations with the master. An individual quarrel might also, earlier and easier than before, erupt in a larger embroil. Antagonism was rife on both sides but rarely resulted in a solid front of all stakeholders. Domination versus subservience was still the name of the game. In their management of village affairs, the landed elite firmly refused to act as interlocutors for the Halpatis in the government agencies. Social workers in the Gandhian mode brokered when a conflict suddenly flared up, and inspired by a mixture of social compassion and political ambition, tried with little success to cater to the needs of the down-and-out for a better way of life. Their so-called 'constructive work' failed to find fertile ground in the quarters of the Halpatis. The disappearance of the functions of patronage supposed to have been inherent to *hali pratha* in its capitalist phase was not substituted by the presence of economic reforms generating decent employment with payment of fair wages and social policies for proper health care, housing and education of the labouring poor. The politics and governance of the Congress party in the post-colonial decades paid lip service to the pledge to end their deprivation but refrained from implementing its pro-poor stance.

In my 1962–63 round of fieldwork, I had found the tribal and landless caste of Halpatis despondently stuck at the bottom of the village economy and society in rural south Gujarat. What happened next? I went back to south Gujarat in 1971 for another round of investigations as a member of a larger team of Indian and Dutch social scientists. Our study focused on the economic and social changes at the regional level, and those which were apparent in the district headquarters in particular. In Valsad town, then still called Bulsar, I explored the set of urban labour relations in this growth pole situated on the main railway line, and wrote up my findings based on the distinction that was becoming fashionable between waged work and employment in the informal sector as against the formal sector of the urban economy (Breman 1979). I took time off to make trips to Chikhligam and Gandevigam to understand what was going on at the polar ends of these villages a decade after my initial fieldwork. The first time I returned to Chikhligam, the village headman (*sarpanch*) kept away from me because he thought he recognized the vehicle in which I had been given a ride as the jeep of the district family planning unit. The *sarpanch* did not want to be pestered again about the quota set from above for sterilization of males in the reproductive age range. It was still a voluntary scheme which targeted the village poor. For undergoing the operation, Halpatis were offered Rs 80, more than twice their monthly wage. When Indira Gandhi declared Emergency in 1975, enforcement would be brutally exercised in various parts of India.

More of the same for everyone, was how I summed up the impressions from the visits I made to my earlier sites of rural research. It implied steady prosperity higher up and ongoing pauperization down below. The *sarpanch* of both villages were still Anavils. The one in Chikhligam boasted of his influence in the government administration at the district level. As chairman of the public works committee, he had been able to set himself up as the contractor for various infrastructural projects. His cousin, with whom he shared the large residence they inhabited in the village, was the secretary of the district branch of the Congress party. After the 1969 split in the party's top ranks, he sided with the conservative wing led by Morarji Desai against Indira Gandhi. Horticulture had remained the main activity in Gandevigam. The chairman of the cooperative society selling the yield of its members happened to be an Anavil from my second village of fieldwork. The sociocultural homogeneity which the members of the dominant caste publicly demonstrated expressed their awareness and pride at being the backbone of the social order.

About half the Halpati households had left Gandevigam to settle down at some distance on wasteland belonging to an adjacent village. Their low-lying hamlet would get inundated each and every monsoon. A heavy flood in 1968 completely destroyed their shacks. Only the households of farm servants stayed back to rebuild these hutments while the casualized workforce moved out to jointly settle down some distance away, on the territory of a neighbouring village. Employed as daily earners, they remained dependent on the farmers of Gandevigam and other nearby villages. The most important change in waged work was undoubtedly the increased spatial mobility of labour. The seasonal migration of Halpatis from Chikhligam continued as before, driven not by choice but by need. The diminished use that landowners made of the local landless was a consequence not only of the growing mechanization of farm operations, but also the influx at harvest time of land-poor and landless peasants who had no means of existence during the dry season in their home area. For the harvest of sugarcane, which had become a major cash crop, the cooperative factories set up by the main landowners recruited many thousands of labourers each year from faraway places. The small farmers among them brought along ox-carts to transport the cane they had cut to the mills. Similarly, the owners of orchards and grasslands or dealers harvesting their commodities brought labour from outside for the duration of the season.

Labour supply and demand was less and less determined by local conditions. Better connectivity – due to road construction and motor transport – facilitated seasonal migration over growing distances, and enabled landowners to replace local labour with even cheaper and more pliable workers from outside. It was a shift accompanied by a more contractual mode of employment: piece work by gangs led by jobbers who agreed to carry out a specific amount of work at a pre-arranged price. Economic gain was no doubt the main motive for the majority of landowners to change the identity and character of waged labour. But it also reflected their growing aversion to rely on the local landless who had become less pliable and docile then before. The clear distaste with which both stakeholders treated each other meant that the dominating Anavils no longer acknowledged the right of the subordinated Halpatis to share and participate in the agrarian economy of their domicile. Among the latter, class animus was certainly activated, but under the existing power structure it would have been imprudent and injudicious to display their anger and hatred too openly. Total bondage to a single landlord had for most Halpatis been substituted by fragmented and partial dependency on farmers, shopkeepers, jobbers, petty government officials and politicians presenting themselves as social workers. These diverse forms of dependence, although distinct in their *modus operandi*, were brought under the common denominator of subjection by those who suffered from them.

CHAPTER FOUR

Fieldwork Findings, 1986–87

CHIKHLIGAM AND GANDEVIGAM REVISITED

To monitor the drift in the ongoing transition of the economic and social fabric in the two villages of south Gujarat which I had investigated in 1962–63, I carried out a re-study of the inter-relationship between the bottom and top castes–classes in the same research sites twenty-five years later. The starting point for this new round of fieldwork was a household survey, which showed that the Halpati population in both villages together had increased from 632 to 889 between 1962 and 1987, and that the total number of working males had gone up by 60 per cent from 180 to 288. In Table 4.1 below, I have listed the number of Halpati men according to their employment, mainly within or outside agriculture.

The identification of Halpatis with agricultural labour could no longer be maintained. Households in this landless caste now depended for their livelihood mainly on non-agrarian activity, in a ratio of nearly 2:1. Rural labour seemed to be a more suitable term for their full-time or part-time occupational diversity. A noticeable change was that in the quarter of a century which had passed since my first round of research, the countryside

Table 4.1 *Employment of Halpati men, 1962–87*

	Agriculture		Non-agriculture	
	1962–63	1986–87	1962–63	1986–87
Chikhligam	38	32	57	132
Gandevigam	62	72	23	52
Total	100	104	80	184

Source: Fieldwork surveys, 1962–63 and 1986–87.

had become more accessible and, conversely, was easier to leave. In the past, it used to take much time and trouble to reach Chikhligam, situated in the less densely populated and arid hinterland. In the rainy season in particular, the rough country road between the village and the only town of the subdistrict would become impassable for weeks on end. Since then, connectivity had much improved with better roads and introduction of a regular public bus service running in various directions. Situated along an asphalt road between two nearby towns and railway stations, Gandevigam did not seem to have experienced the sense of isolation and backwardness that could still be felt in Chikhligam. The main landowners and the landless alike derived a steadily growing component of their employment and income from non-agricultural sources in both villages. The figures that I reported to substantiate this trend, however, conceal major differences between them. The decline in the importance of agriculture in Chikhligam implied that barely a quarter of the male Halpati workforce could still be classified as agricultural labourers. In Gandevigam, their absolute number showed a marginal increase but 70 per cent of them were still at work in the primary sector of the economy.

The agricultural profile of both villages was consolidated along the same lines, which meant that the contrast which already existed had intensified. As before, the main Anavil landowners in Chikhligam were not prepared to behave as agricultural businessmen interested in running a well-equipped, up-to-date farm enterprise. Several of them had started to grow sugarcane but all the labour needed for cultivating and harvesting this crop was managed by the cooperative mill in the subdistrict town where the cane crushing took place. Some other Anavils outsourced their land partially or wholly to persons whom they called partners, in an attempt to avoid the word 'tenant' because of the legal implications this term involved. If paddy was grown under such an agreement, the costs and yield were equally divided between owner and cultivator.

In Gandevigam, fruit orchards, which did not require much labour input, had driven out nearly all other crops on the land of Anavils who were the main landowners. The cooperative society set up by them was booming as never before. The modest accommodation of the early 1960s had been replaced by a two-storeyed office building with a compound and several sheds, together with a store located on the border of Gandevigam and the neighbouring village. In the store, members could buy fertilizers, pesticides, agricultural tools, cement, wood for construction, roof tiles, durable and non-durable consumer goods. The cooperative also owned a rice-mill, a jeep and four tractors, which were hired out with a driver to members for field operations, transportation or land-levelling. What I saw was an impressive agro-industrial undertaking which had remained a citadel of Anavil power and prosperity. The chairman was habitually chosen from their ranks, and so were eleven of the fourteen board members in the late 1980s. When farming was so profitable in Gandevigam, why were more Halpatis not absorbed in producing the much higher yield? Because of their replacement by outside labour in the peak period of the annual cycle. Also, in the early 1960s, I had noticed the arrival of work gangs for digging and levelling of land in my sites of fieldwork, but their number had much increased in the late 1980s.

Seasonal agricultural labourers came mostly from the arid and hilly zone bordering Maharashtra. In Chikhligam, Anavil farmers found these migrants, driven from their homes by a severe famine in the early 1970s, prepared to work for a pittance. In 'normal' years, such footloose gangs consisting of ten to fifteen young men and women would turn up to harvest paddy and other crops in order to meet their urgent need for cash income. All food rations for the duration of their absence were carried by them. I used to meet them on the roadside, walking in single file. The adults carried pots and sacks on their heads, tools in their hands and sometimes a small child on their arms or hips. Their movements should not be seen as aimless drifting. They went straight to the villages where they had been the year before and were directed to other employers through earlier established oral contracts. Neither did they migrate for an indeterminate time, but for a period lasting not more than a couple of weeks until the millet supplies they had brought with them were finished. Then they would return home before making another sortie with the same gang or another one. Arrangements were made and sometimes clinched long before departure with a down payment given to a jobber who came in advance to close the deal. This constant coming and going characterized the spasmodic rhythm of seasonal mobility. Such nomadic work gangs were also employed for fruit picking, though in a way that made the differences in farm management manifest. In Chikhligam, urban traders bought the mangoes from the farmers while still in flower. They stationed a couple of guards in the orchards and sent ambulant work teams to harvest the fruit. As members of the cooperative, the Anavils in Gandevigam were not supposed to sell the yield of horticultural products to outsiders. Responsible for their own harvesting, they engaged migrant gangs which for the duration of their stay set up camp along the Ambika river bank.

What changes had taken place in the agrarian employment of the local landless caste? Table 4.2 illustrates the shift in the pattern of engagement in the process of casualization which drastically reduced the proportion of

Table 4.2 *Mode of employment of Halpati men in agriculture, 1962–87*

	1962–63			1986–87		
	Total	Farm servants	Day workers	Total	Farm servants	Day workers
Chikhligam	38	21	17	32	13	19
Gandevigam	62	50	12	71	30	41
Total	100	71	29	103	43	60

Source: Fieldwork surveys, 1962–63 and 1986–87.

Halpati men at work as farm servants. In Chikhligam, the percentage of daily-wage earners had risen from 45 to 60, and in Gandevigam, from 20 to 58. Combined, their number doubled from 29 to 60 in the two villages. Moreover, the casual labourers were hired not only to work in the fields, but also employed to do odd jobs in and around the village, such as wood-cutting, well-digging and extracting sand from the riverbed. Agricultural employment also provided for these Halpatis a major part of their annual income but the way of life of this dispossessed class in the rural economy could only be understood by stressing their occupational multiplicity. Many of the tasks allotted to them were based on contract (*udhad*), a system to which other modes of wage payment applied, i.e. not based on time but on piece rate or job work.

Farmhands had succeeded the former *halis*. They worked in ongoing and close interaction with the farmer and had a longer working day, starting early in the morning and staying on after the daily wagers had gone. Farmhands were responsible for the farm equipment, looked after the cattle, transmitted orders from the boss to the casual workers, and did a variety of chores on slack days in the employer's house and yard. Their female equivalent was as before domestic maids, Halpati women employed in the farmer's household to tidy the house and its premises, clean pots and pans, do the laundry, fetch water, and be at the disposal of the farmer's wife in the morning hours.

Between 1962 and 1987, the total number of farm servants had decreased by almost half. Of the male Halpati workforce, less than one-fifth – 43 out of a total of 288 – were engaged as permanent hands. The landless in Chikhligam had found an option other than agricultural labour. The prospect of seasonal migration provided them a living and became an alternative to staying put, in view of the scarcity of employment, in the village for the larger part of the year. Work as a day labourer yielded too little and the large majority of them refused to become engaged as farm servants. However unattractive toiling in the brick kilns or salt pans might be, the younger generation preferred that kind of footloose existence to the dependency which was the essence of work and life as a farm servant. The small number of them still locked in this plight under the control of Anavil landowners were from Halpati households which in the past had stayed back in Chikhligam. Members of their caste who had gone to live in the new colony established just outside the village unanimously rejected the idea of such attachment. Their defiance was actually a major reason for their removal.

Although agriculture in Gandevigam needed far more workers throughout the year, the main landowners insisted that they had an ample supply from which to select both regular and casual hands. In addition to the local supply, they had also seen that migrants from elsewhere could easily be recruited and, being more docile and pliable, at an even lower cost than what the local Halpatis used to be paid. The only drawback was their unpredictable behaviour. Quite often they would leave without advance notice and for no good reason, according to their employers. Or they would not show up after the rainy season, in spite of a prior agreement sealed with some earnest money. All outsiders were untrustworthy, was a complaint farmers often voiced, implying that they had a much better hold over the local landless. Even while always finding fault with the Halpatis, the Anavil landowners seemed to realize that, in the end, they would to have make do with them. How did the landless react to the annoying perception that their labour power was tolerated rather than appreciated in Gandevigam? Until so far at least, by not opting out of employment in agriculture and the village in large numbers. Lack of experience regarding where to go in search of either seasonal or permanent employment elsewhere might have played a role. Such opportunities at great distances were beyond their vision and reach.

However, the enlargement in the scale of the rural economy with the ongoing infrastructural development and better connectivity that had come about informed them about ways and means to sell their labour power away from the village for the larger part of the year. Industrial estates located in or near the district towns offered daily wages to newcomers at rates that were only a little above the wage rate of agricultural workers. Halpatis coming from remote villages would have to spend most or all of that extra money on bus travel. Besides, ups and downs in the manufacturing workshops differed little from the equally uneven rhythm in agriculture. Apart from seasonal peak and slack in production that gave rise to hiring and firing alternately, the terms of employment were not much better than those in the primary sector of the economy. Illiterate and unskilled Halpatis would qualify for no jobs other than the most menial ones. Once engaged as 'helpers', it was a grade in which they were bound to remain stuck for years on end. The terms of employment were characteristic of conditions in what had come to be labelled as the informal sector of the (urban) economy. It meant the absence of regulations other than those imposed by their employers and arbitrarily exercised by them. It boiled down to an absence of stability, security, protection against adversity and other features of fair and decent employment, including the inability to bargain for a better deal.

In my assessment, it meant that in Gandevigam, where waged work used to be available all the year round, the push away from agriculture and the village was not strong enough for the landless Halpatis. Neither was the pull of outside employment options sufficiently attractive to try and get access to a better alternative. Conversely, for the large majority of their caste mates in Chikhligam, labour migration to faraway destinations for a major part of the year had become inevitable in view of the scant use that was made of their labour power in or outside agriculture, at home or nearby. The difference does not explain, however, why the main landowners in Gandevigam still found nearly half the members of the landless caste willing to work as farmhands. Why did these Halpatis not prefer the greater independence enjoyed by casual wage earners? After all, permanently employed labourers were not eligible for the slightly higher wages paid to casual workers at the peak of the agricultural cycle. On the other hand, in their steady engagement, farm servants did not need to bother about fluctuations in their daily rhythm, trying to find out in advance from whom to get a wage on consecutive days.

Not all Halpatis weighed the pros and cons in the same way. In the new colony on the fringe of Gandevigam where many Halpatis resettled in 1968, I found a mood similar to the one I detected in the new colony adjacent to Chikhligam. In so far as the members of the tribal caste living there were concerned, they did not mind continuing work in agriculture because alternative employment beyond their immediate reach did not yield high enough wages to warrant the trouble and expense to seek it. They combined selling their labour power on a casual footing to landowners with other waged work in the near vicinity. Occupational multiplicity was not an easy choice as it carried the risk of remaining unemployed for many days. But they were firm in rejecting the possibility of greater security by being dependent on a single landlord. They tried to avoid attachment to a single Anavil household just as much as their caste fellows in Chikhligam did. The promised advantage of continuous employment, as they emphatically reacted to my questioning them on this issue, could not compensate for the restrictions on freedom which was also the fate of the successor to the erstwhile *hali*.

A Proletarianized Consciousness

In my analysis of the trajectory of servitude, I have argued that both patronage and servitude were of formative significance in dispossessing agrarian labour from ownership of agrarian property and tying landless households in bonded indenture. The rights of the master were the duties of the bonded servant and vice versa. This inter-relationship did not mean, of course, that the exchange was an equal one. It was structured in its successive manifestations along a vertical axis of domination and subordination. I have indicated patronage as the social–political dimension of a pre-capitalist system of subservience which was immanently exploitative. To suggest that I gave a positive slant to labour bondage which prevailed earlier in south Gujarat, as Tom Brass maintains, is a grotesque misrepresentation of my writings on the subject (Brass 1990, p. 41).

Closely resembling how *hali pratha* had been instituted, Max Weber highlighted the political economy which was a precondition to this setting in his seminal study on the plight of the landless class on the Junker estates in East Germany during the feudal era. In his conceptualization of patrimonial rule, he phrased pre-capitalist servitude as follows.

> The master 'owes' the subject something as well, not juridically, but morally. Above all – if only in his own interest – he must protect him against the outside world, and help him in need. He must also treat him 'humanely', and especially he must restrict the exploitation of his performance to what is 'customary'. On the ground of a domination whose aim is not material enrichment but the fulfilment of the master's own needs, he can do so without prejudicing his own interest because, as his needs cannot expand qualitatively and, on principle, unlimitedly, his demands only differ quantitatively from those of his subjects. And such restriction is positively useful to the master, as not only the security of his domination, but also its results greatly depend on the disposition and mood of the subordinates. The subordinate owes the master assistance by all means available to him. (Weber 1924, p. 682; translated from the German)

In the transformation to capitalism of the rural economy which in my region of research, started to gain momentum during the last quarter of the nineteenth century, the features of patronage eroded while exploitation intensified in an accelerated process of commercialization and monetization.

In line with the emerging mode of production, subaltern dependency was reduced to a mere employment contract when the farm servant received on his engagement, a 'loan' which obliged him to work until the 'advance' was repaid in labour. During the first half of the twentieth century, the terms of agrarian employment in south Gujarat became increasingly impersonal, contractual and casualized. Attachment in debt had been the means by which landlords manoeuvred their *halis* into bondage. In the changed political economy, the dominating caste of farmers secured the labour power of the landless caste by keeping them locked in a state of dire improvidence if not destitution.

The work provided and wages paid were simply not enough to cover the costs of rites of passage and of illness, physical or mental handicaps, old age, shelter repair or other adversities which occurred without fail in the Halpati household. The deficient income implied that livelihood was impossible without going into debt. Farmers refused to advance money for major expenditures, knowing the risk of default of such an investment in future labour power reduced to a commodity and over which they lacked the control formerly exercised by them. But they could not ignore the frequent requests regular workers made for small cash 'loans' to pay for sudden and unexpected purposes. Daily and close contact with his employer enabled the worker to bring more pressure to bear when in urgent need of money. This was why some Halpatis chose to enter into permanent labour contracts even when these restrained their freedom of movement. Credit for daily purposes amounted to no more than a few dozen rupees at a time and was granted in a niggardly fashion. At the same time, it was precisely this constant need to bargain for even small favours which caused a steadily growing proportion of the landless community, young persons in particular, to prefer the more risky but less curtailed life of a daily-wage earner.

It was no coincidence that the Halpatis in Chikhligam and Gandevigam who resettled in newly-built colonies beyond the reach of their employers were more militant and less submissive than members of this tribal community who stayed back in their old village habitat to work as farmhands. Accumulated dependency occurred when a male servant's wife was also required to work in the employer's house on a continual or rotating basis. Although my findings showed that this linkage was no longer as automatic as in the past, the combination of farmhand and domestic maid was nevertheless fairly common practice. The term *gharni Dubli* meant a female Halpati who belonged to the master's household, an arrogation that arose from payment of money needed by her husband or his father at the time of the couple's marriage.

The main landowners certainly endeavoured to retain their hold over the landless workforce and advance wage payment, though in small amounts, was instrumental to achieve this. But such tactics were only partially successful since even farm servants emphatically refused to consider themselves as bonded because of outstanding debts. An indication of their basic freedom of movement was that they showed no scruples at all in deserting their employer. They were wont to do so irrespective of the debt they left behind, whenever a more attractive alternative cropped up or when their insistent claims for further advance payment were curtly denied. A clear sign of the farmers' diminished leverage was their grief and anger about their inability to get back what these absconding workers owed them. The hand-to-mouth existence in which they toiled made it implausible that anything of value could be redeemed from them. Actually, the petty loans that employers regarded as a claim on future services and which were meant to be met on first-call priority were, in the perception of their creditors, compensation for the shortfall in wage payment – money due to them for the undervalued labour power they had rendered in the past.

If Halpatis could indeed move around freely, why did not more of them do so instead of allowing themselves to get entrapped, and for minimal remuneration, in a subservient relationship with a member of the dominant caste? This question was pertinent especially in the case of the agrarian workforce in Gandevigam. Why were the main landowners in this village able to find a ready supply of labour willing to work for Rs 10 per day (the going wage rate by now), when they could earn twice that amount in one of the nearby towns? According to the Anavils, the physical and mental shortcomings of the Halpatis, their deficient body strength in combination with weakness of mind, meant that the illiterate and uncouth landless workers lacked the qualities required for any employment other than plodding in the fields. They fell short of what their urban bosses wanted: a modicum of discipline, a steady working capacity and rhythm, and an elementary degree of intelligence.

Such denigration was, of course, quite without foundation. As a matter of fact, a growing number of males in the landless community had managed to escape to alternative employment. Still, the number of them who were at work in agriculture and not willing to go away in seasonal migration, as in Chikhligam, was indeed quite high – at 72 out of 124. Sufficient lack of connectivity with the urban milieu prevented them from altogether packing up and settling down in one of the nearby towns. Among the younger generation a growing proportion had taken to commuting on a daily basis.

However, accounting for the cost and time involved, the net wages for unskilled and inexperienced newcomers were only a little higher than they were able to earn in the village. The informal sector of the economy, at that stage still considered to be an urban phenomenon, provided neither tenured nor secure, protected and much better-paid jobs. The terms and conditions of waged employment were as exploitative as they had remained in the rural agrarian sector. The more than half the male workforce in the landless community which I came across in Gandevigam in 1986–87 who were still stuck in agriculture did not consist of a residual contingent with disrespected jobs and a social consciousness that was lacking or immature. They were part of the proletariat to which all Halpati households belonged.

The problem of labour bondage was given a new impetus when Indira Gandhi announced its abolition forthwith under the 20-point programme, the agenda devised under the state of Emergency that she declared in 1975 to increase agricultural and industrial production, improve public services, and fight poverty and illiteracy. But among the civil liberties that were suspended was the right to strike. The interests of the working classes were curtailed in other ways as well. The Bonded Labour System (Abolition) Act (1976) addressed a regime of waged work that had already disintegrated in most parts of the country. The objective underlying it was something else: the desire of the ruling government to accelerate capitalist development. As part of the economic strategy that followed, all those elements had to be removed which were seen as relics of the feudal past. The credo that this policy intent concealed was not so much that labour in bondage was degrading, but that it was above all uneconomical and inefficient.

In anticipation of what Indira Gandhi promised to deliver, the Gandhi Peace Foundation reported in 1977 that bonded labour continued to be practised on a large scale in various parts of the country. According to this claim, in the southern districts of Gujarat, 171,000 agricultural workers, almost 10 per cent of their total size, were classified as bonded *halis*. The government of Gujarat decided to commission a number of experts to investigate what had become a politically sensitive issue. Two rapporteurs concluded independently that while the Halpatis lived in deep misery, there was no evidence of labour bondage (Lal 1977; G. Shah 1978). The team instructed to find out conditions in the district of my research confirmed the existence of labour tied up in attachment. It was a difference in opinions that had no basis in facts but was caused by different appraisals of how to define bondage. The maximalists argued that landless dependency was sufficient reason to speak of bondage. The features mentioned in the report were permanent employment without a time limit, low pay in combination with indebtedness, sometimes also accommodation in a hut built on the landowner's property and employment by the same landowner of more than one member from the worker's household. This profile was indeed indicative of the engagement of farm servants in south Gujarat. However, in my opinion, these elements, separately and together, had more to do with fierce exploitation than with bondage *per se*. I roundly refuted the suggestion that entrapment in debt boiled down to a relationship that attached the *hali* to his master. According to me, this view of seeming continuity denied as irrelevant both the material and ideological changes that had evolved over a long stretch of time in the inter-relationships of landowners and the landless in rural south Gujarat.

My conclusion was similar to that reached by V.K. Ramachandran on the basis of his local-level research in Tamil Nadu between 1977 and 1986. The mode of employment of only one man in that village accorded with the definition of a bonded labourer as someone who could not work for anyone other than his or her current employer, except by physically escaping from the coercive power which that landowner exercised. When questioned in detail about their search for work, the majority of the landless interviewed asserted that they were free to choose between alternative employers. The others fell between the polar ends of the bondage–freedom continuum (Ramachandran 1990, pp. 176, 251). Without detracting from my contention that bondage had withered away, it was clear that remnants of what had been passed from generation to generation lingered on and could be detected in the manner in which members of the main landowning caste treated their regular workers. Their abrasive domination appeared to be echoed in the muted acceptance by the subordinated workforce.

In her village-based study conducted in the mid-1980s in the same district as my fieldwork, Uma Kothari pointed to such avoidance of open contestation.

> Men who work as *kayem majoor* [i.e. permanent workers] for a landholding household tend to be those whose parents worked for the same household. Although they are not bonded and are no longer part of a relationship with farmers based on coercion, subjugation and dominance, which was characteristic of the *halipratha* system, they have some 'obligation' through household ties, to work for the same household. (Kothari 1990, pp. 162–63)

In a footnote, she warned that terms such as 'obliged', 'forced' and 'required' were difficult to explain as terms of economic necessity or indebtedness. The wages paid were simply not enough to allow for the gratification of basic needs. Her comment amounted to saying that the ingrained inequality had created a climate which the Halpatis had, to some extent, internalized in an acknowledged dependency. This made it easier to comprehend why the landless community seemed to consider it more or less inevitable that their labour power should be at the prior disposal of a particular landowning household. On the other hand, it should not cause any surprise that Halpatis who worked and lived in their employers' shadow were very cautious when talking to outsiders about what had to remain suppressed.

Verbal compliance might well conceal a recalcitrant mindset which tried to minimize infringement of a deeply felt want to be independent. I referred to James Scott's study for these hidden transcripts of resistance (Scott 1990). Casual wage labourers were less reluctant to discuss why, with all the risks involved, they tried to abstain from becoming engaged as a farm servant. According to them, it was a condition that reeked of subjugation to an employer, and brought not security or livelihood safety but intensified exploitation. On their part, some members of the dominant caste were not wary to admit that the end of close and personal interaction with their landless workers had resulted in a begrudging and embittered relationship of mutual antagonism. The former master had become a ruthless employer, association with whom was experienced as dishonourable and deplorable. It was a subaltern mindset not any longer smouldering in covered-up resentment but expressed in open confrontation. As one Anavil farmer frankly told me when I took his leave at the end of my second round of fieldwork: 'When you came here for the first time, his father [pointing to a worker] spoke about my *wadi* [garden], my paddy and my buffalo as though they were his own. Nowadays his son thinks about me: he has grown rich by our sweat' (Breman 1993, p. 313).

Max Weber completed his empirical study, the only one he ever conducted, on contemporary agrarian relations in East Prussia, in 1892. Based on a comprehensive data-set collated from a questionnaire sent to a large number of landlords, Weber wrote up his findings without taking on board the perception of the agricultural workers. He described and analysed how in the slowly evolving transition from subsistence to market production, the Junker-owned landed estates had fundamentally changed their character from patrimonial domains to capitalist enterprises. Commercialization of the crop schedule and monetization of waged labour had, from the mid-nineteenth century onwards, eroded the system of bondage on which this rural regime was founded. The falling apart between estate owners and their servile workforce, no longer receiving their share of the yield in allowances of kind but remunerated in cash, led to a major overhaul of agrarian relationships during the preceding decades. At the end of his treatise, Weber granted that redemption from subordination was instigated by the impelling magic of freedom (Weber 1892, pp. 797–98). However, he warned that escape from patriarchal domination was most probably not going to result in the self-reliant existence the landless household aimed for. Lasting precarity threatened to condemn the agrarian workforce freed from bondage to remain floating around as daily-wage earners.

Would this footloose proletariat ever manage to rise above that insolvent future to a secure and independent working life? Weber's analysis of how agrarian labour pushed out from the rural economy in the eastern parts of Germany attempted to find a new berth in urban-industrial employment is of limited relevance for our comprehension of the halting development which took place half a century later in India. Later in this essay, I shall come back to this distinct divergence. For now, it should suffice to state that the switch from an agrarian-rural to an urban-industrial type of economy and society, although awaited and designed, did not materialize in South Asia's subcontinent, with dramatic consequences for the working masses stuck in the lower strata of their nation-states. To contextualize the changes that did transpire, I first return to my findings of 1986–87, to further query whether the national freedom attained forty years before had, in the aftermath of release from bondage, created room for manoeuvre and bargaining power for the landless community in the investigated localities.

Balancing on the edge of subsistence, most Halpatis in my recurrent fieldwork sites remained shorn of the decency and self-respect that accompany life in freedom. As I had expected, the younger age brackets proved to be more eager and assertive in expressing their distaste for subjugation. What did not fail to impress me, however, was that both adolescent and older females appeared to be more assertive than their male household members in finding ways and means to dodge lasting dependency. Girls of a marriageable age had a definite fancy for a husband who earned his living away from agriculture, preferably as a skilled and steadily employed labourer.

Covert resistance from below could once in a while explode into open violence. Animosity was aroused when, in the mid-1970s, the main landowners in both villages started to hire guards to protect their orchards and fields from crop theft during harvest time. The use of mercenaries revealed the waning control of the farmers over their landless workforce. The *zimrakhas* were heavy-handed, armed with sticks and took to beating children who gathered firewood. Emotions flared up when one of these guards raped a Halpati woman cutting grass along the roadside. In response to this incident in Chikhligam, the landless marched to the panchayat office to demand that the mercenaries be instantly dismissed. The conflict would have resulted in the Halpatis being maltreated by the police for their militancy, but the Anavil *sarpanch* withdrew the complaint that had been lodged. He described his leniency as a gesture of goodwill intended to calm feelings that were running high. That the farmers decided to tone down their resentment seemed to me to illustrate a shift in the power balance.

As I pointed out earlier, the settlement of Halpatis in their own colonies on the outskirts of the village has strengthened a joint social awareness and a mood of cohesion among the fragmented cohorts belonging to the landless community. In the liminal landscape described, collective forms of resistance did occur although they remained unrecorded. Strikes either to press for improvement of employment conditions or, unfortunately more often, to ward off a further weakening of these conditions frequently broke out, but due to their small scale, short duration, and lack of organized and coordinated action, were more likely to end in failure than success. Vulnerability remained the bane of the largest dispossessed caste and class stagnating at the bottom of the rural order in south Gujarat. Was no reprieve from improvidence bordering on destitution in sight at all for this substantial segment of the population?

The Post-Colonial State and the Labouring Poor

Upon achieving Independence, the ingrained ideology of inequality was meant to lose its social legitimacy. That transformation, firmly laid down in India's Constitution, marked the onset of the struggle for emancipation by the landless proletariat in south Gujarat. My contention about two generations later was that precious little progress had been made. The research that I conducted brought home the lesson that dire poverty was experienced less by referring to memories of past misery which had lingered on, and more by comparing one's own condition to the existence enjoyed by the better-off at present. The Halpatis considered themselves worse off than before because the gap that separated them from the landowners, and their Anavil employers in particular, had further widened. This was one of the reasons why I attached limited importance to the quantitative studies in vogue which, taking an imaginary poverty line as point of departure, tried to determine whether the percentage of the population living below that line had decreased or increased. It was a kind of appraisal that did not bother to find out if the weight given to indicators by which poverty was measured remained constant or had changed over time.

To what extent did the post-colonial government pursue a pro-poor policy? Mostly by paying lip service to this lofty pledge. The design of the developmental state presented itself by propagating a communitarian facade. Interdependence and compatibility of all inhabitants with one another structured in cohesion and harmony were not only praised, but also assumed as constituting the grid of village life shared by the overwhelming majority of the population. Benevolent governance would play a guiding role in the process of community development and reconcile contradictory interests. This strongly populist design gave priority to concepts such as consensus and cooperation in the public interest to create welfare for all and sundry. From the very beginning, the politics and policies implemented – as exemplified by the manner in which land reforms were executed – clarified that the capitalist growth strategy adopted would be adverse to the declared egalitarian objective. Confronted with critical poverty studies and the eruption of social unrest in different parts of the country at the end of the 1960s, the national policy makers belatedly realized that they must address the spiralling inequity in welfare. Under the label of positive discrimination, social identity-based schemes were introduced to stimulate the 'backward' castes to catch up with mainstream development. A setting of political democracy made compensatory efforts of imperative importance. No broad-based party could afford to continue disregarding the majority of the rural population, which consisted of small to marginal farmers and landless labourers. Enfranchisement of these massive vote-banks required an approach that would oppose or at least constrain the built-in tendency of capitalist growth to only cater to the better-off classes of the population. To what extent did this state-directed policy reach and benefit the hamlets inhabited by the landless Halpatis of Chickhligam and Gandevigam?

A proposal of the central government in the early 1950s to fix a minimum wage for agricultural labourers was endlessly debated but rejected by the landowning lobby which dominated most state assemblies. When it was finally enacted in Gujarat at the lowest possible level as late as 1972, farmers flatly refused to abide by it. Successive rounds of revision, usually announced shortly before elections were due, also failed to be implemented. Throughout my fieldwork, farmers paid at best 30 per cent below the statutory amount. Whenever the going wage began to approximate the official rate of the time, rising prices frustrated any positive effect.

Towards the end of the 1980s the daily wage fluctuated between Rs 10 and Rs 12 in both villages. Remuneration below the floor needed for the most basic standard of living meant that indebtedness remained a regular feature of landless households. Calculated on the basis of the consumer price index, the National Commission on Rural Labour recommended in 1991 a minimum wage of Rs 20 per day for the entire agrarian workforce in the country, which was close to double the amount paid in Gujarat. The change from remuneration in kind to cash wages made it easy to trace the extent to which the market price for labour fell short of the legally proscribed minimum. Both farmers and labourers were able to tell me what ought to be paid. The conventional assumption that the landless were ignorant of their legal right to a minimum wage was incorrect. In general, they knew what was due to them but were unable to get it. In both villages, farmers had little to fear from the authorities because the staff from high to low of the Rural Labour Inspectorate which had been set up used the official ordinance not to fine defaulting employers but to receive bribes from them for non-prosecution (Breman 1985c).

As far as education was concerned, at the time of my first round of fieldwork it was quite exceptional for Halpati children to go to school, and among the adults, I came across no one who was able to read and write. Such near-total illiteracy had slowly diminished, but twenty-five years later about two-thirds of male adults and more than three-quarters of female adults were still uneducated. Many more children in the appropriate age-groups attended school now, although most of them only up to the first few standards and even then rather erratically. Girls dropped out earlier than boys as they were needed to do all sorts of chores at home. Low-grade education provided at best elementary knowledge and became more attractive only when the household income consolidated above a critical level. The majority of the landless were nowhere near such economic felicity.

In Gandevigam, the local Anavil elite had seen to it that the primary school was closed down under the pretext that the quality of teaching was inadequate. The real reason, as I found out, was the steady increase of Halpati pupils, who came to outnumber their own children. The latter were then sent to attend the much better private school in a nearby village, taken there by family members on a scooter or moped, or by a servant on a bicycle. It was impossible for Halpati children to shift to that school because the monthly fee charged was Rs 40. Under pressure from the district bureaucracy, the old village school reopened after two years, but was frequented forthwith exclusively by children of the Koli and Halpati castes. The Noon Meal

Scheme subsequently introduced helped to increase attendance of children of the landless at the primary level. From the landless community, only three boys and one girl had by the end of the 1980s managed to achieve the Secondary School Leaving Certificate in Gandevigam; in Chikhligam, none.

A shortage of everything that contributed to good health meant that illness was very prevalent in the proletarian household. Money with which to pay for medicine or to consult a doctor was rarely available. Many temporary or chronic ailments, a range of occupational diseases, malnourishment at a tender and elderly age, poor housing and insufficient cover to protect the body when it was cold or wet, lack of sanitation and hygiene separately and combined, resulting in ill health – these were all characteristic features of the health standard of the landless. Public health centres which had been set up at the subdistrict level were meant to repair this. People from the surrounding villages could report to these clinics for medical help which was supposed to be given free of charge or at a low cost. When deemed necessary, patients were referred to the public hospital in the district town or city. However, the range and quality of services on offer were deficient as well as ineffective; moreover, they were not cost-free but priced by the doctors and paramedics who ran the facility. Those who were able to pay for treatment continued to consult quacks and all the others took to self-medication with shop-bought painkillers. Birth control and sterilization were propagated but practised in a manner that made the labouring and non-labouring poor fearful of public health care.

Between my two rounds of fieldwork in 1962–63 and 1985–87, the landless in south Gujarat were settled in separate hamlets on the village outskirts. In 1972, a district official told me about a task entrusted to him, which was to find suitable plots on which to shelter the Halpatis. His negotiations with the landowners who ran the village panchayat usually ended with earmarking wasteland of negligible value for this purpose. These were sites far away from the village centre, linked only by a country road and difficult to access in the monsoon. The colonies at the outer edge of the village where I found them during my first stay consisted of scattered and self-built huts with overhanging thatched roofs that almost reached to the ground. Accommodation had somewhat improved a quarter of a century later. The Congress party had started, on a modest scale, a scheme to build houses for the rural poor, a few in each village, to maximize its electoral impact. Dispersed over a large number of locations in the district of my research, eight Halpatis in Chikhligam had over the years become owners of an Indira Awas tenement each. Provided with more floorspace than their former huts, the interior was usually one room which could be partitioned by its four to six occupants on average. The walls were made of bamboo lathes covered with mud but the tiled roof in particular indicated that the construction was no longer a hut but a real house. Assembled in their own quarters, Halpatis remained deprived of amenities such as electricity, tap water and sanitation, which were installed in the streets of higher-up and better-off inhabitants. Although living together did strengthen their common caste-class identity, it did little to enable them to engage in collective action. In the course of time, my awareness of the conditions in which the rural poor were forced to live led me to conclude that the majority of slum dwellers are to be found not in urban India but in the countryside.

In various parts of India, attempts have been made to stimulate rural employment with public works. The trend was set by the Employment Guarantee Scheme launched in Maharashtra in 1975. Between 1970 and 1990 a number of pilot endeavours were undertaken with the indirect objective to raise the local wage level for unskilled labour. Gradually shaped up into a national initiative, the Rural Landless Employment Guarantee Programme in 1983 promised to provide 100 days of waged work a year for at least one member of each landless household. In line with the delegation of administrative decision-making to the local level, the village authorities were given direct control over the funding made available for infrastructural projects that would boost productive growth.

I ventured into the corridors of the district bureaucracy to find out about the schemes introduced and the procedure for implementation. It made little sense to try and fix an appointment in advance for collection of the required data. I had to queue up and hang around the corridors before admittance, curtly being told to come back the next day because the official concerned was in a meeting, or on tour or just 'not available'. While petty bureaucrats made do with peons to barricade themselves from direct access, the higher-ranking staff had personal assistants to run the roster of the boss. A multilayered chain of gate-keepers decided who was next and they had to be bribed in order to get a hearing. I came away from such excursions into officialdom convinced that the state and the poor in their subaltern niche remained aloof from each other in separate realms difficult to bridge. Without *olkhan* – the recommendation of a respectable person equipped with social capital reaching up to the district level of politics and administration – nothing could be achieved. Even the handful among the dispossessed crowd that managed to get through and find a hearing high above usually failed to get their work done due to their inability to pay the required bribe. Already then, I was appalled to register in my encounters with bureaucrats the prevailing climate of corruption in the political circuit as well as in all agencies of the government apparatus. It meant that a very high portion of the public budget set aside for poverty alleviation did not filter down to the targeted beneficiaries but was drained away in fraudulent transactions.

The public distribution of foodgrains and some other daily essentials set aside for the labouring and non-labouring poor prevented spiralling destitution due to unchecked hikes in the cost of living. However, the progress made in real wages seemed to be restricted to households living above or close to the poverty line. It was my impression that the lower the income, the less the people profited from price control. The regulation that limited the validity of ration cards to the place of household domicile meant that the growing number of labour migrants who entered or left the village were cut off from subsidies on daily necessities. The Gujarat government had introduced various social insurance provisions aimed at reducing the threat to survival of the most vulnerable categories – the aged, the chronically ill, the physically or mentally disabled and widows with young children – but without much impact, as I concluded in my research on this issue (Breman 2013c).

The need for a more comprehensive system of social protection was obvious. As the National Commission on Rural Labour had pointed out, a mere 2.5 per cent of India's GNP was expended on social security (GoI 1991, p. x). Moreover, this budget tended to be spent on organized labour in the formal and largely urban sector of the economy. Extension of these schemes to the large majority of the workforce living and dependent on informal employment in the countryside was evidently not a high priority. The greatest political capital was made out of the state pension to be paid to all aged and handicapped workers without adult children and fully dispossessed. The monthly entitlement amounted to Rs 50 for single males or females and Rs 100 for a couple. Although considered insufficient for survival, the stipend could have alleviated the plight of living in dire circumstances. But the chance of this cash dole ever reaching them, let alone on a regular basis, was infinitely small. In Chikhligam, only one old Halpati woman had once been favoured with this amount. She, as well as others (including the official in charge), saw it as a once-in-a-lifetime stroke of luck rather than a right she could claim in future. In the sociopolitical climate that existed in my villages of research, it was unthinkable that an aged Halpati would be able or allowed to claim to the powers-that-be his or her right to survival. While employers denied any responsibility to provide even an elementary quality of life for their workers, the state showed itself unwilling to ensure and enforce the social reproduction of the rural proletariat at a minimal level.

The trend that I observed in Gandevigam and Chikhligam mirrored the capitalist transformation of society. These dynamics, which put a premium on landed property and other assets of value, explained why most members of the dominant caste had forged ahead while the large majority of the landless community had fallen hopelessly behind. The conventional idea that economic growth is a process starting at the top of the heap and gradually trickling down to incorporate lesser-endowed segments of the population, ignored the reality of a dialectic interaction between improvement and impoverishment. The gist of the development strategy followed in post-colonial India was to keep the price of unskilled labour fixed at a very low level. I found no evidence in my fieldwork locales of the persistent assumption that the main beneficiaries of economic growth in the end were prepared to share the resources they had managed to accumulate with the lot who had started with nothing at all. When I asked those who had gained why they were not discomforted about the polarizing trend, the answer was either that all those at the bottom of the pile stagnated because of their inferiority and, moreover, had lesser needs in comparison to those higher up. Or that, because of their defective behaviour, these lowly contingents simply deserved no more than they got.

During the decades which spanned my fieldwork a wide range of new amenities and facilities had been made available in the countryside of western India. The degree to which people were able or not to own or to use them was an important yardstick for the awareness created about one's station in life, expressed in strongly contrasting standards of living. Social standing had come to depend on material comfort or the lack of it. Not being able to enjoy the pattern and level of consumption regarded as basic, which implied much more than just caloric intake of food, increased the infamy that characterized life in the underbelly of society. With the ingrained ideology of social inequality on the wane, a trend that was emancipatory in nature, relations between high and low were couched more than ever before in factual terms of prosperity and poverty. I was inclined to attach more importance to the growing consciousness of the underprivileged, preconditioned by the rise of free labour, than to the wavering improvement in their material condition. Such a change of mentality was particularly noticeable among the younger age-set, and was expressed in the ever-louder demand that the inferior quality of life and work should be ameliorated. The increasing employment opportunities outside agriculture and the village had reduced the proportion of the landless workforce dependent solely or mainly on income earned in their own habitat.

Novel patterns of communication such as transportation by truck, bus or bicycle played an important role in opening up the countryside. No doubt, migration was due above all to economic compulsion, the need to hunt and gather for cash wages away from the village. However, such labour mobility simultaneously enabled the landless class to escape the dependency in which they used to be attached permanently or occasionally to the main landowners. Employers were not alone in insisting on fluid and impersonalized interaction, in line with their consistent strategy of keeping the subordinated flock at bay. In order that their identity and self-respect not be impaired, the younger generation among the landless also favoured more depersonalized labour relations which would release them from the denigration and discrimination they were exposed to at home.

The members of the dominant caste deeply resented the political constellation which had come about after Independence. From the height of their privileged position the Anavils gave vent to a deep aversion to democracy, a system in which they felt outvoted by an illiterate, irresponsible and inert mass. Suffrage, the right to vote, should have been reserved for those who were qualified to judge because of their purity, parentage and education, they felt. In this biased view, the inferiority of the lower ranks remained an article of faith. Already in 1971, the shift towards Hindu fundamentalism was noticeable at the top of the ritual hierarchy. In my second round of fieldwork, this trend had definitely become more prominent. I found Anavils now to be dedicated believers of this gospel, blaming Congress politicians for the way they pampered their vote-banks of lower castes and classes. The policy of reservation had, in their view, further spoilt these indolent and ignorant people who were immanently unfit to help themselves and did not deserve to be helped by others. In order to widen its narrow caste base, the Bharatiya Janata Party (BJP) had managed to attract segments of the upwardly mobile backward castes (Other Backward Classes or OBCs) – for example, the Kolis in Gandevigam – to join their cause as proper Hindus.

Initially, this broadening of the BJP's electoral strategy was less successful in the case of Scheduled Tribes such as the Halpatis, which had not yet distanced themselves to the same extent from their original identity and were, in their state of sustained landlessness, denigrated and despised. This landless community had from the very beginning sided with the Congress party and became even more motivated to do so when their employers turned to oppose this ruling plank of politics and governance. But this mood of defiance ebbed away when Halpatis, stuck at the bottom rung of the tribal communities, derived little advantage from the programmes of affirmative action. Annoyed with the absence of progress so often promised, their political loyalty to the Congress waned. With it, their earlier interest in politics at large declined, and from muted consent, evaporated into indifference.

How do we label this eclipse? I would argue that this avoidance of taking sides should not be regarded as opting out in surrender to the powers-that-be. Contrary to received wisdom, my conclusion was that the social mobilization I observed had no basis in primordial sentiments entrenched in either a forlorn tribal identity or an emerging casteist platform. The widening horizon inherent to the extension of scale in social relationships drained away the existential boundaries in which they were straitjacketed. The changed shape of dispossession in the capitalist era in which I found them stuck in the course of my fieldwork so far had created a proletarian consciousness. No doubt, as a class in itself and not for itself. Not yet, since preconditional to that transition was the ability to speak freely, to engage in collective action, and to get organized in economic associations and political parties. The space to do all of that had remained absent due to the lack of local-level democracy blocked by the unwillingness of India's post-colonial politics and governance to grant it.

CHAPTER FIVE

A Profile of the Rural Proletariat

POSING THE AGRARIAN QUESTION IN POST-COLONIAL INDIA

The debate waged during the 1960s–70s on the nature of capitalism in the predominantly rural economy of India coincided with the period of my research in south Gujarat. The contrasting opinions expressed were often inspired by preconceived notions on how to comprehend the inroads capitalism made among the peasant masses, which were highly differentiated along caste and class lines. These views had an implicit bias because the argumentation regarding the ongoing transition was based on the shift which had materialized in Europe one hundred years earlier, in the restructuring of an agrarian-rural way of life. While contributing to the deliberations on the shape and direction of India's political economy in the post-colonial era, Daniel Thorner firmly rejected the idea of a straightforward repeat of the European path of change written up as a copycat turnaround from feudalism to capitalism. Following up on his denial that India's past could be labelled as resembling Europe's feudal middle ages, he pointed out the missing economic regime held to be preconditional to a capitalist mode of production. The tours he made around the landscape inhabited by the peasantry induced him to assume that the anticipated course of capitalist development was blocked by a built-in depressor. Thorner termed this stultifying obstacle a 'complex of legal, economic and social relations uniquely typical of the Indian countryside' (D. Thorner 1976, p. 16). He clarified its meaning on the basis of observations which had struck him and which he had noted down in his travelogue of rural tours.

Thorner's explanatory notes described a relationship of domination versus subordination which split up the peasantry into a three-tier class composition that ran parallel with the caste hierarchy – major landowners (*maliks*) at the top, self-producing smallholders (*kisans*) in the middle and the landless (*mazdur*) as the largest contingent at the bottom. Relevant for the problematic which I confronted and investigated in my anthropological fieldwork in south Gujarat was the appraisal Thorner made of the plight of landless labour. According to him, labour bondage which had been widely prevalent did not exist any more. This unambiguous supposition was put forward already in his early analysis of the character of the peasant economy at the dawn of India's Independence, which he published jointly with his wife Alice.

> There may be a few pockets or enclaves of India where bond[ed] labour persists, but these are small. By and large the force of hired labourers in Indian agriculture is now made up of free men. One could not say this a generation ago. If we go back to the turn of the century, it is probable that the bulk of the agricultural labourers were unfree men, men who were in debt bondage or some other form of servitude. No one to my knowledge has yet traced the transition in Indian agriculture from a force of hired labourers who predominantly were unfree men (and women) who today are free. This is a change of immense significance, and is likely to have wide ramifications and repercussions in the next few decades. (A. Thorner and D. Thorner 1962, p. 8)

In his subsequent writings, Thorner elaborated on the lack of capitalist acumen among the dominating caste-class of landowners who, instead of attempting to increase production and productivity, indulged in conspicuous leisure. Without engaging themselves actively in the management of their considerable landholdings, they were interested in agriculture only to the extent of earning the highest possible income from it. Their efforts to distance themselves from becoming caught up in the demeaning business of tilling the land were driven by the adoption of a lifestyle which allowed them to disengage from the bothersome and physical side of cultivation. The rentier form of landlordism he observed during his field trips would, according to Thorner, delay if not default the transition to farm management capitalism, which the country needed to boost growth and development.

With regard to Thorner's analysis of the agrarian question in India, my different perception concerns the assumed absence of agrarian capitalism in his initial writings on the issue. The peasant elite at the apex of the rural economy was since long accustomed to avoid manual work – more specifically, to refrain from tilling the land and other menial toils. However, a preference for conspicuous leisure does not necessarily signify the absence of behavioural traits conducive to the emergence of capitalism. My fieldwork findings in south Gujarat showed how a broad spectrum of landowners had, in due course, transformed themselves into capitalist farmers without surrendering a lifestyle in which they substituted their own labour power by subjugating a tribal community, deprived from agrarian property, in bondage. The blinding poverty at the dominated end of the spectrum of inequality that Thorner observed in his travels through the subcontinent persisted because the ruling caste-class in local settings refused to provide the land-poor and the landless with adequate income for their basic existence. Exposed to naked exploitation, the large masses of the workforce at the bottom of the pile remained deprived of the minimal humane treatment required to safeguard their livelihood and protect them against the adversities that put their social reproduction at risk.

Another set of local-level visits of field trips several years later led Thorner to reconsider his earlier conclusion about the absence of agrarian capitalism. Having first noted its incubation at a modest level and with a new set of stakeholders, often from non-agrarian origin, he then reported with more adamance its appearance on an all-India scale (Thorner 1980, pp. 224–53). If indeed the depressor had been lifted, what did it mean for the largest segment of the working class in the country, that of agricultural labour? A mixed bag, was his short answer. To start with, the Congress party, which had ruled the roost in the early decades of Independence, had dismally failed to act upon its socialist rhetoric. Practically nowhere in the country was any land redistributed to the landless tillers of the soil, although this had been a promised reform announced with much fanfare during the struggle for national freedom. The policy of privileging the already privileged inevitably led to staggering inequality. This did not prevent Thorner from noting the other side of the coin, the surge of rising expectations:

> I do not mean that the poor are getting absolutely poorer. I would be the last to deny, or try to minimize, the hardships at the bottom of one-third of the rural population – India's millions of small cultivators and rural labourers who do not earn enough to eat regularly three square meals a day. My contention, nonetheless, is that even they have been affected by the prosperity of their neighbours, and by the changed conditions of life generally since 1947. Their actual level of living may still be miserable, but the level to which they aspire has risen. (D. Thorner 1980, p. 233)

As against the setback of remaining dispossessed from agrarian property, the class of landless peasants which had been subjected to servitude had gained the right to cast their vote. Suffrage, the organizing maxim of political democracy laid down in the Constitution, would be the crucial weapon to gain social leverage and increase their bargaining strength vis-à-vis capitalist employers. In the offing were also more opportunities for non-agricultural work in construction, road-building and diversification of occupational activity, which would ease the pressure on the exceedingly low wage rate in the primary sector of the economy. And finally, the spread of education would put paid to the culture of ignorance which stifled the voices of the down-and-out in disenfranchised marginality.

Important in Thorner's reconsideration of the turning tide of agrarian policies was the role ascribed by him to the state. He minced no words when he summed up the course adopted as pro-capitalist in a mandate which remained covered up behind a façade of socialist jargon. The improbability of squaring such a practice of governance with the declared intent to promote well-being for all in an emancipatory trend away from a heritage of ingrained inequality induced him to critically review the prospects for future development. This ultimately led him to stress the bewildering complexity of the situation. It was actually an open-ended conclusion which stemmed from the double bind in which Thorner had landed himself. His stocktaking of the nature of the agrarian question in India did not differ from the conventional wisdom that claimed bondage and capitalism to be incompatible. He backed up this contention by suggesting that 'to speak of capitalism in the nineteenth century, when the agricultural labourers were largely unfree, may be quite misleading' (A. Thorner and D. Thorner 1962, pp. 11–12). Similarly, his assertion later that 'in every major region of India today there is a boom in capitalist agriculture' (D. Thorner 1980, p. 238), probably followed on his reiterated conclusion that apart from a few pockets, landless servitude no longer existed (ibid., p. 246). The conclusion reached boiled down to the argument that bondage and capitalism cannot coexist, but instead, tend to exclude each other.

My dissenting view of the trajectory investigated relates to the question of how to evaluate the character of India's political economy in both the past and the present. In my early research, I have attested to the intrusion of capitalism into the agrarian economy during the second half of the nineteenth century in (as well as beyond) south Gujarat without, at that stage, releasing labour from attachment. Capitalism had come to India as an incarnation of late-colonial dirigisme that culminated in sustained subjection of the land-poor and landless peasantry. The depressor which Thorner held accountable for the long-lasting lack of capitalism was actually the gestalt in which capitalism began to manifest itself in the peasant landscape of late-colonial India. The system of bondage as it used to be practised slowly evaporated in a stretched-out trend of mutual detachment during the first half of the twentieth century. The substantial class dispossessed from agrarian property was now exposed to a process of commodification, which meant that agricultural labour remained at the behest of employers who either permanently or casually hired their labour power in an increasingly exploitative relationship. However, the further advance of capitalism in the post-colonial era also did not result in an agrarian proletariat that had become doubly free in the classical Marxist sense – free from means of production as well as free to sell its labour power at the best possible price in the labour market. Why this awaited outcome did not materialize, and how the equation between capital and labour resulted in a spiralling of accumulation versus immiseration at polar ends, will be dealt with in the next chapter.

LABOUR MADE MOBILE

I went back to south Gujarat every year for not less than three to four months between 1977 and 1982, to monitor the changes going on in the rural economy. My later round of fieldwork was conducted in Surat district and mainly concentrated on Bardoli *vibagh*, the fertile area around the urban headquarters of the subdistrict bearing the same name. There were several reasons why I decided to shift my research to this district. In the first place, the more general boost in the capitalist nature of the agricultural economy was clearly demonstrated in this central plain of south Gujarat. The advent of canal irrigation towards the end of the 1950s, made possible by the construction of a dam upstream in the Tapti river, and rural electrification which allowed for digging borewells gave rise to a more intensive cultivation cycle throughout the year. Sugarcane became the new cash crop and this commodity drove out most other produce. Having its origin in the region I selected for my local-level investigations, its tillage as a money-spinning monoculture propelled a different form of farm management which had major repercussions for labour relations.

A second reason for my focus on the vicinity of Bardoli was the presence in most villages of Kanbi Patidars as a dominant caste-cum-class of landowners. As already discussed, their ascendancy from the low to the middle rung of the peasantry dated back to the end of the nineteenth century, when they became economically better off from growing cotton as an early cash crop. The profits earned enabled them to adopt a lifestyle that reshaped their improved economic standing by moving up in the caste-class ranking – ritually by endorsing in their behaviour belief practices prescribed by Hinduism, and materially by replacing their own labour power and that of their wives and children by engaging farm servants and all members of their household. The Anavil brahmins may have followed a similar route to upward mobility but in a more remote and unrecorded past, and were therefore much longer anchored in a pre-capitalist mode of peasant production and existence. The seigneurial code of conduct I discussed in their handling of labour bondage in that setting stood in marked contrast to the harsh treatment which the Kanbis meted out to landless labour in the late-colonial era. The sources to which I referred portrayed an exploitative relationship not at all diluted by the features of patronage which were reported to still linger on in the code of conduct of Anavil masters when the process of commercialization and monetization was making headway. Both Anavils and Kanbis engaged *halis* from the same tribal community. In the subdistricts of the central plain, Halpatis comprised not less than one-third of the population, even adding up to half the inhabitants in many villages. Finding out how this landless caste-class of agricultural labour fared in the upscaled and upgraded mode of capitalist production which had taken shape in the booming agro-industry of Surat district was a major incentive for locating another round of fieldwork in its rural landscape.

Labour mobility was the main expression of the state of flux in which I found the terrain to which I had come. The spatial fixity of the peasantry in the past has been much overstated in an imagery of a bounded village community which disregarded the existence of economic, social and political networks reaching out in a much wider arena of interaction. This does not deny, however, that the opening up of the countryside by the middle of the twentieth century was much facilitated by large-scale infrastructural extension of road construction and motorized transport which shortened the time required for bridging distances and lowered the costs of doing so. Naturally, the economic acceleration going on had a major impact on the magnitude and nature of employment and livelihood. Finding out how the regional labour market reacted to the rural transformation in progress would be the common formula for the collection of data required. What I actually put on record was how, in the remoulded mode of production, labour was either exploited to the hilt, or had become displaced and bypassed from contributing to capital accumulation within and outside the agricultural economy. Squeezed from their labour power at excessively low pay were the labour migrants moving into the central plain from outside, while the local landless were ousted from the employment niches they used to occupy. My investigations focused on the triangular relationship between migrants, the local landless and dominant landowners who were the beneficiaries of the upswing in agrarian capitalism.

In my estimate – given that official statistics on circular mobility were either lacking or highly unreliable – at the peak of the annual cycle, labour moving into the main hub of the central plain from outside accounted for about 30 to 40 per cent of the total workforce. This multitude consisted of two separate streams, of which the first came from the area without irrigation bordering the eastern side of the central plain. These were small and marginal farmers driven out in successive sorties lasting a couple of weeks each, to earn cash wages which they needed to bolster their depleting livelihood at home. Trekking around in small groups, they carried their own foodstuff, made night halts wherever and for as long as they found work, and went back when they had exhausted the rations they had brought along. The second stream, of an even larger size, was the tightly organized mobilization of labour by the main agro-industry for harvesting and transporting sugarcane cultivated on the land owned by the farmers to the mill of the cooperative society they had joined. They added up to about 75,000 workers at the time of my fieldwork, recruited by jobbers who, acting as agents for the mill management, contracted *koytas*, work teams of two to three members. Less than half came from the same catchment area as the first stream of migrants, while the larger part was inducted from the Khandesh region of neighbouring Maharashtra and Madhya Pradesh. The jobber was also the gang boss for the duration of the campaign, which took about four to six months. Having handed out advance payment, he also settled the wage bill with his gang at the end of the season. Before completing the monograph which attested to the main gist of my findings (Breman 1985b), I wrote up this major operation which big agribusiness instigated and managed from beginning to end in a separate and earlier published essay (Breman 1978). It turned out to be the stepping stone for my conceptualization of neo-bondage.

The Dissolution of *Hali Pratha* in Bardoli *Vibagh*

The invasion of a huge army of labour migrants coming in and going away again with the tide of the seasons indicated a changing pattern of employment which had major repercussions for the very sizeable landless community living in the central plain and working in the fields of the main farmers. The greater intensity with which land was being cultivated with the extension of well and canal irrigation increased the scope for employment. On the other hand, the simultaneous replacement of draft animals – bullocks in particular

– by mechanized equipment (motor pumps, tractors, sprayers, electrical threshers) had reduced the need to engage farm servants for handling and taking care of them. While overall employability still showed a significant net rise, it was also clear that the more demanding cropping scheme did not require such a massive influx of labour.

To find out the impact on local labour, overwhelmingly Halpatis, I lodged myself in a village at some distance from Bardoli town, which had been surveyed by a team of agricultural economists at the beginning of the 1960s when the changed social relations of productions had not yet set in. In this locality, which I named Bardoligam in my subsequent publications, of the 255 inhabiting households in 1961–62, Halpatis comprised, with a number of 166, nearly two-thirds of all inhabitants; and of this number, 142 or 86 per cent of Halpatis obtained their living from agricultural labour. They were nearly exclusively employed by Kanbi Patidars who constituted one-third of the local population. Members of this dominant caste-class of landowners were accustomed to engaging Halpati men either permanently or casually, and made use of their wives and children for menial jobs in the house and around the courtyard. As noted in the survey findings, the landowning households refrained to the extent possible from being engaged in agrarian work. 'Working on farms is considered an "inferior activity". Women of these households, in particular, take very little interest in farming and they look upon themselves as merely managers of the farm' (Patel 1964, p. 101).

It was an oblique reference to *hali pratha* as an institution, long practised in Bardoligam as well as in other villages in the vicinity. Already in early colonial reports, Kanbis were mentioned as having settled villages and opened up land for regular tillage by attaching Dublas in bondage. Probably only a small minority which had taken the lead in what managed to become the main landowning caste of the region, they could afford the luxury of engaging farm servants while their less well-to-do caste fellows continued to work along with the landless labourers they had hired. The increasing prosperity which resulted from growing cotton as a major cash crop during the last quarter of the nineteenth century enabled most of these peasant cultivators to attach permanent labour. One chronicler pointed out that the desire to be exempted from themselves working in the fields was observed as having stimulated the acceptance of the new crop in the ranks of the middle peasantry by setting free about 3 lakhs of them from onerous toil.

> It is even asserted by careful observers that the keenness of cultivators to grow cotton is due not only to the fact that they can usually make good profits from

it, but also to the fact that it is an easy crop to grow and leaves them plenty of leisure. (Keatinge 1921, pp. 145–46)

This observation was shared by Shukla, who also concluded on the basis of his village research in the early 1930s that the extension of cotton cultivation had enabled farmers to maintain more and more *halis* (Shukla 1937, p. 124). It was this information that led me, already at that stage of my fieldwork, to argue that the relation between the emergence of agrarian capitalism and the disappearance of unfree labour might not be so self-evident and straightforward as commonly assumed (Breman 1985b, pp. 131–32). The upward mobility of Kanbis aiming for Patidar status coincided with the penetration of capitalism. However, they did not aspire to the kind of gentrified and ostentatious lifestyle which the Anavil brahmins wanted to achieve by surrounding themselves with a retinue of clients. The value Kanbis extracted from labour was, from the beginning of the upswing in capitalism, meant to increase their cash incomes and implied the avoidance of expenditure not conducive to that over-riding priority. When and where market production was maximally advanced and nurtured, the benevolent care with which the master was supposed to have treated his *halis* in the past, an affection which colonial accounts had exaggerated, gave way to a relationship marked by distrust and animosity on both sides.

A striking example of this process of commodification was reported during the Bardoli *satyagraha* launched by the Kanbi Patidars in 1928, to protest against the higher land tax imposed by the colonial authorities. Having been asked to supply information on the cost of agriculture, the farming lobby submitted calculations which included not only the wages of hired labour – much higher than were actually paid – but also interest on the *halis'* debt, as well as an amount for depreciation of his wear and tear during lifelong maintenance (Broomfield and Maxwell 1929, p. 57). Not surprisingly, the same report made mention of the growing resistance of agricultural labour against their naked exploitation. Bardoligam was listed as one of the villages where the Halpatis went on strike. Reacting sharply to the 'untrustworthiness' of the landless community, their employers wanted to see labourers prosecuted and punished for not working off the debt they owed. The government did not give in to this adamant pressure to legalize unfree labour formally, but neither did it end the agrarian bondage that continued to be widely practised in south Gujarat. The agrarian trade union which sprang up in the 1930s found fertile ground in the restiveness, which marked the turning of the tide in the power balance between big farmers and landless labour.

This movement initially remained mainly focused on the tribal peasantry's claim to regain land rights lost through usurious sharecropping and tenancy contracts. But Indulal Yagnik and Dinkar Mehta who had dissented from the Gandhian fold insisted that the community, which had been deprived already in the remote past of agrarian property, would be similarly mobilized in the struggle that challenged the prevailing regime of landlordism. In chapter 2, I have highlighted how the Congress stalwarts, backed by Gandhian 'constructive workers' who had established *ashrams* in and around Bardoli, tried to prevent the agitation of the tribal communities from spreading. Through coordinated action, they effectively blocked the call to redeem the landless underclass from bondage. In the early 1940s, this episode of a swelling agitation of agricultural labour ended when the Congress government of Bombay state outlawed the *kisan sabha* and got its leadership arrested.

Converting the Adivasi communities to the tenets of Hinduism was, for the Gandhian disciples, a higher priority than strengthening their bargaining power against exploitation. Bardoli became the headquarters of the Halpati Seva Sangh. This was an association set up to promote their integration in the lower ranks of the caste hierarchy. The Halpatis were instructed to abstain from confronting their high-caste masters in a code of conduct increasingly rooted in proletarianized consciousness. Jugatram Dave, Mahatma Gandhi's acknowledged representative in south Gujarat, desisted from fighting against the exploitation and derogation to which Halpatis were exposed, and claimed instead that that their bondage continued because the landless underclass showed itself reluctant to end it. 'As a woman without having married a husband has no prestige in the society, similarly a Halpati without a *dhaniyamo* [landlord] as his master has no prestige in his community' (Dave 1946, p. 18; my translation).

The missionaries of pretended emancipation were actually subscribing to an ingrained ideology of social inequality which affirmed the superiority of the dominating caste-class and the inferiority of the subjugated contingent. They failed to register that the time for subaltern compliance in expected docility had run out. Refusal to do so was matched by a growing resentment among the main landowners to depend on a workforce unwilling to be depleted of basic livelihood provisions that were a precondition to their social reproduction.

The mutual distancing of farmers and labourers from their former relationship which I had observed in my preceding round of fieldwork in Chikhligam and Gandevigam was confirmed, and even more forcefully so, by the findings I derived from the changed fabric of the agricultural economy in Bardoli *vibagh*. Likewise, as in my earlier sites of investigation in Valsad district, the team of agricultural economists that surveyed Bardoligam in the early 1960s reported that the Halpatis had been collectively shifted away from their employer's land and household to a hutment colony on the outskirts of the village. The farm servants among them moreover were no longer permitted by their master to cultivate a small plot for their own food requirements, and were also deprived of other allowances in kind that were crucial to their upkeep. Whatever congeniality might have formerly existed had drained away, to be replaced by a mood of class hatred.

The casualization of employment had progressed greatly at the time of my stay in Bardoligam one-and-half decades after my first round of fieldwork. The younger age-set in particular did not believe in the dubious advantages offered by a more steady and regular relationship, and were inclined to weigh the accompanying setbacks of greater subordination more heavily. At best, one-fifth to a quarter of the large majority of Halpati males at work as agricultural labourers were still engaged as farm servants, while not less than three-quarters of them were hired, if and when their labour power was at all required, as daily-wage earners. Moreover, being engaged as a *kaim majoor* (worker in permanent service) was no longer of lifetime duration but a much looser arrangement that could be discontinued on the initiative of either labourer or farmer. While the Halpati worker did not want to be constrained in bondage, the Kanbi landowner had become wary of investing in the maintenance cost of his farmhand by advancing 'loans' to pay for lifetime events or to cope with adversities such as illness or debilitating health. Neither could expenditure of such livelihood eventualities be met from the earnings received.

Weber's conclusion that agrarian capitalism had depressed the standard of living of the landless workforce in East Germany (Weber 1892, pp. 790–92) was applicable to Bardoli *vibagh* as well. In Gujarat, the Minimum Wage Act was introduced as late as 1966 and was enacted only in 1972. It set the minimum wage at the lowest rate possible, restricted to the most basic daily needs. The hike to Rs 5.50 per day in 1976 was meant to meet the cost of inflation but the going remuneration remained stuck at Rs 3 or below two-thirds of the pay required for sheer survival. While debt held the *hali*s locked up in attachment, the latter-day farm servants complained about having forfeited their creditworthiness. Roughly one-quarter of the women from the landless caste were employed as maid servants in the main landowning households for cleaning out the byre, washing clothes, fetching water, sweeping the house, cleaning the eating utensils and other menial chores from which the Kanbi Patidar women exempted themselves. The earlier bond that cemented landless households to landowning ones in a beck-and-call relationship had broken down. Halpati women working as *vasiduvali* (housemaids) were no longer employed as a matter of course by the same boss for whom their husbands used to work. When the maid servant felt slighted by her mistress, she did not hesitate to offer her services to another household. The high turnover indicated that short-term and contractual relationships predominated, reflecting the pronounced capitalist nature of the agrarian economy.

In his analysis of the changing agrarian relationship in East Germany, Weber pointed out how the intrusion of capitalism had destroyed the common bond of interest which tied the rural labourer to his landlord when the latter was not yet a commercially minded entrepreneur. The employer was held accountable for the maintenance of his workforce, though not as a commodity paid for in cash. With the withdrawal of subsistence allowance and the substitution of payment in kind for a money wage, their community of interest collapsed.

> The labourer then becomes a proletarian and for the sake of his freedom he needs a money wage. . . . They [the labourers] sacrifice their accustomed conditions [secured livelihood in bondage] in their aspiration for emancipation; their apathy is shattered. The oft-lamented 'mobilisation' of the rural labourer at the same time sets in motion the beginning of class struggle. (Weber, as quoted in Tribe 1979, pp. 184–88)

However, the class war I found raging in Bardoligam was one in which the farmers had the upper hand. The Kanbi Patidars cowed down the labour they required by fixing the wage for their ready availability at an abominably low rate. When I questioned their niggardly behaviour, they reacted sharply with the argument that the deplorable work morality of the Halpatis was not worth even the three rupees they were paid. '*Kaam chor, dam chor*', they said, shrugging their shoulders: 'they cheat us in work, we rob them of money.' The Halpatis were thoroughly proletarianized but shorn of the bargaining power needed to raise the cost of their hire. Nevertheless, the ire and disdain the landowners gave vent to derived to a large extent from the loss of something they had always taken for granted – total control over labour. The landless staunchly refused in their commodified gestalt to internalize the stigma of inferiority in which they had been entrapped by their employers in the past. Although helpless against being exploited, they withstood the treatment of denigration and discrimination as much as possible by avoiding any interaction with their bosses other than work-related. Wrestling free from the subservience they had been forced to comply with also signalled rejection of the claim to superiority of the dominant caste-class. It was an assertion kept under wraps, but one that the Kanbi Patidars were aware of and which annoyed them immensely.

The distancing went on from both sides and resulted in a marked separation of residential domicile. In their drive to economize on labour cost, the farmers also found ways and means to avoid daily confrontation of workers unwilling to exert themselves in strenuous acquiescence. Distracting themselves from this face-to-face contact, they took to contracting out field operations to middlemen who brought along their own work gangs. Conversely, the recruited labourers felt freed from the pressures inflicted by a bullying boss who always found reason for complaints about the quantity and quality of the tasks performed. Not required to live any more in the shadow of the Kanbi Patidars, the Halpatis congregated in a neighbourhood inhabited only by members of their own community. This self-built hutment colony stretched along a country road at the periphery of Bardoligam and remained deprived of the amenities – electricity and tap water – that lent comfort to the lives of the Kanbi Patidars residing in opulent mansions on both sides of the main and paved street in the village centre.

The slumlike character of the quarters of the landless expressed the immense poverty of its inhabitants. It was a consequence of lack of regular work aggravated by too low a wage. The household inventory summed up in the 1961–62 survey earlier mentioned showed no more than a few low-value assets, and in that year of enquiry, more possessions were lost than gained. With 86 per cent of all expenditure incurred on food purchase, the degree of malnourishment, for which this study provided detailed information, was alarmingly high (Patel 1964, p. 113). During my stay in Bardoligam in 1977–78, the local Halpati workforce remained hugely underemployed throughout the agrarian cycle due to their displacement by outside labour. They had become proletarianized but in a pauperized condition.

THE SWITCH THAT FAILED TO MATERIALIZE

In the concluding part of his study of the agrarian question in East Germany at the end of the nineteenth century, Weber characterized the accelerating influx into Prussia of seasonal migrants from Poland as a weapon in the class war which was directed against the growing proletarian consciousness of the local workers. Redeeming themselves from the lord of the manor to which they were attached, the agrarian workforce had been granted by Bismarck's government the right to association with which to bargain in collective action for a better deal. Weber showed himself quite pessimistic about its effectiveness. According to him, the sizeable agrarian workforce did not have the same interests, fell apart in disunity and would remain unable to build a joint front. The rural labour question, he argued, boiled down to the problem whether upward mobility for this landless contingent would ever result in escape from dependency and be able to attain the self-reliant existence aimed at (Weber 1892, p. 798). Missing in his doubtful assessment, however, was the transformation from an agrarian-rural to an industrial-urban economy and society in Germany which had already reached an advanced stage towards the end of the nineteenth century. The subordinated workforce on which the Junker estates depended found escape from remaining stuck in agriculture and rural distress. Workers left the countryside in increasing numbers to settle down in towns or cities, where they found jobs in industries or other sectors of the developing economy. The terms of employment were better than those they had left behind, in the first place because labour was in short supply in the rapid expansion of urban trade and business, and in the second place because the new way of life of the swelling working class – despite Weber's scepticism – successfully managed to get organized and fight for higher wages and secondary benefits. Assembled in proletarian assertion, economically in trade unions and politically in party formations, a modest degree of emancipation changed the balance between labour and capital. Of pivotal significance for the outcome of the tussle that arose was the interference of the Bismarckian state in solving the social question which had erupted. Granting the right to associate had not been the only ordinance which Germany's emerging nation-state issued to defuse the class war from taking a violent turn. The government acted, or pretended to do so, as an 'honest broker' between both stakeholders set on a confrontational course with each other. The labour legislation introduced included a spate of social policies – banning child labour in industry as early as 1839, health insurance, old age pensions and coverage against the risk of unemployment – to bridge the spiralling gap between wealth and poverty which threatened to twist the nation out of its designed shape of integrated unity.

I have referred to Weber's historical treatise repeatedly because of its relevance for taking stock of the social question that I encountered in south Gujarat in the course of my fieldwork three-quarters of a century later on. My appraisal endorsed the correctness of his conclusion to regard the mobility of labour as an expression of an ongoing class war, but this was where the similarity ended. To begin with, and of crucial significance, the setting I found in Bardoli *vibagh* during the late 1970s was markedly different from that in East Germany in the early 1890s. In my research area, the further intrusion of agrarian capitalism did not lead to a flight of the landless underclass away from the agricultural economy. This was because the transformation that had changed the landscape of labour in Europe failed to materialize here. The massive influx of seasonal migrants on which I focused did not drive out the local stock of agricultural labourers they replaced. A ferocious mixture of relentless exploitation and underemployment meant that in their proletarianized identity they fell victim to pauperism.

In 1961–62, merely 14 per cent of the Halpati workforce in Bardoligam had partially or wholly managed to find work away from agriculture, and this contingent increased to at best between one-fifth to one-quarter of them during my stay in this village in 1977–78. While the urban economy in particular had become to a certain extent diversified and although the nearby towns offered a variety of job opportunities, Halpatis in the rural hinterland seldom qualified for these newly opened rungs of upward mobility. They were held back from competing in many ways: lack of doing anything else had been their habitual way of life hampered by illiteracy and shorn of *lagvag*, the imperative need to claim recommendation from somewhere higher up to be accepted for employment that was regular and secure. Only about one-fifth of the Halpatis in Bardoligam had managed to filter through into the menial, unskilled and low-paid occupations at the lower end of what had become classified meanwhile as the informal sector of the non-agrarian economy. Acquiring skills for off-farm employment took place on the job but was not cost-free. Rather than receiving an apprentice allowance, candidates had to pay a hefty price for the training they received.

It was next to impossible for a Halpati household to free a member of working age from contributing to the common budget of the household. Virtually everyone in proper control of their hands and feet – from children who were eight or ten years old to more or less able-bodied adolescents – had to at least provide the labour power required for their own upkeep. In an average household of agricultural workers, about three out of a little more than five members were assumed to participate in the waged labour process. This law of minimal survival dated back to the days of *hali pratha* (Hali Labour Enquiry Report 1950, p. 28), but was equally vigorously upheld after its demise. Retirement was an unknown blessing for the elderly. Self-provisioning by hook or by crook forced them to carry on irrespective of their drained stamina to do so. Decrepit and with loosened ties of kinship, they failed to maintain themselves at the level of bare subsistence. On the opposite side of life's arduous cycle, the need to contribute to the collective but deficit income highlighted why children soon reached working age rather than going to school. Progress was absent in the milieu of the landless in this respect as well. Bardoligam's primary school, established in 1867, had for more than a century remained a higher-caste enclave of learning to read and write. In the early 1960s, only 7 per cent of its pupils were Halpatis (Patel 1964, pp. 76, 80). Fifteen years later, this proportion had not increased by much. Even if these boys and girls went to school at all, they dropped out after the first few classes to join their parents at work. It meant that the new generation would stay put in occupations where those they replaced had remained stranded.

In the course of my investigations across the region at large, I happened to come across rare instances of Halpatis who had somehow succeeded in accessing a steady job with a fixed income and labour protection in the public sector: as a guard on a railway crossing, a watchman or peon in a government agency, a field labourer in a state-run model farm, and the like. In the habitat of the landless, they were beacons of hope for betterment, but, at the same time, stoked bitterness for having missed on such accidental strokes of luck. Moreover, members of this tribal caste disappeared altogether from the horizon of progress as soon as the work got slightly more skilled or better paid. Next, there were the semi-skilled and self-employed craftsmen at the lower end of the caste ranking who set up shop seeking clientele, of whom little was expected by way of technical proficiency but who were also paid less for work done: tailors, bricklayers, painters-cum-plasterers, tailors, etc. Their earnings were higher than that of agricultural labourers but they were dependent on assignments which were obtained irregularly. The one exception was the brewers of country liquor. Distilling (and drinking) alcohol was prohibited but very profitable with a range of customers which stretched from the landless to landowners of the dominant caste-class. Payment of a regular bribe would allow them to operate illicitly but once in a while their business-cum-stock was raided by the police for having stepped beyond the fold of legality. Income-wise, they stood at the top of the landless section, but their trade did not set them apart in terms of a contrasting lifestyle.

Finally, a contingent endeavoured to find non-agrarian self-employment beyond the village in peripatetic ambulance on bicycles or pushing a cart on foot in the vicinity or along the roadside in the service and transport sector of the economy: as a vendor of cheap commodities, tinker, scrap collector, railway station porter, bicycle repairer, tea-stall boy, shop assistant, garage hand, or, the best paid of all, a lorry or tractor driver. In principle, they were so engaged the year round, although in these occupations too, the rainy months were difficult to live through. Even though their economic condition was far from satisfactory, they at least escaped the demeaning existence of agricultural labourers. This did not apply to the large majority of the landless who continued to toil on the fields, but without shying away from other employment they accessed off and on, like joining a gang engaged in roadwork, digging wells, riding on lorries as loaders–unloaders. All said and done, off-farm employment was an imbricate and untidy amalgamation of various sources of income missing from or inadequately recorded in occupational surveys. Added up, they reflected the growing diversity of the rural economy, expressing a trend that gradually would reshape what had been an agrarian workforce into a rural proletariat of occupational multiplicity. Congregated in hutment colonies on the village outskirts and sharing their tribal caste identity, they did not build up a joint front capable of articulating their class-based interest. There was much they had in common: an improvident habitat lacking in basic amenities and facilities in confirmation of an existence which was considered demeaning; income that was too low and irregular to provide an acceptable livelihood; inability to read and write; and no skills other than that gained by experience. The households which inhabited this milieu of deficiency and scarcity were incapacitated from teaming up and breaking out of their marginality in collective action. They fell apart in fragments in their attempts to sell the only surplus value they had, labour power, in a buyer's market which drove down both the demand as well as the price for their instant availability to the lowest possible level.

Why did this landless proletariat, displaced from increased employability by a tidal wave of circular migrants, not emulate these intruders and move out from Bardoli *vibagh* to find better employment than at home? Urban growth poles such as Navsari and Surat along the Mumbai–Ahmedabad railway line and highway were thriving and easily accessible. Surat in particular was a booming city nearly doubling its population every decade. A multitude of settlers and transients came from all over the country to join its thoroughly informalized economy. On arrival they were met by kinsmen or caste-mates from their places of origin who arranged for their board and lodging, and introduced newcomers to the jobs found for them in one of the many workshops. Without a bridgehead at their destination site, labour migration was a forlorn option when it meant moving to unfamiliar territory. It was this lack of connectivity which prevented the Halpatis from giving up their paltry residence in the countryside. They had become habituated to roam around for daily work in the immediate vicinity of their village, joining labour gangs recruited by a jobber to work away from home for shorter or longer spells of absence, but had neither the contacts nor the means required to settle down in towns or cities.

A survey of members of the main tribal caste living in Surat city reported that many of them had become citizens of the municipality when their village was absorbed within its spreading borders (K.I. Desai 1979). These Halpatis had not benefited much from their incorporation into the urban economy. A quarter of the households covered by the survey had to maintain themselves on less than a rupee a day per head. Child labour was an absolute necessity to add to the income of this primary unit of cohabitation, which explained why only one-fifth of the children attended school. For their kinsmen and caste-mates in the hinterland, to rely on this shallow network for mediation to the urban labour market was useless. But if settling down in the city was out of reach for the landless underclass, would commuting from the village not offer a better option? Bridging the distance and daily pay for the fare by bus or train might reduce the attraction but was still less of a problem than finding the mediation required for access to a somewhat steady niche of work. While in Bardoligam not a single Halpati had been on this route of escape, in an adjacent village I came across a few such cases though not very successful so far. These ventures into the urban landscape of informality had resulted in a job of sorts but at a wage level only somewhat higher from what they got on a regular workday in the village. Adding the expense on travel and additional cost of commuting, it meant that persevering in this effort was not attractive. It denied the conventional assumption that availability of non-agrarian employment would ultimately raise the wage level in the agrarian economy. The other way around, implying that the sweat of agricultural labour kept wages stagnating at low levels in all realms of informalized employment, seemed closer to the mark.

THE STATE AND RURAL LABOUR

The changing mode of agrarian capitalism had been pushed through by a dominant caste-class of farmers. The footloose workers pouring into the villages of south Gujarat ousted the indigenous stock of landless labour from the work they had always performed. Their expulsion formed part of a wider marginalization following the disintegration of the former dependency institutionalized in *hali pratha*. Mutual antagonism, initiated aggressively from above and answered defensively from below, expressed a polarization which discharged itself in social tension and conflict. The art of domination was premeditated and relied on the ability of the main landowners to close ranks and unite on a shared platform. The build-up to this began with the construction of a common social identity.

The Patidar Yuvak Mandal was set up in 1908 and its widely circulated periodical, *Patidar Hitechhu*, advocated a uniform and sanskritized style of conduct to adhere to in family life and social interaction within the fabricated community. Advancement of education was an important priority in the agenda of self-improvement to gain recognition of their collective elevation to the aspired twice-born status in the ritual hierarchy. Having succeeded to establish themselves as the chief landowning class, they played a leading role in the process of economic transformation. Their elevated ranking extended to political power, which was made manifest in the no-tax campaign launched from Bardoli in 1928. The *satyagraha* had been a training school on how to defy interference from the centre of the state at loggerheads with the interests of the dominant caste-class. Resistance from these quarters blew up once more in 1973. The Khedut Samaj, a Patidar-controlled union of the better-off peasantry, agitated successfully when the government wanted to push through a new round of land reforms aimed at a lower ceiling for agrarian holdings. The Patidar lobby perceived Indira Gandhi's declaration of Emergency as a threat to its regional dominance and hegemony in the political arena. This anti-government caucus was firmed up with complaints about the support the landless class received from officialdom. Immediately after the Emergency was lifted, the revived peasant union demanded the repeal of the ordinance regulating enforcement of the minimum wage law.

How did the state machinery intervene in rural labour relations? By backing the power elite at the local level, would be my short answer. Right from the beginning of Independence, agrarian policies were tuned to the interests of the main landowners, to which those of the land-poor and landless proletariat were invariably subordinated. The disappearance of the mutual involvement between the main stakeholders at the polar ends of the agrarian hierarchy did not result in public provisions intended to compensate the proletariat for the loss of their right to survival. The reluctance of state governance to upgrade labour relations in the primary sector of the economy was obvious in the faint attempts made in the late-colonial era, and again during the first quarter of national freedom, to declare labour bondage out of legal bounds. Even when enacted in 1976, the bureaucratic apparatus abstained from enforcing abolition where it was still practised.

The government also dallied when, as a consequence of the progressive conversion from payment in kind to payment in cash, wages consistently lagged behind the rising cost of living. A minimum wage for agricultural labour was only decreed when strikes and clashes between farmers and workers reached a boiling point. Even this legislation was callously abused in its wily implementation by officials from the top to the bottom of the Rural Labour Inspectorate (Breman 1985c, pp. 1043–55). Illustrative of the absence of social care arrangements was the abominable quality of public health, education and housing. Growing political awareness of escalating inequality resulted in the floating of so-called target group schemes. Also, this policy of positive discrimination did not produce the desired outcome due to inadequate efficacy and underfunding as well as adamant resistance from established quarters. Ideologically a premium was put on the Gandhian recipe for addressing 'backwardness': class collaboration, conciliation and compromise, i.e. on strategies presumably contributing to the restoration of a much praised social harmony which had never existed. It was an approach which rejected demands for social justice that reflected impatience and called for militant action.

Had the state become an instrument of the main landowning class? This was not how the Kanbi Patidars in Bardoli *vibagh* appraised public governance and its policies. The landed elite took pride in having gained hegemony by fiercely pushing their class interests and in confrontation with colonial authority. The notion of a common weal guarded and promoted by the state was alien to their power-mongering habitus. Members of the dominant peasantry took their supremacy for granted and any official attempt to remedy the lopsided balance, however weak or feigned, was perceived by them as an impediment to their freedom of action. The Patidars considered themselves as the social pivot around which the rural order revolved. Their upward mobility was founded on the backbreaking toil of Halpatis, but they had come to regard this underclass not only as ignorant and useless, but also as redundant to regular and regulated demand. A stereotyped opinion among the rural gentry was that the declaration of suffrage had given political weight to a non-deserving class of people who should remain confined and repressed by sharp discipline.

On their part, my informants in the Halpati neighbourhoods showed themselves to be familiar with the provisions on paper meant for them – such as the prescribed minimum wage – which the landowners refused to comply with. The frustration of being denied their rightful due was fed by the disdainful treatment meted out in the corridors of government to customers who hailed from the landless class. The obtuse manner of dealing with them indicated the prevailing attitude of officials towards this clientele. Conversation with them would all too soon turn into an interrogation in which condescending affability alternated with snapped orders. Small wonder that the Halpatis felt uneasy in the domain of officialdom, and when that encounter was unavoidable, they affected an air of ignorance, helplessness and submissiveness. While Patidars were rarely pursued for transgressing the law, Halpatis were fined or arrested out of all proportion. A bounty from the farmers provided the incentive for the police to adopt this form of persecution, which in the last resort could be waived when 'the culprit' was willing to settle disorderly demeanour with a cash bribe. In this biased setting, any protest against disregard of the existing labour legislation would be seen as an act of defiance. Farmers did not pay the minimum wage but could be prosecuted only when labourers dared to lodge a formal complaint. Who in his right mind would dare to risk that? Such impudence would result in boycott from further employment by all landowners.

It would be incorrect to judge state intervention in rural labour merely by pointing out the discretionary power resting with officials staffing the regional bureaucracy. Most of them were recruited from higher up the caste spectrum, and were prone to act and behave in accordance with the norms and values of their social identity. At issue more fundamentally were the institutional moorings of the state machinery. The inescapable conclusion is that the impact of agrarian capitalism as practised in Bardoli *vibagh* had tilted the balance of costs and benefits in a major way. The administrative apparatus, which was so reluctant and reticent about introducing policies that ran counter to the interests of the caste-class which ruled the roost, acted with firmness and brutality when claims were voiced from the bottom of the pile for decent employment and dignified life. Too little and too late – and even then promised but not practised – is the only way to sum up official attempts to effect a different distribution of gains and losses in the process of capitalist expansion. The changing lay of the land in the central plain of south Gujarat demonstrated that the disappearance of labour bondage had not led to a better existence for those freed from such attachment. The structural change that was a precondition for this to happen involved a strengthening of horizontal ties of solidarity among the landless. The space required for cementing togetherness in both economic and political association did not emerge. The main landowners persistently blocked such solidarity and its organization in a number of ways. The bureaucratic and political support they received from the top of the statist machinery prevented the awaited tide of emancipation from setting in.

Organization is the device by which the Patidars have converted their local control as a body of main landowners into regional dominance. They call the shots in all social, economic and political associations in Bardoli *vibagh*, which are entwined in a web of overlapping directorates, boards and councils. Their supremacy has materialized in a domain of privilege and prosperity which does not concede room for distributing the spoils of agrarian capitalism in a give-and-take compromise. The business of the dominant caste-class is gaining wealth, for which their entrepreneurial acumen stands them in good stead. But this goes combined with a social Darwinist mindset in their relations with the underclass. Greed has remained the driving force and the craving for more is not gratified with the gain of property but also expresses a lust for power. Rudely scolding a Halpati at work in the field for wayward behaviour, a farmer said in an aside to me, 'We need inferiors around us in order to be able to bully them.' David Pocock defined the same habitus in more polished terms: 'For the Patidar the idea of the good life implies immediate superiority, superiority over someone else' (Pocock 1973, p. 23). The cleavage observed between accumulation and dispossession has an all-embracing social, economic and political character. This mentality signals a heinous climate of animosity boiling over in undiluted hatred. In the arena investigated, I found a class war raging but it was a top–down clash targeting the bottom segment. The domination discerned obstructs at ground level the arrival and spread of a fabric of democracy and equality. Freedom from want and subalternity are mere slogans promised by the commanding heights in order to retain the vote bank among the masses at the bottom of the pile; such symptoms of emancipatory policies stand no chance of being implemented. They are prevented from taking shape and cannot be acclaimed as rights. In the first few decades of the twentieth century, public governance seems to have moved in the opposite direction – of an authoritarian if not fascist state regime.

CHAPTER SIX

Neo-Bondage

COOPERATIVE CAPITALISM

The rise of the Kanbi Patidars to domination was the outcome of a long trajectory. Having settled down in the central plain of south Gujarat as peasant colonists, they opened up the area for regular tillage and established themselves as the main landowners, displacing and dispossessing tribal communities who as shifting cultivators were still nomadic. Between 1840 and 1920, the arable acreage around Bardoli tripled in size producing foodgrains but increasingly also planted with cotton. Millet, the staple food in this era for the majority of the population, remained important but was gradually overtaken by cotton as the major cash crop. Urban traders mediated the contact between the producers of cotton and the market. They bought up the yield at the village level and set up seasonal enterprises for ginning and pressing the picked cotton. Although the income gained improved livelihoods for the main landowning community, the local purchasers acted as commission agents for large trading houses and factories which appropriated most of the commercial value added. When a price fall occurred at the close of the First World War, farmers joined forces in several villages and sold their harvest collectively.

The cooperative society which emerged from this initiative in 1921 was the first of its kind registered in Gujarat. Many more followed, to become federated in 1926 in a cotton-selling association. Soon after this initiative, several of these village cooperatives fused and switched to processing the raw materials themselves. Cotton pressing and ginning became very successful businesses owned and controlled by the leading class of farmers. These establishments set the trend for a model of agro-industrialization which spearheaded the further penetration of capitalism in the rural economy, not along corporate lines from above but initiated from below by producers assembled in cooperatives. The crop has by and large disappeared from the area, but the entrepreneurship remained in practice and resulted in the accumulation of wealth for its privileged stakeholders, mainly members of the dominant caste-class.

The building of the Kakrapar dam across the Tapi river, completed in 1953, made for radical changes in the cultivation calendar of the central plain. The subsequent construction of a large reservoir upstream in the tribal hinterland extended the Ukai–Kakrapar command area under perennial irrigation to 3,38,000 square kilometres. Cotton started to disappear from the fields and within the next twenty years sugarcane became the king of crops. The earlier cultivation schedule had brought about small-scale cotton gins. The introduction and spread of sugarcane required more capital-intensive farm management, and also gave rise to much larger-scale and technologically more advanced agro-industries for processing the produce. Only big landowners could afford to grow cane and buy shares in these cooperative societies.

The fieldwork I carried out focused on three sugar mills in and around Bardoli *vibagh*. The largest and oldest cooperative factory in Bardoli town started operating in 1955–56, and the other two established in 1964 went into production in 1967–68. The acreage under sugarcane in the subdistrict of Bardoli rose rapidly from 583 in 1958–59 to 15,645 in 1974–75, and this crop covered two-thirds of its irrigated area in 1977. Organized as an agro-industrial model of cooperative capitalism, sugarcane production and milling in south Gujarat became a successful formula in imitation of the same initiative about ten years earlier in the neighbouring districts of Maharashtra. Extensive contacts were made with these enterprises prior to the establishment of the first factory in Bardoli. This enterprise prepared for increasing its milling capacity from 5,000 to 7,000 tonnes a day at the time of my stay in the mid-1970s, to keep up with the extension of the cultivated acreage. The farmers who delivered cane to the factory, and only members of the cooperative were allowed to do, were paid Rs 87 per tonne in 1970–71 and double this amount in 1974–75. Indeed, growing sugarcane was very profitable and the price paid for the Rs 500 shares rose tenfold during these years.

Most of the board members of the three factories were Kanbi Patidars, and the few who were not also hailed from the main landowning castes. They were all part of the vanguard of economic power in the region. The same names turned up in the governing boards of other agro-industrial cooperatives. The Patidar chairman of the Bardoli factory was also the secretary of the Surat branch of Khedut Samaj, the farmers' lobby of vested interests in the district. The leading members of those cooperatives were affiliated to the main political parties and had a foot in the offices of the regional bureaucracy as well. The big landowners had the sugar factories to thank for their opulent prosperity, and frankly admitted that these were run by them and for them. More than contributing to their economic standing, sugarcane cultivation enabled the dominant caste-class to behave as supervisory farmers. In addition to supplying all sorts of facilities – credit, seedlings, fertilizer, pesticides and extension services – the monoculture of this crop freed the owner from remaining engaged in the cultivation cycle. Private land ownership was maintained but management of the farm was to a large extent outsourced to the factory. Right from taking decisions about when to start cultivation to the most important operation at the end, which was to cut the cane and carry it to the mill, it was the same method which the sugar factories in Maharashtra adopted. Known as the Deccan system, the management of this agro-industrial cooperative resembled the capitalist model of plantation production based on out-growers.

A decade after my first round of research I went back to monitor the scale and impact of labour migration at the same sites of investigation. The Bardoli factory had remained the largest and was now cutting 7,000 tonnes of cane daily with plans for expansion up to 12,000 tonnes. The members of this cooperative produced on average 40 tonnes per acre, and in 1985–86 were paid a bonanza price of Rs 600 per tonne. Its shares were now sold for Rs 50,000–60,000, again ten times more than a decade before. These were eloquent figures to chart the trajectory of agrarian capitalism and its beneficiaries. Spread over the subdistricts of south Gujarat, nine factories were in operation – six in Surat district and three in Valsad district. During the months of harvest campaign, they were together able to crush approximately 30,000 tonnes per day. The cane was cut by an army of migrant labour roughly adding up to over 1,20,000 men, women and children considered of working age. Their plight of exploitation and oppression highlights the other side of this success story.

Agro-Industry and Migrant Labour

The harvesting season was the high tide of the cultivation cycle. Hectic activity went on in the fields around Bardoli with labour gangs cutting, cleaning and binding the cane into bundles from dawn to dusk. On the roads, heavily loaded trucks rushed day and night to the factory to keep the production lines fed with cane. From the villages nearby, the transporting was done by bullock cart. Pairs of oxen in long rows behind each other dragged their freight at all hours in a slow procession which never seemed to end. As the season changed, winter turning into summer, the big wooden wheels shod with iron bands sank deeper into the melting asphalt leaving behind them a route map of the harvest campaign. On nearing the mill, one would first notice the smoking chimney and the sickly-sweet smell permeating the environment and becoming more noticeable as one got closer. The noise of the machinery, the messiness of the mill's precincts, the access roads jammed with lorries and carts, the myriad wayside stalls and the crush of people around, all signalled the footprint of a massive industrial workforce.

The pressure of activity went with the season. The harvest took up at least five months, from the end of October until early May. Cutting cane has been, from the very beginning, the occupation of an army of migrant labour. The women's garb, the conduct of the men and the Marathi they spoke made it easy enough to distinguish these seasonal migrants from the local population. But what marked them even more as outsiders was the way in which they lived and worked, banded together. The migrants set up bivouac – rows of tents made from a couple of mats held aloft with a few wooden sticks – on the outskirts of villages, in the open field stretched out along the road. These camps were regularly shifted to new sites as the seasonal labour force worked its way through the area to be harvested without interacting with the village inhabitants. The three sugar mills in and around Bardoli *vibagh* located at a distance of 15 to 20 kilometres from each other had contracted 50,000 migrants from Maharashtra in the 1976–77 season, and half this multitude were under the command of the largest factory in Bardoli town.

Seasonal migration was certainly not a new phenomenon in the fabric of India's rural economy, but the character and scale of labour mobility that I came across struck me as indicative of a far-reaching transformation resulting in a new set of social relations of production. The organization of the dominant class of farmers into agro-industrial cooperatives had spearheaded this process of change. My data collection concentrated on its main stakeholders: the factory management, the labour gangs at work or in their camps, and the farmers in the villages. I started by paying visits to the factory offices and went along with its field staff on their daily rounds in the area. The managerial staff provided information about the cultivation of sugarcane, the organization and schedule of production, the crushing of the cane delivered, the recruitment of migrant labour, the harvest operation, labour conditions, etc. This stage of my fieldwork was combined with meeting farmers who had come to the factory to discuss their issues as members of the cooperative. Accompanying them as they went back home introduced me to their villages and to other caste-class fellows living there.

The last and most important phase of my investigations was spent in the fields or in the camps of the labour gangs. At the factory, administrative data on agricultural and industrial production were readily available and it was also perfectly possible to talk about the work performed in the fields and in the mill. But my probing into the conditions of workers failed to evoke the details I wanted. Labour was something to be used but did not merit much discussion as a theme of interest in itself. Also, farmers were forthcoming while telling me about their appreciation of the profit made from sugarcane cultivation without having to spend much time and energy on the labour side of this money-spinning crop. Sitting on the swing in front of their bungalows from morning till evening, their behaviour was that of a rentier class, freed from the onerous task of sourcing the local landless for chores which had to be done. While enjoying the new style of farming, they turned out to be singularly uninformed and uninterested in the presence nearby of the migrants. Where they came from, how they coped with the lack of amenities in their makeshift shelters or what they earned was of no concern to the owners of the fields in which these transient masses toiled. My fieldwork's slow gravitation to sites where the migrants worked and lived did not remain unnoticed. I usually avoided any open provocation of the mill management, but when my hanging out where the migrants toiled and camped became more pronounced and I did not heed signs to lay off doing this, my interaction with the stakeholders in command of the terrain became stressful.

Neither did I receive an immediate welcome when I walked into a bivouac sheltering migrants which I had not visited before. The *mukadam* who had recruited the gang and supervised them for the duration of the harvest campaign also acted as their camp boss. He was the one who came forward as interlocutor when anyone approached his gang. It was but natural for him to be suspicious of me as an unusually inquisitive intruder and to keep me from direct contact with the *koytas* (cutting teams) into which his work gang was split up. All these intermediaries between the mill management and the cane-cutting teams were busy watchdogs who needed to run around continuously. When the jobber-cum-foreman was not on the spot, as could be found out in advance, it was possible to meet and talk unmediated with the cane cutters. This meant an escape from surveillance, since the *mukadams* were also the ears and eyes of the factory's management, reporting on all my doings to their superiors.

My *modus operandi* is known as participant observation: a misleading term because the observations made did not allow for participation. The body of data required for analysis were gathered by meeting, as much as possible, more than once or even often, a large and sufficiently varied number of informants. They were, on the one side, staff and members of the cooperative sugar mills, and on the other, cane-cutting migrants. The axiomatic disparity between these stakeholders gave an unusual tension to the fieldwork carried out, on which I have elaborated in an article entitled 'Between Accumulation and Immiseration: The Partiality of Fieldwork in Rural India' (Breman 1985a). The substance of my findings on the deployment of the huge army of migrants hired for harvesting sugarcane was reported in a lengthy essay published in *The Economic and Political Weekly* while I was still engaged in ongoing fieldwork (Breman 1978). From this early and separate account, reprinted in Breman (1994), the parts are summarized which throw light on the recruitment under duress that forced this workforce to leave home. Contracted by the sugar mills in an exploitative and oppressive relationship, the toil they produced had generated the wealth which the main landowning class in Bardoli *vibagh* came to enjoy.

The preference for migrant labour seemed to be a pervasive feature in west India. In Maharashtra too, workers were brought from far away to harvest cane, and the sugar factories established in south Gujarat followed suit. On the other side of the border, Khandesh was the main catchment area for recruitment. The rural population in this backward region comprised mostly land-poor cultivators of the tribal castes growing rain-fed and low-quality foodgrains. The yield provided the staple diet for their subsistence. Lack of employment in the dry period of the year obligated them to search for waged work elsewhere. Factory agents from Gujarat roamed these districts during the monsoon to engage *mukadams* who agreed to form a gang of *koytas*. This name for the long cutting knife also applied to a team of two to three persons, the cutter and his helper(s), to clean the stalks, bind them together and then carry the bundles from field to roadside. Using the same term for the worker and his tool neatly expressed the commodification of labour. A written contract was signed by the jobber and the factory agent stipulating the number of *koytas* to be recruited and the earnest money – paid in two or three instalments – distributed among his catch. New jobbers were selected on the recommendation of trustworthy ones, but not without checking their work experience, creditworthiness, ability to read and write, and proficiency to head a gang. Candidates who turned out to be successful in the tasks allotted were allowed the following year to contract a larger number of *koytas*.

Using various sanctions, the factories were able to cover themselves against risk upon non-compliance. The jobber had to give his property – land, cattle – as collateral for duly discharging his obligations. He had to return part of the cash advance received from the factory agent if he failed to turn up at departure with the stipulated number of work teams. Even more effective was the pressure on the labour broker with the insistence of the factory that every two or three jobbers stood guarantee for each other. Standardization of the recruitment system for all factories in south Gujarat – informing each other about the workforce contracted and fixation of the maximum cash amount handed out in advance – assured a ready supply of the required magnitude of gang labour at the right time, at the lowest possible cost and without any risk ensuing from the recruitment process. It was a cheap, reliable and efficient system for the large-scale mobilization of migrant labour. Economic dependency, resulting from indebted engagement, continued to be the foundation of the labour system. But the factory management did not shy away from using additional means with which to discipline the army of harvesters. Although it was the jobber's task to call members of his gang to order, it regularly occurred that the factory's field staff resorted to extra pressure if the work schedule did not proceed smoothly. Curses and an occasional blow or kick emphasized the intimidation to which the cutting teams were exposed. Working in an alien environment and leading a segregated life in the camp when not toiling in the fields facilitated the use of non-economic force, which did not necessarily have to be manifested in physical coercion. Still, it would not be an exaggeration to see this army of migrants as detainees of the agro-industry with the *mukadam* acting as reliable warder.

THE JOBBER AND HIS GANG

The labour contract with the *koyta* was binding for the whole season, and was closed when the jobber paid the first instalment of the negotiated amount to the head of the cutting team. Being mostly illiterate, he had to acknowledge receipt of the cash given with a thumbprint. The amount jotted down in the labour broker's notebook was often much higher than what was handed to the cane cutters. The factories discharged the recruitment risks on to the jobbers who in turn shifted these to the workers with whom they settled the contract. With customary brutality, sanctions were applied to force adherance to the deal closed, leaving the cane-cutting teams defenceless against unjust or unreasonable claims. The migrants usually preferred to go with a jobber they already knew but were free to join another gang if a different *mukadam* offered a larger sum. The *mukadams* shelled out more money than the factory was willing to advance to them. They had to supply the deficit amount themselves by taking loans from local moneylenders at usurious interest rates. It was a burden ultimately borne by the contracted cutting teams, and meant that in the jobber's administration they were held accountable as indebted for double the amount than had been handed over to them.

The area of operation of the factory in Bardoli town covered about 15,000 acres. It included sugarcane fields in 170 villages spread over four subdistricts. In order to maintain the progress of harvesting over such an extensive area according to a tight schedule, a well-run field organization was imperative. To see to it that cane-cutting proceeded smoothly round the clock, the factory placed excessive obligations on the availability of the work gangs without recognizing any rights in return. The teams had no set times for eating, sleeping and resting, with the mill operating day and night without any interruption. For work, everything else had to give way. For the duration of the campaign, the factory had to be constantly supplied with sufficient loads of cane brought in by lorries and bullock carts. Every disruption that occurred – stoppage of cutting due to a breakdown in the mill or because of traffic jams on the access roads, sudden orders to cut a double quantity – had to be put up with by the workforce without fail. Wages were settled every fortnight at the factory with the jobber of the gang, and also included a grain ration for the next fortnight. Back in the camp, he distributed the food allowance – 30 kilograms of millet per *koyta* – and split up the wage bill among the cutting teams in accordance with their work performance, after deducting the advances (plus interest) handed out on recruitment. The cane cutters were unable to check what the jobber told them and his malpractices remained concealed, though they created animosity leading to quarrels with the gang boss but also among the cutting teams. The small amounts received had to be spent on buying food items in addition to the grain allowance.

To satisfy their basic needs, this army of migrants were conditioned and confined to an incredibly low wage level. They looked upon their employment during the harvest as something that could not be avoided, and the same applied to the subordination imposed on them. They were well aware of being at the mercy of the 'company' and the gang boss was the link in that chain of attachment. It was he who gave them advances in the slack period, supervised the work, looked after their upkeep and in all these respects, made it possible for them to survive. On the final payday, the management rewarded the workforce for the diligence shown by adding to the last half-a-month's wage, a cash bonus called – in typical Gandhian jargon – *shramphal* (fruit of labour). It was not a contracted emolument but a gratuity which could be reduced or withheld if the gang failed to comply with instructions given and had not achieved the prescribed output. The final set of wage bills that I checked showed that the factory had paid the gang bosses between Rs 225 and Rs 455 per *koyta*. But this was not the amount that the head of the cutting team received. It was precisely in the handling of the last and most important payment that the jobber managed, in addition to his commission fee of 9 per cent over the total wage bill, to take an extra cut by deducting fictitious items along with genuine ones. His way of squaring the advance on recruitment, petty loans taken in between, days of absence at work, costs of illness and additional food bought, etc., ended in fake calculations. The factory management frankly admitted the swindle but regarded the malpractice as part of the discretionary price for the brokerage accomplished.

The *mukadam* was the kingpin in the relationship between agro-industry and the labour migrants. His brokerage freed the sugar factories in south Gujarat from dealing directly with the workforce. Who became a jobber and how? The first criterion was creditworthiness. A precondition was a solid standing of reliability and ownership of assets demanded as collateral for advances shelled out to *koyta*s on recruitment. A modicum of literacy was required as he had to run a simple administration. Candidates were only selected if they had taken part for several years in harvesting and were thoroughly familiar with the ins and outs of the work on the basis of past experience. Ability to follow orders and command obedience from workers who joined his gang were desired personal qualities which could only be found out in practice. He had to prove his skills and was initially permitted to bring only a small gang of eight to ten *koyta*s. Not until the *mukadam* had demonstrated that he could fulfil his role as a middleman to the satisfaction of the factory management was he given permission to increase the strength of his gang the following year.

It took time to move up the pyramid of mediation. At the top was a small core of old hands who, owing to their length of service, supplied the larger gangs of more than thirty cutting teams. Rather than competing with each other in their business of brokerage, the jobbers were related to each other and the senior jobbers helped the juniors to earn their grade. In spite of all this assistance the new and inexperienced jobber was not assured of success, and not performing adequately ended in going bankrupt within one or two seasons. This, it was explained to me, was a result of badly performing *koyta*s having been recruited. Experienced cutters tended to go along with experienced gang bosses and were given a higher advance. Failure to get work done according to schedule, being too easy with or too hard on the workers, and inability to liaise properly with the factory's field staff were not tolerated. Most of these shortcomings could be put under one heading: inaptitude to handle the pressures that a broker faced from both sides.

Most jobbers had risen from the ranks, but having a common origin with the cane cutters did not prevent their differences from becoming more pronounced. Brokerage being a profitable business, they were economically much better off at the cost of the workers who joined their gang. Compulsions of an extra-economic nature were possible because of the collusion between jobbers and factories. It meant that they were able to regulate the labour market in ways most profitable to themselves. While employment under such conditions does not by definition exclude the feasibility of labour being more or less 'free', a capitalist mode of production on the other hand by no means precluded absence of freedom. Being tied down in debt to the head of his team also forced a cane cutter's helpers – usually his wife and a child considered of working age – to join him in attachment for the season.

Observing the cane cutter's toil at close quarters made me realize the burden imposed on women in particular. Although the cutting knife was mostly wielded by men, their female helpers occasionally took over so that the male cutter could take rest. The cleaning, cutting and bundling of the cane stalks were all chores delegated to women. During short breaks, the women also had to attend to underaged children they brought to the field with them, the youngest not yet weaned. The label of industrial proletariat did not apply exclusively to the regime of work, but certainly came to mind also when observing life in the mobile shelters in which the *koytas* were forced to pass their off-work hours. On returning to the camp at the end of the day, and all seven days of the week counted as working days, it was again the women who gathered bundles of wood for the cooking fire. They were also busy in the camp. Waking up in darkness early in the morning they prepared the food to carry to work; and at night, while the men squatted down exhausted, started boozing and gambling, or dozed off, the women arranged the meal and cleaned the utensils.

'Nomadic' is how Karl Marx phrased the plight of this footloose army.

> We now turn to a group of people whose origin is rural, but whose occupation is for the most part industrial. They are the light infantry of capital, thrown from one point to another according to its present needs. When they are not on the march they 'camp'. Nomadic labour is used for various building and draining works, for brick-making, lime-burning, railway-making, etc. A flying

column of pestilence, it carries smallpox, typhus, cholera and scarlet fever into the places in whose neighbourhood it pitches its camp. In undertakings which involve a large outlay of capital, such as railways etc., the contractor himself generally provides his army with wooden huts and so on, thus improvising villages which lack all sanitary arrangements, are outside the control of the local authorities, and are very profitable to the gentleman who is doing the contracting, for he exploits his workers in two directions at once – as soldiers of industry, and as tenants. (Marx 1976, p. 818)

Densely packed in the camps and totally deprived of basic amenities, the cane cutters lacked a niche of their own to retreat to. There was no closed space, however small, in which husbands and wives or adults with their children were able to meet in intimacy, to find relief from their fatigue and to comfort one another. They lived in each other's shadow, perhaps just one square metre apart from the next team. Any private deed had many immediate observers and they were fully aware of the infringement such an existence made on their sense of decency and dignity: '*hum to kutton se bhi kam hai*' (even dogs are better off), exclaimed a cane cutter when questioned by an investigatory committee which, on the basis of my writings on the issue, was set up by the High Court of Gujarat to look into the conditions of the workforce seasonally engaged by this agro-industry in south Gujarat. Although arguing from a non-radical perspective on the preference for migrant labour above local labour, Max Weber had reached a conclusion that was similar to the one Marx had formulated.

> The migrant worker, torn from his family and usual environment, is regarded as simple labour power both by the landlords and himself. The barracks of the migrant workers are the money-economy equivalents of the slave barracks of antiquity. The estate owner saves on workers' housing, since accommodation for the migrant costs little or nothing. He also has no need to allocate plots of land, but above all he is not regulated by laws governing conditions of work and pay. The migrant would not accept at home the kind of living conditions and diet is not the only, or even principal, factor here. (Weber 1893, quoted in Tribe 1979, p. 193)

WAGE PAYMENT AS A DISCIPLINARY DEVICE

In the account of my findings at the revisited sites of migrant labour in Bardoli *vibagh* in 1987–88, I straightaway spoke of neo-bondage. The jobbers had been instructed to recruit only young men and women who were in good physical shape. They were expressly forbidden to allow non-working dependants to accompany the *koyta*s on their annual migration to south Gujarat. A decade earlier, I used to find that non-working dependants, old people and small children who stayed back in the camps, took care of each other and shared the food rations distributed as part of the maintenance allowance. Now the camps were empty during the day when the workforce of adolescents and adults of younger-age sets were cutting cane. Much more than before, the expanded army of migrants were reduced to a commodity pure and simple, locked up in neo-bondage.

Changes made by the agro-industry in the system of labour contracting impelled me to use this term in order to highlight the duress imposed on the workforce. By introducing a new system of wage payment, the sugar mills tightened their grip over the army of labour migrants for the 1980–81 harvesting campaign. Wage settlement was an important instrument used by the factory management to keep the workforce locked in a state of dependency. To pre-empt the rise of labour militancy, the sugar mills decided in the early 1980s to introduce a new method of payment. Until then, wages had been paid fortnightly, subject to deduction in instalments of the advance money paid on recruitment. In this way, around the middle of the harvest, they could clear their debt to the factory, though not the additional amount they owed their gang boss. But from now on the *koyta*s had to make do with a maintenance allowance of Rs 30 twice a month, supplemented with 30 kilograms of millet. The major part of their earnings was withheld until the end of the season. Apart from administrative convenience, this modality gave the agro-industry a considerable financial advantage in the form of bank interest on the unpaid balance. But of crucial significance was that this revision enabled the management to maximize control over the workforce. The combination of advance and postponed payment considerably strengthened the subjection of labour to the employer. It also nullified the outbreak of strikes and other forms of resistance such as threat of desertion when the campaign was in full swing. The explanation given by the factories for the revised payment method was that it encouraged the cane cutters to save money. They could now take much more money with them on their return home. No longer would they succumb to the temptation to gamble their earnings away in the camp or to squander it on drinking bouts immediately after the fortnightly payment.

What then followed showed that instead of reducing the risk of labour trouble, the revision in the mode of payment had the opposite effect of brewing militancy. At the end of the 1980–81 season, labour protest broke out in one of the mills in Bardoli *vibagh*. On the final payday, the *khandeshi*s received far less than they had expected on the basis of earlier promises made by the management to raise the cutting rates. The small amounts of cash and grain rations doled out on regular paydays were insufficient to meet the subsistence needs of the *koytas*. They had no alternative but to ask their gang boss for extra credit, which he readily gave at a high rate of interest. Inevitably, on pay settlement day at the end of the campaign, the cane cutters could not lay hands on a large part of the back pay to which they were entitled. While the jobber was thus able to accumulate profits, the cash paid out to the harvesters fell short of the amount they needed to bridge their income deficit in the forthcoming monsoon months.

A large crowd consisting of gangs from nearby camps trooped together and laid siege to the administrative office, assaulted members of the staff who were busy settling the final wages, and caused havoc in the factory grounds. The alarmed management realized that the *mukadams* were unable to keep their gangs under control or prevent the cutters from closing ranks. Some of them were even suspected of having instigated the trouble. It was the first time that the migrant workers had congregated in collective action. The vernacular press ignored the grievances of the cane cutters, suggesting that their demands for higher pay were excessive and impossible for the factory to accept. The newspapers spoke of 'a reign of terror' and of 'crowds indulging in violence', thus turning labour claims into a question of peace and order. The police were called, and they arrested fifteen 'ring leaders' and cleared the factory premises of the protesting workers.

The turmoil put to an end the myth for which the *khandeshis* used to be praised: their physical stamina and pliability. In comparison, the tribals from the Dangs, a district in the hinterland of Gujarat bordering on Maharashtra, were regarded as being more compliant. Their increasing share in subsequent years in the composition of the army of mobilized migrants should be seen in the light of this reputation. An additional reason for spreading recruitment to catchment areas within Gujarat was the fear that the government would directly interfere in the labour regime. Under the Inter-State Migrant Workmen Act, 1979, footloose labourers coming from another state were shielded from undue pressure and exploitation. Fearing a considerable increase in labour costs, the sugar mills opted for engagement of migrants who remained unprotected. In this way, managements conveyed their willingness to provide employment to labouring sons of the soil within the state.

But recruitment from beyond the borders remained necessary for securing sufficient hands and feet for the booming and expanding business of cutting-cum-crushing sugarcane in south Gujarat. Labour costs remained a tiny fraction of the burden of this industry because the new law, ineffective for the targeted workers, became a boon of wealth for corrupt officials of the state's Rural Labour Inspectorate. A memorandum I came across in the branch office of this agency in Surat district directed its staff, on orders coming from above, not to investigate and prosecute the management of sugar mills for circumventing the regulations of the Minimum Wages Act, 1948. By keeping labour costs down to bare survival levels, the agro-industry, in collusion with the regional bureaucracy, was able to defuse another threat which would have resulted from the implementation of the Contract Labour (Regulation and Abolition) Act, 1970. The Bardoli factory management was in 1987–88 the first one to pretend that the farmers themselves contracted work gangs for cutting sugarcane. Members of this cooperative were obliged to sign forms alleging that they would settle the wage bill directly with the jobber on completion of the harvest. This fraudulent scheme was practised by all sugar factories, not only in south Gujarat but also in Maharashtra.

WHY MIGRATORY LABOUR?

It could be argued that the recruitment of labour from distant locations for the harvesting campaign in south Gujarat occurred because sufficient manpower was simply not available locally. In line with this logic was the consideration that for the army of migrants during these months, there was dire lack of employment opportunities at home. How else could the massive mobility of labour from an area of excess to an area of shortage be appraised in a favourable light? However, this argumentation started from a false premise. Local labour in south Gujarat was both present and in abundant supply – to the extent that when the harvest was in full swing, the main tribal community in the region milled around in idleness. Indeed, the influx of labour from outside contributed to the pauperization of Halpatis. It could be argued initially that the local landless at least were employed in the earlier stages of sugarcane cultivation. But gradually, that suggestion too became invalid. Several operations, especially the preparation of land, were increasingly mechanized. In many villages, ploughing and ridging was now done by tractor. Planting of the crop was still a manual task, but it coincided with the arrival of the *khandeshis* and was outsourced to them. Finally, regular spraying much diminished the need for weeding.

While sugarcane covered most of the arable land, agricultural labourers belonging to the region and adding up to more than half of the total population remained excluded from its cultivation. When I probed this issue deeper with spokesmen of the agro-industry, I was told a different tale. How was it possible to put the cutting of cane in the hands of Halpatis who were not used to this work? Depending on such an inexperienced lot accustomed to a much shorter workday would result in an unacceptable fall in productivity. This argument also lacked substance. The agro-industry in south Gujarat had from beginning disregarded an entirely different alternative, i.e. to utilize the abundantly available stock of local labour. Past experience indicated that this could have been a feasible option worth exploring. Sugarcane was not at all a new crop in the region but had been extensively cultivated in the past wherever sufficient water for irrigation was available throughout the growth cycle. The commercial significance that the crop already had in the first few decades of the nineteenth century is evident from an early colonial report.

> There is no part of Guzerat in which the sugarcane is cultivated to the same extent and perfection as in our own and Gaikwar districts in the *attaveesy*. In a few villages of the Gaikwars the assessment is I believe as high as Rupees 100 a *beega* on sugarcane, and there are some Coonbees in our villages who consume all the other produce of their farms themselves, and pay their entire Revenue from *Jagree* (the end-product made from sugarcane) and who are as rich people in their way as any I have met with. *Indeed they may be called Planters as they have 30 to 40 bond servants and cattle in proportion among them.* Lumsden, Collector of Surat, 9 April 1823. (Breman 2007a, pp. 27–28; emphases added)

Bardoli was also mentioned in the first settlement report as a place which 'yields a fine crop of sugarcane' (Jayakar 1925, para 15). The very high labour intensity of the product, then processed as *gur* (jaggery) on the farm and sold to distant markets, was in colonial reports of the time indicated as explanation for the existence of the *hali* system. The main landowners insisted at the onset of Independence that they needed landless and bonded workers to take charge of all operations from planting to harvesting and processing the commodity at the farm site. 'A capitalistic cultivator keeps one or two Halis for performing field operations. He is bound to maintain them whether he exact work from them or not. He, therefore, deems it wise and profitable to occupy them in sugarcane-cultivation' (Mukhtyar 1930, p. 97).

The factory management, farmers as well as government officials reacted with utter disbelief whenever I drew attention to this historic evidence of the suitability of local landless labourers for employment in what was once, and now on a much larger scale than before, the main cash crop. In the firm opinion of these stakeholders, the factorized production of sugarcane would not be feasible without making use of migrant labour. That assumption too was disputable. Between 1942 and 1945, a privately owned sugar mill in Gandevi milling cane for the production of white sugar had successfully operated with only a local workforce of both field and factory hands.

Labour mobility had become a widespread feature in south Gujarat with the transition to agrarian capitalism. This circular movement contradicted the obstinate belief that landless labourers preferred to suffer hunger at home rather than going elsewhere in search of wages. Assumed shortcomings of the local landless made it possible to bring in workers from outside, notwithstanding the presence of a thoroughly underemployed or unemployed proletariat on the spot. The argument posited for bringing in outsiders was the intolerable laziness, indifference and genetic incapacity to work properly of the Halpatis. Drummed into my ears was the saying, 'On waking in the morning these good-for-nothings tested the pot of *bharku* [a mix of gruel of millet with undermilk] with their toe and if there was enough they stayed supine for the day.' This pathological syndrome of unwillingness to work, instant gratification of a limited set of needs and a total lack of energy constituted the classic justification put forward by the employers for the misery of the dispossessed underclass. Rather, the traits of the pauperized they described were an inevitable outcome of malnourishment and underemployment.

Having rejected standard explanations for labour migration which assumed lack of adequate manpower in both quantitative or qualitative respects, my proposition was that workers imported from elsewhere were both cheaper and allowed for greater command over their labour power. The reproduction cost of *khandeshi*s was of no concern for the cooperative sugar mills in Bardoli *vibagh*. Engaged only for the duration of the harvesting campaign, the *koyta*s were not allowed to stay on after the final payday. The contract signed on recruitment stipulated not only when to report for departure, but also obligated them to return home when the work was done. The income they needed to meet their maintenance cost during the monsoon months, a slack period in the annual cycle, could in no way be charged to their past or future employment. This explained why and how labour cost was a minimal part of the total cost of production. For economic and social reasons, it would have been less easy for the agro-industry to abstain from any responsibility to contribute to the survival of their labour force in case they were bound to employ local agricultural labour. To be assured of a ready supply of cane cutters in a relentless day-and-night work schedule for the next harvest, some sort of protection outside the season would then be well-nigh unavoidable. Even under a blatantly exploitative mode of production it was difficult to see that such an anonymous and ruthless treatment could have been meted to local people. Engaging outsiders enabled the agro-industry of south Gujarat not only to reduce their obligations to the absolute minimum, but, in addition, to confine them for the duration of the harvest campaign. By precluding the local landless from cane-cutting and thus excluding them from the main crop grown, their claims as sons of the soil to a stake in the agrarian economy remained obfuscated.

Thus, the pauperization of the Halpatis was not a result of the indifference – called economic rationality when perceived from another angle – of those who deprived them of access to livelihood. The local landless, it was tirelessly avowed by both factory managers and farmers, lacked discipline. What they actually meant by making this complaint was that Halpatis had set limits to what they were willing to suffer. Just like anyone else, they were disposed to observe the routine of daily life and wanted to honour obligations to their household, to adhere to the cultural norms of their community, to celebrate rites of passage as well as religious festivals. And all this was exactly what the agro-industry did not tolerate. By contrast, it was possible to deny any social life at all to the *khandeshi*s, cooped up in a milieu that was alien to them and in which they were held in isolation. The seasonal migrants were available at all times, working during day and night, and immediately transferable to other sites as and when required. In all these respects, to employ local workers would have diminished the degree of subordination and alienation – in principle, total – of labour in the production process.

My case study, which was the outcome of a new round of fieldwork on migrant labour engaged for the harvesting of sugarcane in south Gujarat, dates back to nearly half a century. The miserable plight of this agro-industrial proletariat as narrated above concerns a recent past. It is important to add, however, that in the subsequent years no drastic change has occurred. Exploitation and locking up this footloose workforce in neo-bondage has been going on as before until now. This was highlighted in a repeat round of investigations undertaken in 2017 by Prayas Centre for Labour Action and Research, a non-governmental organization based in Ahmedabad. The data collected provide detailed information about the findings, summed up as follows.

> Every year, 30-year-old Raghu Thakre and his family – hailing from Nandurbar district in Maharashtra – migrate to southern Gujarat, where they work as agricultural labourers in sugarcane farms for six to eight months. He has been doing this for the past 15 years, ever since he had to drop out of school and join

his parents and siblings to work on sugarcane fields. Raghu says he inherited this work (and the fate of a sugarcane harvester) from his father, and that his father had inherited this occupation from his grandfather. Raghu knows that his children too will be condemned to the life of a sugarcane harvester, he adds, and thus the vicious cycle shall continue.

There are about 1.5 to 2 lakh people who have a story similar to that of Raghu *bhai*. Thousands upon thousands of people from the Adivasi belts of Gujarat and Maharashtra migrate to parts of southern Gujarat to work in the sugarcane fields.

For months, they live with their children on the outskirts of the villages of sugarcane field owners (most of whom are *patidars*), in conditions devoid of basic amenities like clean water, sanitation and medical facilities. As parents and adults toil for 12 to 14 hours a day, the children engage in unpaid care labour – cooking, cleaning and caring for their siblings. For the months that they stay with their parents, these children remain out of school and out of coverage of welfare schemes.

The sugar industry centred around the town of Bardoli (Surat) hosts the factory with Asia's largest sugarcane-crushing capacity, and is also home to the largest cooperative society of farmers. The cooperative has been working for decades to ensure welfare and interests of the sugarcane farm owners. However, there have been no efforts to ensure the rights and well-being of the sugarcane harvesters who fuel the progress of these sugar factories and have helped make India the second largest producer of sugar in the world after Brazil.

Recent empirical studies (2014, 2017) conducted by Prayas . . . say that while the expansion of sugarcane fields and sugar mills on a cooperative basis has become a replica for agro-industrial development in and around Gujarat, the conditions of the harvesters continue to remain highly oppressive and exploitative.

When one compares the findings of the current report with Jan Breman's seminal work on the workers in sugarcane fields in 1978, one finds that the condition of the worker has only worsened over the years.

A second research report published by Leela Visaria and Harish Joshi on the same subject, and also based on investigations conducted in 2017, confirmed that there has been no change for the better in the exploitation of the huge army of migrants attached in neo-bondage for the duration of the harvesting campaign by the sugar factories in south Gujarat (Visaria and Joshi 2021).

Footloose But Not Free

Shortage of income required for the cost of survival and reproduction forces members of landless and land-poor households to accept advance payment for their labour power in a contract constituting unfree labour, which I have defined as neo-bondage. The starting point is an absence of choice which confronts these workers. Earnings are low, irregular as well as uncertain, a situation that leads to a loss of autonomy. Their labour power is the only collateral they have, which they need to sell in a market controlled by a diverse and fluctuating range of buyers. Engagement in waged work on which livelihood depends and which gets expressed in a relationship of indebtedness has become a common phenomenon in India's thoroughly informalized economy. Employers present such arrangements as 'advances' on wages that will be repaid by laying claim on the labour power of the borrower. However, such 'advances' are solely intended to immobilize labour, whether instantly or at a later date. Neither party views the transaction as a loan that will be terminated on repayment.

Debt bondage is by no means a new ploy. Already in the remote past, it was the customary manner by which subordinated workers dispossessed from means of production were attached to landowning households of higher castes. This master–serf relationship was quite common in the pre-colonial and colonial eras throughout the South Asian subcontinent. My first round of fieldwork in south Gujarat led me to qualify such bondage as a pre-capitalist system of unfree labour (Breman 1974b). The bondage was lifelong, could stretch from generation to generation, and also included the servitude of wife and children of the bondsman. The master owning land claimed a broad spectrum of services – both economic and extra-economic, including sexual ones of the female subalterns – that demonstrated the subjugation of the landless household. The social context in which this form of servitude operated was a localized and non-monetary agrarian-rural order, predominantly based on subsistence production.

In the course of my research then and later on, I found that in the transition to capitalism in the late and post-colonial period, the erstwhile system of bondage substantially changed character and ultimately collapsed. Having fought free from constraints, the dispossessed proletariat remained subjected to exploitation and oppression. Indebtedness continues to be a crucial feature of the capitalist work regime that I have called neo-bondage. This modality of employment is not restricted to the much shrunken category of permanently employed farm servants. In more intermittent formats, similar arrangements also pertain to a wide range of labour in the non-agrarian informal economy.

In my continued fieldwork in rural south Gujarat until well into the second decade of the twenty-first century, I have investigated how men, women and children are recruited as circulating migrants. This chapter highlights the plight of migrant labour engaged by large-scale agro-industries for seasonal employment in the cultivation and harvesting of sugarcane in particular. Run along capitalist lines of production, the management of these cooperative enterprises has, from the start until today, relied on contracting the huge workforce required from outside. I have detailed how the recruitment of the labour armies they need, their deployment to the worksite, the labour process in the fields, the camp life during off-work hours, the method of wage payment and their return to their places of origin, are organized from top to bottom and from beginning to end. These organizational features stand out in this model of agro-industrial growth. But in my preceding rounds of fieldwork in south Gujarat, I had already come across the same practice in a less corporate and more petty form of rural-industrial capitalism. Both in 1962–63 and 1986–87 I had followed, and sometimes travelled with, Halpati migrants in Chikhligam and Gandevigam who, during the monsoon, were contracted by a multitude of small-scale entrepreneurs for seasonal employment in brick kilns, salt pans, stone quarries or road construction works scattered over the countryside. Also, this wide range of employers commissioned *mukadam*s to recruit labour gangs in the villages of recruitment with advance wage payment and delayed settlement as a modality of time-bound attachment.

Switching my research to all these rural worksites meant that my village-based investigations were extended to how migrants worked and lived when away from home. My wanderings around such seasonal niches of employment had alerted me already then to the footloose as well as captive character of labour migration. It was indicative of the transition, mainly in the course of the twentieth century, from what in earlier generations had been exclusively agrarian manpower to a rural workforce with a multi-occupational identity. The shift in the next stage of my ongoing research from the countryside to the informal urban economy changed the focus of my fieldwork to diamond-cutting and polishing, fabrication of cloth, processing of gems, and the manufacture of bangles, garments, *bidi*s, embroidery, incense, toys, matches, etc., either in workshops or as home-based industry (Breman 1996). A host of service providers who also fall in this bondage category, such as street vendors indebted to their suppliers, waste collectors, scavengers and domestic servants, are prevented for the same reason, debt, from changing their employer. The work contract would sometimes bind all members of the household who are able to work; in other cases, it specifically applied to a man, woman or working-age child. This meant in fact that the man could demand higher advance payment by expanding his own bondage to include his dependants.

The new bondage differs from the traditional one in terms of the short duration of the contract – often no longer than for one season; its less inclusive character – just labour instead of a more encompassing beck-and-call relationship; and finally, its enhanced vulnerability to non-compliance. Again, it is the labour power which is required by working off the amount of debt. The greater risk of breach of contract discourages employers from being imprudent and generous in granting an advance on wage payment. It is difficult to recoup losses made in this way and it has become useless for employers to appeal to the government for help in taking absconders to task. Moreover, today's bosses lack the natural superiority that made it highly unlikely in the past that a contract would be broken. In contrast to the direct and highly personalized relationship which was a marked feature of the old system of attachment, neo-bondage is often mediated by a go-between to whom recruitment, supervision and wage settlement of the contracted labour is delegated. This middleman is a crucial figure in a highly fluid and erratic labour market, sourcing reserve armies of labour from remote hinterlands and operating his catch on the hire–fire mechanism. The jobber allows the employer to keep a distance from the exploited workers. Often, the social identity of the jobbers is the same as that of the labourers recruited by them, and consequently, their relationship is no longer based on superiority versus inferiority.

As against differences, there are also similarities between the 'old' and 'new' forms of bondage. In both, the unfree relationship does not have its origin in extra-economic coercion. The contract is entered into voluntarily, in the sense that the workers are supposed to work off the advance given, and until then have lost their room for manoeuvre. The prevalence of indebtedness is the second feature of similarity. But the present situation differs from the former one in that the neo-bonded worker who enters into debt repays it with labour power without subjecting himself or herself in any other respect or unconditionally to the creditor. Although the relationship remains an unequal one, the employer is no longer addressed as master but as boss. Then as well as now, labourers are held captive to foreclose alternative options for selling their labour power at more attractive terms and conditions. Adding to the economic vulnerability of bonded labour is their social identity which invariably ranks them in the bottom layers of the caste order. As with the agrestic serfs in the past, the men, women and children prone to fall victim to neo-bondage mainly belong to the Scheduled Castes or Scheduled Tribes. Thus, next to major differences, multiple symmetries and high exit costs continue to be the organizing principle of old and new forms of unfree labour. I have to add here that the molestation of women and children in their plight of neo-bondage has remained much understated in the available documentation, including in my own writings.

Unfree labour has formally been outlawed as it thrives on the vulnerability of people who are driven by economic need to sell their labour power in advance and, by doing so, are exposed to sustained dependency. It is an outcome which is much understated in official records and statistics. In a report titled 'The Cost of Coercion', the ILO (2009) has drawn attention to millions of people worldwide who are entrapped in work regimes of coercion – ranging from slavery, forced or bonded labour to human trafficking. The South Asian subcontinent is indeed identified as having a high prevalence of debt bondage. The relationship between an employer and an employee can only be referred to as one of debt bondage if the loan is provided at the outset with the clear intent of disposing of the labour power of the borrower, and if the amount happens to be disproportionate to the terms imposed in scale and duration. Debt bondage is a form of servitude which does not need to be enforced with extra-economic sanctions. Out of economic distress, workers turn to this mode of employment because they have no choice but to sell their labour power in advance. The paucity of estimates of the magnitude of debt bondage in India has its roots not only in the reluctance of official agencies to gather data on the phenomenon, but it is also related to the problem of establishing a clear dividing line between free and unfree labour. The lives of the working masses at the bottom of the labour hierarchy without means of production are conditioned by far-reaching deprivation, denigration and discrimination, making the distinction between working voluntarily and involuntarily a spurious and elastic concept. Modalities of free and unfree labour cannot be described in a clear-cut dichotomy but have to be seen as a sliding scale, a continuum on which only the extremes on both sides are in sharp contrast to each other, as Lerche (2012) has argued. It means that debt bondage needs to be classified as belonging to a whole gamut of decency-deficit labour practices.

To cope with deprivation is a full-time occupation and most people living precariously do not have much energy left for engaging in joint action leading to redemption from indigence. I am not suggesting that the tribal caste of Halpatis in south Gujarat is enmeshed in a 'culture of poverty', as Oscar Lewis long ago framed it (Lewis 1966). Their behaviour is marked by improvidence but this is mainly because the demand for their labour power is intermittent, and the employment for which they qualify as unskilled or self-skilled workers is casual rather than regular and is paid on piece-rates at the lowest possible level. Due to a chronic shortage of income, many Halpatis have no other option than to ask for payment in advance. They refuse, however, to consider themselves as subservient to one or a succession of employers who have bought a prior claim on their labour power at some later stage. Nevertheless, using debt as a device for what I have called practices of neo-bondage adds to the dependency which is a major feature of poverty. Resistance against oppression and exploitation is difficult to organize when the supply of labour is structurally much higher than the demand for it. The vested interests, on the other hand, face fewer problems in taking a united stand when their dominance is challenged.

This does not mean that the Halpatis accept with docility the harsh treatment meted out to them. The agrarian relations are fragile as well as tense, and what begins as a quarrel may escalate into a regular fight. I have reported one such incident that began when an agricultural worker was beaten to death to punish him for his impudence (Breman 2003b, chapter 2). Strikes do break out every now and then to articulate claims for a higher wage. But they tend to be spontaneous rather than planned, remain localized rather than spreading to other villages, and are short in duration because the landless have no reserves to live on. Lack of food brings them back after only a couple of days. If this does not happen, the landowners back their refusal to bargain by bringing in outside labour. No doubt, the opening up of the rural economy has made labour more mobile, but going out of the village or trying to gain access to regular non-agrarian work is not so easy. Instead of changing their occupational profile to other sectors of the economy, the landless masses remain footloose, but in a fluid and already saturated labour market. It is a workforce without acknowledged skills, social capital and political leverage, a reserve army stuck in rural slums, pushed out for some time and then pushed back again. They remain fragmented over a wide range of short-term niches and continually rotate between them. The pretension that they are self-employed in whatever they do at any moment needs to be addressed critically. Their modality of employment is a contractual and casualized wage–labour relationship, but one that prohibits them from uniting in solidarity for concerted action.

To sum up, the disappearance of agrestic servitude in most parts of South Asia, in the manner in which it operated in the pre-capitalist past, has not done away with exploitation and oppression of the swelling proletariat. The wage-dependent workforce in the nether echelons of the economy and society is not in a position to themselves determine when, where and for whom to work. That conclusion contradicts the classical assumption that capitalism is marked by a mode of production based on freedom of labour in a double sense: free from the means of production, as well as free as to when, where and to whom to sell their labour power. Reporting on my fieldwork findings in rural south Gujarat during the late 1970s and mid-1980s, I pointed out in various publications that 'a capitalist mode of production . . . by no means precludes certain forms of absence of duress, emanating for example from the necessity to enter into debt' (Breman 1978, p. 1350; Breman 1988, p. 21). As also argued by Robert Miles, amongst others, bonding mechanisms which restrict the liberty of the worker do not necessarily diminish the capitalist character of the production process (Miles 1987). I still stand by the way I have phrased the proletarian consciousness of the workforce stuck at the floor of the informal economy.

> The need to accept a cash advance on wages entails the obligation to subject oneself to the orders of an employer for the direct future. Back payment has a similar binding effect. The loss of independence that adheres to such a labour contract explains why it is only entered into through lack of a better alternative. That so many nevertheless have recourse to this last sort of employment indicates the enormous pressure on resources of livelihood in the bottom echelons of the economy, Even that disenfranchisement is subjected to restrictions of durability, range and intensity. The work agreement is not entered into and continued for an indefinite time, as was the case with the *hali* of former times. The neo-bondage is further strongly economic in nature and restricts the imposition of the employer's will and his claims of superiority *per se.* The behaviour of wage hunters and gatherers not only expresses their longing for material improvement but also manifests their basic unwillingness to seek security in bondage. Theirs is a type of social consciousness that might be expected from the proletarian class. (Breman 1996, p. 237)

The debt bondage of today might even be practised on a scale larger than traditional agrarian bondage ever was. My estimate is that at least roughly 15 to 20 per cent of South Asia's urban and rural workforce in its close to totally informalized economy are employed on terms that amount to debt bondage. This system of waged work typical of non-liberal capitalism strongly displays a form of dependent attachment in which provisions of protection and security are largely or completely absent. The boss for the moment is not interested to use the relationship to gain power, extract deference or enhance his social status, nor does he feel obliged to guarantee that his employees can meet their basic needs, irrespective of how the employment contract lasts. He lays claim to their labour power and that, not the need to act as a patron, is why he is willing to provide a 'loan' which results in indebtedness of the worker. The reduction to a labour commodity pure and simple is also apparent from the specification of who falls under the contract. Especially in the case of the footloose classes of labour, the lifelong or intergenerational attachment that was characteristic of traditional agrarian bondage is lacking. I am inclined to attribute the loosely structured duration of neo-bondage to the unwillingness of employers to hire labour any longer than strictly necessary. By leaving the exit from arrangements of neo-bondage unspecified but open-ended, they make sure to insist on their right of instant dismissal. The regular replenishment of the workforce is not motivated by any voluntary limitation of the employer's span of control. Workers are hired and fired when and to the extent that the monetary benefits exceed the costs.

CHAPTER SEVEN

Circulation of Labour in the Informal Economy

FROM SEASONAL TO PERPETUAL MOBILITY

My extensive and protracted research into the changes that had occurred in rural and urban Gujarat over a period of half a century was inspired by persistent accounts during the last quarter of the twentieth century claiming that deprivation was on the decline. Poverty alleviation worldwide was declared a policy objective in the Millennium Development Goals pledged by the United Nations. The adopted target – a massive reduction of extreme poverty – was indeed reported to have been successfully met by the deadline that was set. While in 1991, close to half the workers and their family members in the developing countries had to make do with less than $1.25 per person per day, this proportion had dropped to 11 per cent in 2015. The decline in the number of extremely poor workers was from 900 million in 1991 to 300 million in 2015. Although South Asia lagged behind this global falling rate, in this subcontinent too the size of the workforce forced to cope with extreme poverty was, at 23 per cent in 2015, less than half of the 53 per cent subjected to that predicament in 1991 (United Nations 2015, pp. 14–15).

However, as argued in my writings, I found it difficult to reconcile this optimism with the gist of my fieldwork findings. In 2005, Deaton and Kozel warned against accepting at face value the claim of India's government that the neoliberal reforms introduced in the early 1990s had not only boosted economic growth, but also, in that upward swing, resulted in a sharp decline of poverty. 'Although there is no consensus on what happened to Indian poverty in the 1990s, there is good evidence both that poverty is falling and that the official estimates of poverty reduction are too optimistic, particularly for rural India.' (Deaton and Kozel 2005, p. 177). In the opinion of these two economists, wishful thinking has played an important role in what was announced as 'The Great Indian Poverty Debate'; they urged caution to make sure that the methods, which are sometimes less than transparent, are not in effect assuming the answer at the very outset.

My return to sites of earlier investigation in the countryside of south Gujarat from 2009 to 2011 enabled me to report on how economic growth and diversification had impacted the rural proletariat. Connectivity with the outside world had accelerated. From the early 1970s onwards, an infrastructural extension of scale had been launched, leading to installation of electrical grids, road-building, motorized transport and communication – all of which made it easier to enter the village or depart from it. The bridging of distances in less time and at lower cost resulted in a rapid widening of the labour market. The rural economy became more diversified, and activity in sectors such as construction, transport, trade and services created new employment opportunities also for the landless and land-poor classes. This happened at a very opportune moment, because the squeeze on resources at the congested bottom of the agrarian ladder was preventing any further absorption of the expanding workforce in what had been since time immemorial the primary sector of the economy. The extremely skewed man–land ratio was made manifest in increasing bouts of underemployment and unemployment, leading to a further worsening of the already very insecure livelihood of marginal owners and landless labourers.

The earnings from off-and-on work in the cultivation cycle are not enough for the daily needs of the land-poor and landless classes, and they have to search for means of additional income in the vicinity or far away. They commute to work on foot, bicycle or paid transport by jointly hiring autorickshaws, leaving home early in the morning and coming back in the evening. Most of the commuters are men; women mostly when they are young and unmarried, and even then – to avoid sexual abuse – often not on their own but in the company of others, preferably male kinsmen. As a result, agricultural work steadily became feminized. When more distant worksites began to be accessed, daily travel became cumbersome and overnight stay away from home was practically inevitable. The schedule of regular travel to destinations outside the district could stretch to a week or so. To reach distances beyond that, the term commuting is not considered appropriate any longer – particularly when the duration of the absence is erratic and not known in advance. Short-term labour circulation would seem to be a better label for such type of mobility.

Fluctuations in the slack and peak seasons of economic activity are usually addressed under the heading of seasonal migration. But seasonality does not any longer cover the mobility of labour forced to remain afloat throughout the year. The distance to destinations and length of absence closely correspond with each other. Migration to faraway localities may last for several years, or even for the best part of the working life. But in the end, when labour power has been spent or wasted, many migrants have hardly any other option than to head back 'home'. It means a return to where they have left behind the dependent members of their household. Most of those who go away happen to be males. Women and children accompany them only if their labour power can add to the wages earned, as for instance on construction sites, in quarries, brick kilns, road-building or harvesting of crops. In migration to urban worksites, dependent family members may go along but only if they are likely to be gainfully employed. At these urban camps there is no room for free riders, and also not enough space for dwellings. The village has thus become a transit house for the rural underclasses, a place to halt once in a while, to rest and recuperate, to enjoy the comforts of family life, but then to depart again.

Labour circulation, which became a major theme of both my rural and urban research, is a prominent feature of the regime of informality characteristic of the economy at large and on which I have elaborated in successive publications (Breman 1994, 1996, 2007b, 2010a, 2010c, 2013a and 2019). The sexual abuse to which working-class women and children are exposed, not just at home but even more so when cut loose from the protection of settled life, should alert us to the extra-economic coercion that rampant practices of neo-bondage entail. The distinction made between mild and harsh forms of working under duress is often restricted to conditions of employment – wage payment, hours of work, etc., which differ in the degree of exploitation (Breman, Guerin and Prakash, eds 2009, p. 5). However, when confronted with migrant workers being manhandled – beaten up, kicked around – and the rape of females and minors, it is implausible to insist that the use of extra-economic force is missing from neo-bondage. Such instances are anything but rare, as a recent case of heinous attachment details (Shanta 2022). The dismissive reaction of the state machinery to the reported crime once more affirms the tight collusion that exists between employers and authorities.

The struggle for social emancipation of the lower classes had an early start in the southern states of Kerala and Tamil Nadu, while this trajectory of progress was much less detectable in other parts on the subcontinent. It is only since the last few decades that the assertion of the downgraded segments of the population in northern India, the Gangetic plain in particular, has shown signs of becoming more vocal and visible. Tracing the history of these divergent social dynamics is beyond the purpose of this treatise. My more limited objective here is to consider how a comparative perspective may help us to identify the kind of changes required for the rural proletariat of south Gujarat to share more equitably in the overall progress that has been made. No doubt, substantial segments of the land-poor and landless classes have already found access to waged work outside agriculture and the village. But the progressive diversification of economic activity cannot be taken for granted. While jobs in the formal economy are hard to come by and candidates from the lower castes stand no chance of accessing them, there are also indications that making a living in the informal economy has become much more difficult. For many decades policymakers have held on to the idea that the regime of informality has an infinite elasticity to absorb labour pushed out of agriculture. It is a myth and a charade, cherished because it implies that nothing needs to be done about the ebb and tide regulating the flow of the reserve army of labour. They will go wherever work is available even if for a short while, and move on to other sites when their presence is redundant to demand.

The large majority of the rural poor have not left their tenements in the countryside. From the villages of my fieldwork in south Gujarat only a small segment has managed to resettle in a town or city, land-poor households more than landless ones. The primary reason for staying put in their slum colonies on the village outskirts is the uncertainty of regular and secure employment elsewhere. Crowding is already apparent in several sectors of the non-agrarian economy, the tertiary sector above all. This problem has aggravated because employers prefer to opt for higher capital intensity. In their perception, the advantage of labour at minimal cost is no longer outweighed by the difficulties posed to sourcing a workforce of the desired quality as well as docility – that is, to engage this commodity in a permanent state of flux, hired and fired according to the need of the moment. The mood among industrialists and other owners of capital is turning in favour of mechanization and robotization in spite of the availability of a huge quantity of labour at short notice.

An associated signal is growing resentment among the better-off classes against the influx of so many newcomers, particularly the out-of-state ones. The better-off and well-settled urban citizenry hailing from higher up castes-classes are quite vocal in showing their intolerance of a multitude of labour nomads with whom they share no common ground. The dislike with which these floating outsiders is treated is compounded by a social consciousness that is antagonistic to the labouring poor. That caste-cum-class-biased angle finds expression in drives to clean the city of an underclass considered to lack the stamina to work and behave 'properly'. Eviction of squatters and slum demolition resorted to by municipalities in campaigns to beautify the urban habitat are not resented but get strong backing from better-housed and well-to-do inhabitants (Breman 2016, pp. 74–107). The enclosure policy of the Indian city is exemplified by the Smart City drive which the Ministry of Urban Development launched in 2015. The Urban Renewal Mission speaks of a mindset with social Darwinist overtones, implying that the poor are defective and unfit to become rehabilitated. Instead of joining mainstream society they should be kept apart, locked up in their own niches. It basically means that inequality and inequity are justified since the segments of the population held in exclusion from mainstream society do not deserve a better deal.

Boasting to be the state with the highest rate of economic growth, Gujarat has a lower wage level for the workforce in its thoroughly informalized economy than in India as a whole. In the accounts of my research in rural as well as urban localities, I have consistently commented on the lack of social justice and the absence of a democratic frame. The uneven representation of class interests cannot remain covered up behind a constructed facade of benign development. The cherished notion of a village community, a well-knit and harmonious collective, as the cementing format of local governance does not exist. How could it be if about one-tenth of the inhabitants own over two-thirds of the agrarian capital, while the large majority has no or hardly any land or any other means of existence? Still, politicians and policymakers want to stick to their delusion because it allows them to pretend that governance is in the service of all, rather than driven by the interests of a privileged minority.

Poverty is so persistent in contemporary India, Parry argues, because of the manner in which politics and policies are shaped. His disconcerting but justified conclusion is that the way in which democracy is fabricated and operates may be as big a part of the problem as it is of the solution (Gooptu and Parry 2014, p. 3). While still in office as the Chief Minister of Gujarat, Narendra Modi launched the idea of the village as a corporate body which prefers to keep its ranks closed and cultivate a consensual spirit rather than instigating the sort of disunity and open conflict to which political rivalry would inevitably give rise. *Samaras* was the name he gave to the social assimilation initiative with the intent to discourage local elections to the village council. It means that a small caucus of domination decides who will be nominated next. In the name of development, his campaign aimed at depoliticization of governance at the local level.

In the early wave of post-Independence developmentalism, it was taken for granted that caste would wither away, to be replaced by class as the main principle of social organization. This reversal was considered to be part of a trajectory of change which implied that 'developing' societies such as India would follow in the path of already 'developed' nations. But it is a makeover well-nigh impossible to discern in the political, economic and social fabric of India today. Not much thought seems to have been given to the predicted dynamics in the course of time. It was mainly non-economists who brought up the issue in their writings. That glaring misconception needs to be repaired at least to some extent. After all, shifts in the relations of production have to be contextualized in the wider canvass of the social order. Caste in its emergent setting was inclusive, in the sense that its multiple ranks from top to bottom were supposed to live according to their prescribed status in ritualized separation from each other. The notion of impurity has not lost its hold in the occupational restructuring which marked the passage from a pre-capitalist to a capitalist economy. The village notables have not been dislodged from their privileged position, although they cannot take their domination for granted. The claim to superiority of those at the top by those down below has moved from covert to overt contestation. Neither has the inferiority imposed from above on those at the bottom ever been internalized. It means that the social system has graduated from one based on a top-to-bottom hierarchical ranking to one that is structured on a compartmentalized plane of separation. Social inequality as it exists and operates lacks an ideological underpinning of acquiescence across the whole gamut of differentiation. Its matrix is stretched along a horizontal axis of graded contrasts. The class dimension was not missing in the caste order of the past too, but in the conversion to the capitalist mode of production, economic rank, concretized in terms of power and property, has gained in prominence, while ritual and religious status has not receded in the attribution of cultural identity. The concordance that earlier existed between the distribution of social and economic dominance has broken down, and that dissolution has major political repercussions.

The imperative need is for a social consciousness and political assertion in which the land-poor and landless coalesce and engage in collective action. Neither class nor caste identities are strong enough for closing the ranks. In the informal economy, the spirit of solidarity breaks down by segmented niches of employment. The lack of steady and regular jobs, fragmented rather than concerted action and rife competition in a very tight labour market figure as obstacles which pre-empt the need to take a joint stance in the emancipatory struggle for freedom. The problem is one of representation. The rural poor pass their life in marginality, hidden away in colonies on the village periphery or urban outskirts, and remain without agency. In the worst case, they are coopted by the local elite and petty officials to serve interests other than their own. Although conflicts flare up again and again, defiance against exploitation and oppression does not yet find expression in organized social movements or any other form of orchestrated action that succeeds in redressing the balance of power so heavily tilted against the rural proletariat. Nevertheless, the clamour instigated from below is beyond the stage connected with the weapons of the weak. In faint attempts at social revolt, the antagonism expressed has sparked off a backlash of counter-violence from above, which is made manifest in flashes of atrocities reported from all over the country. The village has become a terrain of contestation.

THE PROMISE TO GET RID OF POVERTY AND THE CONSISTENT FAILURE TO DELIVER

In the long transition to a monetized and more diversified economy managed along capitalist lines of production, a small contingent of the workforce found access to the slowly emerging formal sector of employment which qualified for provisions meant to improve the plight of the working class. Mahatma Gandhi, as the founding father of the Textile Labour Association in Ahmedabad, insisted that the worker's pay be enough to meet the basic needs of his household. Gandhi's demand for a fair wage included social care benefits such as pension and health insurance, as well as a dearness allowance to compensate for the rising cost of living. The labour rights introduced in the first decade after Independence were meant to strengthen the bargaining power of the small segment of labour which had managed to get organized in trade unions. The industrial legislation introduced remained restricted to a vanguard of the non-agrarian workforce which benefited from the statist objective to calibrate the interests of labour and capital. The National Planning Committee set up in 1938 and chaired by Jawaharlal Nehru wrote the draft for the transition to an industrial-urban society, heralded as the ultimate trajectory for the multitude of land-poor and landless peasants made redundant in the rural economy. The regulations the state planners proposed were modelled on those practised in the developed world and included a variety of social security benefits. The progress promised did not filter through to the huge workforce outside the public sector and the mills.

In Gujarat, the committee charged in 1966 with the fixation of a minimum wage rate for agricultural work turned down the suggestion that the cash needed to meet the daily cost of living should be the yardstick. The panel argued that the recommended pay scale should not negatively affect agricultural productivity and profitability. But the statutory wage finally enacted in 1972 and periodically revised since has consistently remained below the level required for bare livelihood. Farmers bluntly refused to pay even that minimum rate. Increasing clashes between the main landowners and the landless proletariat forced the Gujarat government to introduce various social insurance and welfare schemes aimed at reducing the threat to survival of the landless class. These schemes were announced as a first step towards a more comprehensive system of social protection. The need was obvious. The National Commission on Rural Labour, 1991 reported that a mere 2.5 per cent of India's GDP was set aside for social security. This budget was nearly exclusively spent on organized labour in the formal and largely urban economy. There has been no change for the better in the subsequent decades. The approach taken was not meant to address the problem but to provide immediate electoral gain with minimal pressure on the budget of the Congress government.

The strategy of informalization which followed in the late twentieth century – although in Gujarat it was already practised much earlier on – paved the way for the regime of neoliberalism. It meant that capital was set free from the onus to ensure the welfare of labour. The closure through the 1990s of about 50 textile mills in Ahmedabad, once called the Manchester of India, led me to investigate the impact of the turnaround in the city's economy on the dismissed workforce of at least 1,20,000 mill hands. A deep fall in income, erratic but long hours of work in casual engagement or self-employment, deskilling, the end of collective action and lack of representation together with loss of social welfare benefits were major features of their forced exit from formal employment. My next round of fieldwork concentrated on these issues (Breman 2004). Its main focus was to find out how the fall from the formal to the informal economy had affected the proletarian consciousness of the dismissed workforce.

Sliding down from what was stymied as unduly tenured and protected terms of service in the doctrine of the free market, these victims had come to share the plight of labouring masses which had never enjoyed job security, income security or social security. This huge workforce had consistently been exempted from the body of labour legislation which, under pressure of trade unionism, together with a broad range of civil associations canvassing for social reform, had been promulgated for the well-being of labour in the formal sector of the economy. However, in the previous decades labour relations in the informal sector had not been totally left to the discretion of the employers. This attempt at regulation led to a number of labour laws which targeted employment practices considered unfair or abusive in official eyes, and became enacted from a social justice perspective. The most important of these were the Minimum Wage Act, 1948, the Contract Labour (Regulation and Abolition) Act, 1972, the Bonded Labour System (Abolition) Act, 1976, the Equal Remuneration Act, 1976, the Inter-State Migrant Workers (Regulation of Employment and Condition of Service) Act, 1979 and the Child Labour (Prohibition and Regulation) Act 1986.

A Rural Labour Inspectorate was set up in 1981 to check on the employment conditions of both agrarian and non-agrarian workers. Government labour officers were appointed at the district and sub-district levels to monitor the implementation of the legislation. But these officials used their mandate of inspection to line their own pockets instead of exposing and prosecuting employers for non-payment of minimum wages (Breman 1994, pp. 291–331). Under pressure also from the World Bank and the International Monetary Fund (IMF) – operating as the high command of globalized capitalism – the state has stepped back from guaranteeing minimal protection and security to the labouring poor. In order to avoid *inspection raj*, which is supposed to have led to 'unnecessary' litigation, and to promote amiable collaboration between the government's labour department and private business, a policy of self-certification allows employers to just declare that they abide with the labour laws applicable to their enterprise. Inspection of worksites has reduced to a trickle compared to what it used to be – much to the chagrin of officials who received hefty bribes for not prosecuting the large majority of employers unwilling to comply with the rules and regulations. The agency charged with checking on the terms and conditions of labour has become moribund and might as well be shut down.

The widespread practice of informalization is aimed at weakening and cheapening labour for the greater benefit of capital. In the changed scenario, social welfare for the worker remained a far-fetched illusion. Pushing through the politics and policies of neoliberalism in the 1980s as a win-win strategy for all stakeholders, the Congress government astutely abandoned the role it had claimed from the very beginning as a protector-cum-provider of the common good. Under the Hindutva regime, this retrogression was confirmed and further promulgated in the form of four labour codes which boil down to withdrawal of the body of labour legislation that had earlier been fought for. The new legislation is part of a strategy of reducing labour costs, aimed to depress both wages and social benefits, and driven through with despotic labour control mechanisms to pre-empt trade unionism (Jose 2022).

The insistent and prolonged denial of the social question in post-colonial India (Breman 2010c) would seem to be impossible to square with the reported trend of poverty alleviation. Of course, not for politicians and policymakers who changed track and became ardent proponents of the shift from a formal to an informal economy. This turnaround gained momentum in the 1970s and was postulated by the advocating lobby as a win-win strategy for both capital and labour. At the beginning of this section, I have already referred to the sobering words of an essay authored by Deaton and Kozel (2005), which signalled that India's poverty guesstimates were politically tailored and that the rapid decline of deprivation was less than officially reported. The Bharatiya Janata Party (BJP) government, since 2011–2012, has obfuscated the measurement of poverty. The National Sample Survey Organization (NSSO), which was the main statistical agency, is no longer a semi-public body. It was incorporated within the Ministry of Statistics and Programme Implementation and in that repositioning, lost its reputation of professional competence and rectitude. There is solid evidence to conclude that major segments of society hovering around the poverty line – mostly those of OBC (Other Backward Classes) denomination, equipped with skills and owning some means of production – were able to work their way out of hardship. On the downside, however, many of the unskilled and dispossessed households have further slid down in their deficient way of life to destitution.

The controversy that remained a raging one, on how to figure out the changed magnitude and composition of indigence, induced in-house consultants of the World Bank to keep the gospel of neoliberal bliss alive. Persevering in the charade of a progressive decline of indigence, their statistical analysis shows a steady shrinking of poverty between 2011 and 2019 among roughly 10 per cent of the population – but, as they are belatedly forced to concede, 'not as much as previously thought' (Roy and van der Weide 2022). Without this cautionary afterthought, an IMF working paper wants us to believe that by 2019, India had succeeded in almost eradicating extreme poverty, a feat that is reported to have remained unspoilt even by the explosive impact of the pandemic (Bhalla, Bhasin and Virmani 2022). These are brazen claims in the light of the multiple livelihood disasters that befell the labouring poor in these years more than any other social class.

Big data torn loose from their socio-economic and political context run the risk of becoming flawed in statistical fabrication to big errors and, framed in preconceived and wilful expedience, are bound to result in big lies. The evidence for my claim is to be found in a World Bank report, *Poverty and Shared Prosperity: Correcting Course*, which the World Bank released in autumn of 2022, amending its earlier estimates (The World Back 2022).

The lack of official data on poverty which the Government of India has stopped publishing since 2011–12 and a major reappraisal of its own flawed fact-finding has impelled the Bank to upscale the number of people who fall short of income for their bare livelihood. Stuck in extreme poverty – a level of indigence I have addressed as pauperized – their daily earnings are less than $2.15. For an average working-class household, this would add up to roughly Rs 750 to Rs 1,000 per day. According to its new tally, not 23 crore (230 million) but 56 crore (560 million) people, or about one-fifth of India's population, are now documented as living in destitution. In its resetting of these figures of a sub-human existence, a retrogression for which the Covid-19 pandemic raging in 2019–20 is held accountable, the World Bank study records that out of the 70 crores globally, 80 per cent live in India. While, in my perception, most of the people in the world living in these dire straits are Indians, those in other countries (spread over the global South in particular) face a similar predicament which has remained wilfully unrecorded and glossed over.

A Transformation that Did Not Materialize

Propelled by the forces of capitalist production, large masses of the people are driven out of what, since time immemorial, has been the mainstay of the peasantry, and away from their village habitat in the countryside. The great transformation was how Karl Polanyi analysed the capitalist onslaught that disentangled the economy from the political, social and cultural framework in which it was embedded. Industrialization, in tandem with urbanization, had become the organizing principle of the market-driven transformation that started to take place in the North Atlantic basin about two centuries ago. Polanyi insisted that the emerging new order had global ramifications, an observation that led him to label its remote fringe zones as the colonial and semi-colonial jungle. Europe, and Great Britain in particular, was the capitalist heartland on which his seminal work focused. He described the landscape that shaped up as a veritable abyss of human degradation and comments: 'Before the process had advanced very far, the labouring people had been crowded together in new places of desolation, the so-called industrial towns of England' (Polanyi 1944, p. 39).

The exodus of rural labour began in Europe around the turn of the late eighteenth to nineteenth century. In the wake of decolonization in the second half of the twentieth century, a similar spatial mobility spread to what came to be called the Third World in the southern hemisphere. The loss of employment in agriculture escalated globally and resulted from a process in which people deprived of decent standards of living became redundant in primary production and were converted into a huge reserve army of labour. The opening up of the countryside and reduction in the cost of transport accelerated the footloose character of labour on a larger scale than ever before. The blockade of passage to the developed zones of the world, mainly located in the northern hemisphere, implies that labour migration by and large tends to remain restricted to movement within the same country. Intra-rural migration has remained quite significant, but the emphasis is on the trek from rural to urban destinations. Most migrants who manage to reach the urban labour market are not absorbed in permanent jobs but end up in casualized waged work which keep them roaming around or make do with what passes for self-employment in the lower echelons of the informal economy.

Labour nomadism is a major feature of the swelling proletariat pushed out of their agrarian-rural abodes. The footloose nature of their employment is matched and aggravated by the unsettled character of their means of livelihood. Going away and coming back was initially also a major trend in the west, when the exodus from the countryside began to accelerate. However, fairly soon, such circular mobility decreased and sojourners settled down in their new habitat at or close to their site of work, usually towns or cities. They left their rural dwellings behind to become urban citizens, often as industrial workers. As Polanyi commented, what started as a catastrophe turned out to be the dawn of economic progress and social emancipation that signified the recouped control of human society over markets. The great transformation which changed the character of the Atlantic world eventually succeeded in harnessing the forces of runaway capitalism but not in the world at large, and also, as we have come to realize with the wisdom of hindsight, not forever. The triumph of the market has had a dire impact on what Polanyi called the 'native' economies.

The three or four large famines that decimated India under the British rule since the Rebellion were thus neither a consequence of the elements, nor of exploitation, but simply of the new organization of labour and land which broke up the old village without actually solving its problems. While under the regime of feudalism and the village community, *noblesse oblige*, clan solidarity, and regulation of the corn market checked famines, under the rule of the market the people could not be prevented from starving according to the rules of the game. (Polanyi 1944, p. 160; see also Davis 2000)

Tearing the labouring poor out of their village abodes in India, as also elsewhere in the global South, has indeed for many of these subordinated classes so far not been a trajectory to a much better destiny. The desperate search for waged work which forces a large part of the agrarian workforce out of their village habitat drives a high percentage back again after a season, a few years or at the end of their working life. Labour migration is thus, for all intents and purposes, a spasmodic form of labour circulation. For over half a century, my fieldwork has consistently focused on these footloose contingents in rural and urban Gujarat, a state marked by high economic growth. The pattern of constant movement has become an important feature of the informal economy. The regime of informality and labour circulation are closely interdependent. The endless trek to other destinations is a direct consequence of the inability of this reserve army of labour to qualify for regular jobs yielding higher income at home or elsewhere. For the large majority of these landless and land-poor people, poorly educated if not totally illiterate, labour circulation is not a free choice. It is a strenuous and tiresome venture that has to be repeated again and again. This ongoing mobility back and forth is rarely rewarded by getting skilled or bringing back earnings that can be saved and used for productive investment leading to improved livelihood.

Circulation is at best a survival strategy, a route taken to cope with the threat of underemployment and the lack of basic means needed to keep the household going. The labour power of migrants is required off and on, but not their cumbersome and defiling presence. The urban arena has turned markedly hostile to newcomers bereft of assets, skills and social capital, who have come not only to work but also to occupy space for living. Finding access to government agencies charged with issuing permits for urban citizenship is next to impossible for the footloose nomads. The space they encroach upon is either required for expanding infrastructure, or is taken up by housing colonies for people with higher and regular incomes. The squatters are chased off before the construction works begin. Drifting around the city's periphery, they have to keep a low profile because they cannot afford to buy or hire the plot on which they erect a bivouac of sorts. These aspiring settlers do not qualify for property rights and tenured security. They are what I have called 'nowhere people', adrift in a nowhere, nebulous landscape. Those who manage to gain a foothold in one of the more regularized urban slums belong to the somewhat better-off category of migrants. It does not mean, however, that they have found a more permanent niche in which they are safe from eviction. Even when they are enlisted in the municipal records, their dwellings get demolished because the waste land they occupy becomes a target for the real estate mafia which terrorizes the slum dwellers to vacate and move away.

The senior official in charge of Ahmedabad's urban renewal programme for poor households told me that labour nomads do not qualify for residential rights in the city – 'we allow them to come but for staying on they have to make their own arrangements'. What he meant to say was that these people are free to come and go for work but are not allowed to camp in public or private spaces for shelter, even if such spots are lying waste and not utilized for any other purpose. When they invade such spaces it is considered as trespassing, and dealt with as illegal occupancy that even after many years gives no right to entitlement. A Supreme Court order in 2009 mandated large cities in each and every state of India to set up night shelters – one for every 1,00,000 inhabitants – to cater to the needs of those who have no shelter to stay at the end of the workday. In 2015, I went around to check on these public dormitories in Ahmedabad, and found that they have either not opened up or do not provide the services promised. The transient customers for whom they are meant were dwelling on the pavement in front of these hospices (Breman 2015). The inability of these homeless people to seek each other out in mutual support to change the rule of casualized hire-and-fire, to claim higher pay for their labour power and to get permission to settle down with their dependants where they find work, is caused by a total lack of political representation and drives them in an abhorrent state of lasting anonymity.

David Harvey has foregrounded the habitat rather than the worksite as the focal point of social struggle. In his view, the accumulation of capital has destroyed the urban commons, understood as public space, public institutions and public goods. The rise of the Paris Commune of 1871, he argues, did not revolve around work and labour but prioritized the right to reside in the city: 'It was not a proletarian uprising or a class-based movement at all, but an urban and social movement that was reclaiming citizenship and the right to the city' (Harvey 2012, p. 211). Its reversal has taken shape in today's India: the right to come for work is acknowledged or even insisted upon, but not the right to live and to livelihood, as the outbreak of the pandemic in 2019 vividly demonstrated. The urban employers of this footloose proletariat closed shop when the lockdown was announced and left crores of hapless workers to fend for themselves. The social drama that unfolded saw masses of this reserve army of labour in agony, trying to get away from imminent disaster caused by the mix of instant loss of income, lack of hope for access to informal social safety nets at home and fear of the pandemic looming ahead (Breman 2020). Suddenly, the flight away from land and village of this huge multitude was made visible, as well as the demarcated segregation between their 'for the time being' site of work and their domicile at a great distance.

Civil rights activists have put the plight of the fugitives on record with much compassion. But on another wavelength the vagrancy of a footloose multitude that became so noticeable was alarmingly written up as the manifestation of a dangerous class. For sure, their massive presence at the bottom of the informal economy does constitute a threat to peace and order. This eventual risk is forestalled by not only chasing this multitude away from where they live, but also by withholding them permission to settle down wherever they go, hunting and gathering wages. Being spread out over a vast hinterland in communal colonies prevents these restlessly mobile sections from congregating in slums on the outskirts of urban areas, where they might eventually team up in collective protest against their exclusion. Acting on behalf of vested interests, the authorities would want to keep a watchful eye on the people being uprooted. Indeed, there is no dearth of historical evidence which suggests that roaming around without being allowed to stay put may generate restiveness that escalates in an attempt to escape from control and discipline. This, however, is not the peril associated in India with the more than 100 million adults, adolescents and children incessantly driven out and back again for sheer survival at the bottom of the pile. Fragmented and segmented in communal niches, theirs is a way of life that does not crystallize in a joint platform from which to bargain for a better deal. The menace their obnoxious presence spells is the risk of contagion with the filth and squalor and viruses that fester in their impure ranks, from which the better-off classes must be protected. However, instead of discerning a dangerous class, the public lens should be on their authentic identity, which is that of an endangered species.

Homecoming

The ravages caused by the pandemic have been mainly documented in the mainstream media from a class-biased perspective which highlighted how the better-off segments in the mega-cities were able or unable to cope with the cataclysmic event. Away from this highlighted gaze, reliable information on what transpired in the vast hinterland is difficult to come by. The uneven spread of Covid-19 reflects, much more than differences in the real incidence of the disease, its lack of detection in many quarters. Public health care, never easily accessible or cost-free was, together with several other pro-poor commitments, subject to far-reaching cutbacks from the end of the twentieth century onwards. The labouring poor were accustomed to consult quacks or make do with self-medication paid out from their own pockets in case of failing health. The death toll of the pandemic was high, but often neither the nature of the fatality nor its occurrence was duly notified and recorded. The contingents deprived of access to formal medical care were often found to be more afraid of starvation than of catching the disease. The labouring poor passed away as undocumented persons in their informality, just as they were when still alive. Mortality has been heavily and consistently undercounted to an extent that is impossible to estimate. Even the figure of 5 million deaths for India alone out of a worldwide total of 15 million, as reported by the World Health Organization, is a conservative one. Still, it is ten times higher than the government count, and telling proof of how politics and governance have failed in the protection and care of the country's citizenry.

Conducted by the Centre for Labour Research and Action based in Ahmedabad, a rapid assessment survey in May 2021 across eight streams of 590 rural migrants in Gujarat and Rajasthan recruited for seasonal work in agriculture, brick kilns and construction, found that more than a third of the workers themselves or members of their families fell sick during the second wave of the pandemic in early 2021 with Covid-like symptoms. This figure is an underestimate since respondents showed extreme reluctance to talk about pandemic-specific matters. Many workers would stop talking as soon as Covid-related questions were asked. Almost none of those who fell sick were admitted to government hospitals for medical care, but went instead for treatment to quacks and private infirmaries. About one-fifth of the respondents made mention of positive cases in their villages, and the same proportion also reported deaths which remained unregistered. High mortality, especially in tribal districts where outmigration is huge, was a consequence of the strong vaccination hesitancy amongst the workers. While a large number of deaths did occur, these communities avoided public health facilities like plague. The people were scared of being tested and if found positive, of being confined to isolation wards from which, they feared, chances of coming out alive were slim. The hearsay was that the vaccine itself caused the disease (Katiyar, Vijeta and Rose 2021). The rumour mills abounded suggesting that the disease was being spread by the state to kill off old people and pensioners, in order to remove their organs.

The disconcerting tales of anxiety, distrust and dislike demonstrated how the labouring poor had come to detest the wanton refusal of the state to provide protection against adversity, and instead contributed to their immiseration. Since they were excluded from the officially collected statistics, the feelings they voiced could be discounted. This lapse allowed the government in January 2022 to claim that three-quarters of all adults were fully vaccinated against the virus. In his acknowledgement of this proud achievement, the country's Prime Minister went public claiming that 'the faith of our people in our nation's vaccine is a great source of strength'. India's ruling caucus had adjudicated to cover up the social drama played out in the rural milieu of people driven to vagrancy. As part of this policy of abandonment, the National Statistical Office charged with the compilation of statistical data has severely curtailed shedding of light on the deprivations of the labouring poor. While its forerunner, the National Sample Survey Organisation, had been commissioned with finding and reporting factual data-sets, the restructured NSSO operates from within the state apparatus and does not disseminate all the collected information – or goes to the extent of fabricating fake data-sets to cover up the appalling conditions of the massive workforce in the nether echelons of the economy.

Many land-poor and landless households at the bottom of the rural heap had already, since many years, become split up in off-and-on multi-localities. This falling apart of the basic fabric of social life in varying frequency and duration cannot be avoided, because those who go in search of income elsewhere do so on the strength of their labour power and without co-residents either too young or too old to work. Not able yet or any more to at least reproduce their maintenance cost, the underaged as well as overaged, with their usually female caretakers in the household, have to stay back and somehow vie for their own subsistence. They receive support from the earnings made outside, which are sent or brought back on home visits of the migrants. The news of the lockdown declared at short notice at the start of the pandemic drove the footloose workforce in a stampede away from their worksites back to where they were supposed to belong. The fugitives not only arrived penniless, but often had to shop around for loans to settle their much-inflated travel fare. Oftentimes, this cost added to a much larger debt which was already outstanding on their departure to faraway worksites. In the functional interpretation of labour migration, the emphasis is on how the income made away from home is put at the disposal of dependent members in the village of origin. It is the perception of the male provider eager to contribute to the well-being of the household in which he is an absent stakeholder. In the account of my last round of fieldwork in 2014–15, I have discarded this assumption. Footloose workers selling their labour power on an early morning at a labour market on the outskirts of Ahmedabad told me that they could not afford to give priority to household needs. They were obliged to set aside a very large part of their earnings as payback instalments to usurious moneylenders (Breman 2016, pp. 168–94).

The ceaseless coming and going of both adults and adolescents to engage in waged work elsewhere in short or long intervals displays the fragility of this primary unit of cohabitation, which results in a weakening of social cohesion and mutual care within it. The main protagonist in Aman Sethi's novel, *A Free Man* (2011), is the archetypal tramp or hobo. His perambulations in work and life keep him on the road and free from becoming bogged down in dependency. He has also cut ties with other household members on his departure and does not contribute to their cost of living. As against the portrait of the footloose provider anxiously caring for resourceless dependants at home, the careless hobo is at the other end of a spectrum; the average case may be the majority in the middle ranks, stuck between caring for the household left behind to some extent, but caring for themselves first and foremost. However, the cherished image of 'home' as a social safety net that is always there as a fall-back option in case of adversity needs to be corrected. When footloose mobility is of working-life duration, this average modality predominates, ending only when labour power is squeezed out of the debilitated body. Homecoming then means heading back to stay put, likely in a hybrid identity, at a loss with whom to share and where to 'belong'. This countervailing evidence leads me to emphasize how circular migration fosters individuation and tears apart the social fabric of the proletarianized household.

FROM BEYOND TO WITHIN THE PALE OF INCLUSION?

Between 2004 and 2006, I went back to the sites of my earlier investigations in the countryside of south Gujarat to monitor the pace and direction of change in which the land-poor and landless communities were enmeshed. Summing up the common denominator of my findings in these rural localities over a period of close to half a century, the still-widening gap between the dominating and the dominated caste–classes was my focal point of concern (Breman 2007b). The spiral which I described highlighted a growing polarization in the context of what had transpired in the politics and policies of neoliberal capitalism. These dynamics of an intensified divide were harshly visible at opposite ends of the village scale which separated more from less, high from low and better from worse. What in the recent past had been different circuits with off-and-on interaction and involvement on both sides, had solidified to segregation which came close to institutionalized apartheid. The progressive distancing was quite noticeable in starkly differentiated spheres of life: housing, health care, education and, of course, the ability to participate or not in the process of economic growth. My comments on this trend concentrated on the swelling magnitude of the rural proletariat. It was clear that agricultural labour, which had been their mainstay in the past, was for the large majority of them not any longer their occupational identity. They had become fragmented in the provisioning of their livelihood, although they were almost without exception amassed in the informal economy. Their spread in heterogeneity made it impossible to rank them together under this heading, as I have argued in a previous publication.

> It is misleading to focus on the contrasts between two extremes of the labour hierarchy. Instead it is the enormous diversity, not only between formal and informal sectors, but also within them, that should above all be stressed. . . . Thus, a unidimensional hierarchical stratification does not exist. Confusing heterogeneity characterizes the broad middle range. At the top of the range is guaranteed job security, at the bottom multiple vulnerabilities. (Breman 2007, p. 418)

In a more recent essay, I elaborated on the distinct character that splits up labour in several subclasses (Breman 2021). Occupational multiplicity has become the hallmark for the footloose contingents among them, either in separate bouts throughout the year or even within their lengthened working day. Clubbing them together as the labouring poor is also a classification too simple for this huge mass which ignores structural and lasting differences that exist between them. Construction of a poverty line has been the customary watershed to identify segments of the workforce unable to live within means too shallow and failure to cope with adversities that are bound to happen. Engagement or not in regular employment is a major indicator for identifying the class status of workers. The better-off workers among the self-employed, those who own or hire some means of production, as well as wage-earners who have become semi-skilled, are more steadily at work than in constant rotation; also in receipt of steady pay, they are found to be hovering around the poverty line. Consolidation in this endeavour opens space for some upward mobility in a trajectory of further improvement. My appraisal in the last round of investigation was that, taking together the four localities in south Gujarat that I had covered over nearly five decades, at best, one-third of the land-poor to landless households can be classified in this segment. Less than half of them have also managed to set up households with their dependants in the vicinity of their worksite. It means an escape from the ordeal to remain circulating between where they are employed and where they live. Half the marginal landholders and even more of the fully dispossessed from property constitute the massive hardcore of the labouring poor, coping with not enough work and very low pay to meet the basic needs of their household, let alone being able to invest in expense required for finding a way out of their improvidence. To arrange for mere survival, most of them are entrapped in relationships of neo-bondage. Loans contracted at usurious interest rates that they have to work off usually forces them to circular wage hunting and gathering nearby or far away from home. They are only familiar with accumulation as staggering indebtedness, which is the bane of their existence.

Destitution is the predicament of the residue at the tail end of indigence. It is an underclass which, in the villages of south Gujarat I researched, adds up to between one-sixth and one-fifth of the indigent workforce. These people are commonly classified as the ultra-poor but are in my lexicon written up as paupers (Breman 2016). For lack of creditworthiness, they are not eligible to fall into debt and are therefore free from neo-bondage. Extreme vulnerability prevents them from finding regular work but severe underemployment, of course, aggravates their downward slide. There is a contingent within this class that is least paid attention to, which has been driven out from the shelter it had established in villages, towns of cities without being able to settle down somewhere else. I have come across such destitute hordes on the pavement, along the roadside and in the open field. This modern form of nomadism is not circular but begins without coming to an end: nowhere people in a nowhere landscape. The degree of poverty and pauperism I have distinguished above dates back already to fifteen years ago. Neither does it take into account the employment and income loss in the wake of the disastrous demonetization drive in 2016, and the subsequent surge in the collection of black money under the randomly declared Goods and Services Tax which ravaged the informal economy. Nor does it register the havoc caused by the pandemic between 2019 and 2021 which disproportionately affected Indian households in the bottom ranks of the working classes.[1]

A topic that never failed to come up in my encounters with workers who were forced to remain shuttling between domicile and worksite was their desire for a settled life that would redeem them from drifting in loneliness. This aspiration would warrant the ability to establish their household where the search for livelihood forced them to go, and thus combine working and living without being driven back and forth in perpetual mobility. But to satisfy this desire would be at cross-purposes with India's policy ambit to cheapen the cost of labour by keeping the lower classes of the workforce flexible to demand and pliable in casual conditions of employment. This nefarious dictate sees to it that the majority of the labouring poor are bound to remain footloose. To cope with recurrent adversity and lifecycle events, cumulative indebtedness becomes inevitable. It is a liability that drives many of them down a spiral of dependency from which recovery is next to impossible. The two handicaps together – remaining adrift and in debt, having mortgaged control over one's labour power in a state of neo-bondage – dampens protest against ruthless exploitation and prevents these workers from engaging in collective action. In the informal economy, trade unionism comes close to being prohibited, more so among the lower ranks whose struggles for a better deal are stringently opposed. It does not mean that dispossession leaves no room for dissent, which, in the multiple ranks of the labouring poor, finds expression in a rejection of the claim to superiority from quarters high above. This resilience speaks of a mood of muted assertion, an anxiety and unwillingness to being held down in subordination, and makes their shared consciousness manifest in proletarianized demeanour. The spirit of defiance is articulated by will power and courage which refuses to bow down under the weight of domination.

Such a contrarian guile of demurral is exemplified in the autobiographical narrative of Gidla's *Ants Among Elephants* (2017). It is an audacity which sets the stage for transcending from defiance to a class-for-itself consciousness. No doubt, economic need is the main reason for going in search of employment elsewhere. But amongst youngsters in particular, the appetite to strike out to faraway and often unknown destinations should also be understood as an escape from boundless derogation and discrimination at home. It may not lead to redemption from exploitation and dependency, but such harsh treatment is meted out more anonymously than in personalized and face-to-face interaction that is common practice in the village setting.

The Hindutva ideology has expanded beyond the social pool of the upper castes, the milieu in which it had its origin (Breman and Shah 2022). The wide variety of communities in the lower echelons clubbed together as OBCs were the first to articulate their Hindu identity and lead the way in the electoral swing in favour of the BJP. The Scheduled Castes (SCs) and Scheduled Tribes (STs) followed suit to the extent that a sizeable proportion of them – the creamy layer above all – followed suit and deserted their label as loyal clientele of the Congress party. What made them change their political stance and join the BJP bandwagon? Thorough disillusionment with the promise to relieve them from poverty, a pledge repeated again and again but deficiently if at all practised, had fuelled animosity. The appeal to cultural nationalism, to be properly affirmed in their Hinduized status, also played a major role. Mahatma Gandhi and his upper-caste disciples, a strong lobby in Gujarat, never gave up persuading the Adivasi communities, under proper guardianship of the upper castes, to forsake their tribal lore as a precondition for getting access to mainstream society. Inroads were also made into the ranks of the Scheduled Castes via the Bharatiya Mazdoor Sangh, a trade union established by the Rashtriya Swayamsevak Sangh (RSS) in their campaign to build cohesion and harmony between the higher and lower castes. The objective of gaining hegemony required the BJP leadership to compromise their *savarna* purity and coopt the majority of shudras and *avarna*s. It is a classic dichotomy segregating the small minority of twice-born castes from the majority belonging to the lower orders. As Ghanshyam Shah reported, in the quest for domination as designed by Hindutva's caucus, apostles were engaged to spread the Hindutva gospel in the terrain of impurity.

> In the late 1990s, some Dalit youths were recruited as members of the Bajrang Dal. They received training not only in the Hindutva ideology but also organizational management in winning over people. Some of them were given positions like local president or *mantri*, i.e. secretary. Their responsibilities were to coordinate and supervise activities such as celebration of festivals and meetings organized from time to time in the area. Along with these activities, they distributed literature – pamphlets, leaflets, journals, and audio and video cassettes published by various organizations of the Parivar. Swords and *trishuls* [tridents] were distributed among the members. The office-bearers also worked as brokers between government functionaries and the residents to solve day-

to-day problems of the people with the government. (Breman and Shah 2022, p. 203).

It would seem that in Gujarat, the state operating as a 'laboratory' for the BJP's holy mission of a Hindu *rashtra* has achieved what it set out to accomplish: to welcome into its twice-born vote-bank not only shudras (as common people), but also segments of the nation which from generation to generation were kept beyond the pale of inclusion. My reservations are regarding the bottom end of this compressed social differentiation. Acceptance of downgraded social categories as Hindus does not imply their treatment on par with those of twice-born vintage. It is an alliance steeped in apartheid between the dominating and the dominated. Admittance to the grail of belonging to the fold is not meant to impinge on the distancing that is pivotal to the caste order. In their turn, the communities stuck as before in subalternity may fall in line with what is expected from them, i.e. a veneer of compliance. Lacking the space and the means to escape from overt submission, they have in a long-winded trajectory tenaciously resisted internalizing dependency in their social consciousness. Speaking from his personal experience of village life during his childhood as a member of a Dalit community, Ambedkar denounced the 'beyond the pale' label, and insisted that these downtrodden communities were part and parcel of the Hindu society and thus strongly interconnected with the mainstream fabric.

> The Hindu society insists on segregation of the untouchables. The Hindu will not live in the quarters of the untouchables and will not allow the untouchables to live inside Hindu quarters. . . . It is not a case of social separation, a mere stoppage of social intercourse for a temporary period. It is a case of territorial segregation and of a cordon sanitaire putting the impure people inside the barbed wire into a sort of a cage. Every Hindu village has a ghetto. The Hindus live in the village and the untouchables live in the ghetto. (Ambedkar 1948, pp. 21–22)

Much has been made of the sweetmeats that Narendra Modi distributed in the quarters inhabited by the lowly classes. In their colonies where civil amenities often fail to reach, social goods such as gas cylinders, tap water, toilets, food rations and other freebies are distributed not as a right but as a generous donation by the head of the state. These are gimmicks of populist welfarism, needed in a show of benevolence when elections are due to raise expectations of better days around the corner. Behind the fanfare massively propagated, checking on fact and fiction is required to monitor the spread and impact it has had on the targeted recipients. My scepticism of people having been solidly accommodated beyond the pale of the BJP frame by handing them doles and stirring them to follow the path of duty they owe to the Hindu nation stems from what I have observed during my fieldwork in Gujarat where Narendra Modi held power as Chief Minister from 2002 to 2014. As Prime Minister, the supreme leader of the nation started to practise the same demeanour he had adopted when in command of the state which became the model to acclaim BJP's majoritarian rule for the country at large.

In a final round of research from August 2010 to February 2011 in four villages of south Gujarat which I have investigated time and again, the focus was on the implementation of the Unorganized Workers' Social Security Act which the Congress-led United Progressive Alliance (UPA) government legislated in 2008. My grassroots findings clarified that the stipends budgeted for the labouring poor rarely reach them; those who do receive only get a fraction of what is paid out in their name. To understand why and how it was so difficult to qualify for entitlement, I frequented the corridors of officialdom and came back from these ventures with the strong feeling that the state and the poor belong to different realms, are caught up in separated circuits, and do not speak the same language but operate from an incompatible logic. More is at stake, however, than just unfamiliarity on both sides. The political and bureaucratic machinery is from top to bottom not only ineffective, but also thoroughly corrupt and engaged in large-scale fraud. Nothing has changed, also not under Modi's tutelage, since 1985 when Rajiv Gandhi flippantly confirmed that out of every rupee spent on pro-poor schemes, 15 paise is what the intended beneficiaries have to make do with.

In my efforts to get a closer understanding of the political and policy manipulations at play, I kept myself informed on Modi's vision for and outreach to the ultra-poor to secure what they badly needed, and summed up my observations as follows. In his capacity as the Chief Minister of Gujarat, he announced a scheme meant to improve the plight of the non-working poor. The welfare agencies were instructed to arrange camps at the sub-district level and present themselves there in order to facilitate the distribution of social benefits to the needy in the villages around. Under the banner of '*Garib Kalyan Mela*', this initiative was promoted with fervour in the regional newspapers and in a short time, became quite popular. Long before the event was going to take place, the local authorities were briefed to spread the word in colonies of the landless and make sure that the targeted beneficiaries were assembled and fetched to the *mela* grounds. The idea was to deal with the deserving cases on the spot, but that turned out to be too difficult to realize because of the formalities which were required. It meant that several files got duly prepared in advance, but the successful applicants only came to know about their entitlements in the course of the festivity. Narendra Modi was not shy to make an appearance on such occasions to read out the list of benefits granted. The impression created was that the non-working poor were blessed with endowments due to his benevolence and largesse, even when the source of funding was not the state of Gujarat but the central government (Breman 2013b, pp. 314–15).

At the sites of my fieldwork, I met with a handful of men and women who had received their pension or handicap allowance (for a variety of physical or mental disabilities) when a *mela* was held nearby. They told me that they owed their windfall – that was how they perceived their good fortune – to their own tedious efforts of many months, spent running around at no little expense to collect all papers required and for the indispensable *olkhan* (mediation) from somebody higher-up, rather than to the personal blessing of the man wont to proclaim himself as the saviour of all deserving Gujaratis, right up to the very least and last of them. Hence, to conclude that the discretionary and wily dispersion of relief would have swayed the people at the bottom of the heap to toe the BJP line is in my view a misplaced notion of the popular mood among them, which, in my reading, was sulky and abrasive rather than docile.

Tanika Sarkar's incisive approach in *Hindu Nationalism in India* (2022) stresses and highlights the frantic efforts that the band of front organizations set up by the RSS make to attune to Hindutva as the obligatory radar for the meritorious citizens of the nation. Her well-documented and subtle inquiry zooms in on the larger unnamed struggle. She correctly points out that that the Sangh Parivar is eager to reorient the discursive order of power relations in the Hindu *rashtra* of its dreams. Its emissaries are sent to the landscape of impurity to invite these communities to join hands with the bearers of the majoritarian gospel. But how plausible is the appeal made by these zealots to an all-embracing Hindu brotherhood and sisterhood, for an audience that is accustomed in day-to-day experience to negligence, derogation and discrimination? There is a dearth of information on the caste composition of these front organizations. To assert that all among the dominated masses are welcomed as members, in my opinion, is a façade, behind which not social mixing but communal and ranked separation has remained the organizational device. The Congress party's approach never penetrated deeply into the milieu of the labouring poor; instead, they outsourced these vote-banks to usually high-caste agents at the local level. The idea that the RSS has managed to do this more effectively by relying on its organized cadre needs more factual proof than the doctored evidence put out on its social media channels. Of more critical portent, however, is the systematic effort to 'cleanse' schoolbooks and the educational curriculum at large from information which negates and sullies the record of the sponsors and acolytes of Hindutva in the past and present. It is their writing of history in the Big Brother mode of Orwellian newspeak.

Yogendra Yadav's *Making Sense of Indian Democracy* (2021) despondently illustrates that getting democracy embedded in a backward society with a lopsided economy is a near-impossible task to attain. His book argues that the political canvas which Jawaharlal Nehru and the Congress courageously tried to foster in a top–down approach has floundered due to the chasm between the elite and the masses. A democratic fabric was duly instituted with suffrage installed right from the beginning of Independence. But the rural-agrarian habitat in which the large majority of Scheduled Caste and Scheduled Tribe communities all over India continued to dwell prevented escape from the domination to which they have been subjected from the remote past. Fieldwork investigations conducted over half a century enabled me to get a firm hold on the power configuration in the countryside of south Gujarat.

The subaltern mindset has drastically changed in the period covered. The need to engage in labour circulation contributed to widening the social horizon for the classes at the bottom of the agrarian pyramid and kindled aspirations of shedding life-long subalternity. In the Dravidian parts of the country, a surge of emancipatory assertion flared up much earlier than in the Hindi belt. It has taken more time to become manifest in the vast Gangetic plain and adjacent regions, but here too, the village has become an arena of contestation. The constitution of the village council is meant to reflect the local caste hierarchy, and Scheduled Caste or Scheduled Tribe members are frequently elected to chair this lowest rung of public governance. As pointed out in my writings, these candidates are often manipulated to act as stooges for the high-caste elite, the main landowners, who continue to call the shots. A political mandate levelling down rampant inequality as a precondition for a frame of democracy is a far cry in the contemporary village setting. Ambedkar's grim perception holds true even today, that from the vantage point of the lower castes and classes, the village is a den of narrow-mindedness and communalism, a site without equality, liberty and fraternity (Jodhka 2002, p. 3351). At the same time, to conclude that undiluted authoritarianism is as prevalent as before and binds the proletarian segments as foot soldiers to Hindutva's chariot of cultural homogenization is to overstate its reach and impact.

My scepticism about the popularity that, it is suggested, the BJP enjoys among the proletarianized masses, urban as well as rural, stems first and of all from mismanagement of the economy by the ruling party and its hallowed leader who has from day one of his reign taken charge of this portfolio. A short phase of catering to the needs of the lower castes and classes in the late 1970s and 1980s – which saw the first state-level experiments with employment guarantee schemes and some thinly spread social security benefits – broke down when the Congress under Rajiv Gandhi's charge uncompromisingly swung to neoliberalism in the early 1990s. As Chief Minister of Gujarat, Modi was even more ardent in hailing the same recipe with corporate capitalism of his home-state brand in particular as the main engine of economic growth. The agenda drawn up and executed by him implies a stringent denial of the social question (Breman 2019, pp. 258–65). When canvassing as the BJP's candidate in 2014 for his shifting ground of power to the national level, Modi announced in his usual blustering style that he would create 10 million jobs as India's Prime Minister. It was a promise like so many others which he did not deliver.

The problem is that the proletarianized masses so far have failed to come together in a common front. The multifold barriers put up against getting organized in class-based action has forced them to articulate their primordial identity to shop around in the labour market in order to secure a minimal livelihood. The caste culture is deeply embedded also within the lower echelons of this stratified zone of inequality, and results in communal separation instead of a social consciousness shaped in solidarity among the victimized majority of this inhuman regime. A platform of working-class unity on an anti-caste platform is urgently required to escape from remaining entrapped in both poverty and exclusion from mainstream society, as Anand Teltumbde has rightly advocated in his *Republic of Caste* (2018). This is an arduous task, more so because all those who want to practise it – as Teltumbde himself does – have to face the wrath of the surveillance state and are taken into political custody.

Relentless and progressive inequality should be acknowledged as the hallmark of neoliberal capitalism. The rapid rise in underemployment and unemployment among the low-skilled or unskilled workforce in particular is due to the replacement of labour by capital in the informal economy as well. The magnitude can only be guessed at since official figures are either unreliable or unavailable. The worsening plight of the labouring poor is the outcome of much more than merely economic tribulations. The political democracy acclaimed and installed with the declaration of Independence in the country's Constitution has remained a facade and restricted to the top end. Although suffrage was mandated for India's adult population and incorporated the working classes in the electoral lists for national and state-level assemblies, a democratic fabric has failed to materialize at the floor of society. Daniel Thorner's hope that political democracy would enable the labouring poor in their rural habitat to gain social leverage and strengthen their bargaining power has, in retrospect, turned out to be a pipe dream. While, during the decades of Congress rule, at least lip service was paid to poverty alleviation, under the ruthlessly authoritarian Hindutva regime, the promise of eventual inclusion of the down-and-out has been converted to rigorous exclusion. The Prime Minister found, a few years down the line, another solution for the raging problem of unemployment, now threatening the intermediate castes and classes also. In 2020, shortly after the outbreak of the Covid-19 pandemic, he launched the Aatma Nirbhar Bharat scheme with much fanfare. Making clear that job creation cannot be the business of governance, the CEO of Hindutva politics stipulated that the people should be held accountable for their own livelihood.

In the brand of neoliberal capitalism, self-reliance is the prescribed remedy for the workforce to find incomes high enough to maintain both themselves and their dependants. The required ethos is a code of conduct which combines self-employment with self-representation and boils over into self-exploitation. The dictate aims to avoid the need for state-provided protection against adversity and the right to public relief for the labouring poor. In this gross policy of social eviction, destitution is blamed as the outcome of defective behaviour and lack of commendable virtues such as industriousness, sobriety, thrift and self-discipline. Solving or at least alleviating indigence through the public budget is considered to be counter-productive, as it would, in the logic of self-provisioning, only stifle the non-deserving poor in their immorality. It is a recipe of undiluted social Darwinist vintage on which I have elaborated in a monograph on pauperism (Breman 2016).

The Prime Minister's speech on Independence Day of 2019 signalled alarm over what he indicated as a high rate of population growth. This incorrect assumption, which was meant to blame the Muslim minority for outbreeding the Hindu majority, led him to hold forth on acceptance of the small family norm across the board as invoked by the national interest. In support of this expression of political concern, a few members of parliament from his party then wrote the draft of a population bill with penal sanctions for anti-social segments which are wrongly supposed to fall short of the set target of family planning. These improvident and undisciplined contingents should not be allowed to participate in elections, be exempted from the public distribution system, and deprived of all state-provided relief such as subsidized food and participation in the public works programme. This safety net, meagre as it already is, should be restricted to 'the deserving poor' who, because of their diligent and disciplined way of life, duly qualify for admission to citizenship.

The disconcerting initiative and its political rhetoric express serious misapprehension of the mounting economic and employment crisis. Nevertheless the proposed coercive population control has found broad endorsement. It fits with the more general trend to deprive abused communal identities of citizenship rights. The constitutional right to have rights and practise them is blatantly sacrificed for the greater glory of Hindutva's ideological frame. Dalits, Adivasis and Muslims in particular stand accused of lacking the distinct qualities required for joining the majoritarian fold, either for confessing to a different creed – Islam or Christianity – or because of failure to find succour in self-reliance. Inclusion versus exclusion is a dichotomous divide which segregates the dominating shepherds from the dominated sheep. Nationhood has come to be defined in terms of cultural symbolism and the obnoxious policies adopted have resulted in a system of apartheid culminating in the ghettoization of the excluded identities (Breman and Shah 2022). Such an enclosure of despised otherness signifies a new form of rank untouchability which denies its victimized multitude aspiring to live not beyond but within the pale of mainstream society and instead condemns them to remain stuck without public voice, visibility and representation.

Is then the Hindutva juggernaut indefatigable and bound to endure indefinitely, in a weird twist of India's civilization away from tolerance, secularism and pluriform diversity with respect for the inclusive rights of its citizenship? I am in full agreement with Yadav's suggestion at the end of his treatise that counter-hegemonic politics need a new political instrument. Clearly, none of the established political parties are fit for this purpose. But the need is not merely to create a new party or a new alliance. What we need is a new kind of political formation that subsumes a party, which is a party but not just a party (Yadav 2021).

In other words, we need a social movement which aims and succeeds to mobilize the massive segments excluded from participation in mainstream society and economy against the hegemonic and authoritarian order. Modi and his peers are alert to this looming danger of restiveness, and react to it by keeping a close watch over subversion. The rallying cry to unite against the main religious minority as 'the enemy in our midst' has targeted not only this sizeable contingent of the population. The hugely expanded surveillance apparatus is also instructed to hunt down 'urban naxals'. This pejorative label concerns anti-establishment protesters and other dissenters who, with the help of vigilantes, are tracked down and kept in detention at the state's discretion, accused of left-wing extremism. This attempt to stamp out civil protest and resistance in an ideology of hatred tends to be the final phase of dictatorial suppression, which also in this instance will hopefully mark the fall of an abominable regime. One can only hope that despite the efforts made to malign social and human rights activists, the causes they fight for are not blunted but will be raised and spread beyond the quarters in which they have their origin.

NOTE

[1] See, for example, Centre for Sustainable Employment, *State of Working in India 2021: One Year of Covid-19*, Bengaluru: Azim Premji University, May 2021. A total of 1,12,000 daily-wage earners committed suicide between 2019 and 2021, according to recent statistics from the National Crimes Record Bureau. On the occasion of the third anniversary of the lockdown, we must remember the lives lost due to starvation, exhaustion, financial distress, accidents during migration, lack of adequate medical care, suicide, police brutality, and crimes during the Covid-19 crisis and its aftermath. These three years underscore the pressing need for an inclusive framework that prioritizes the dignity and security of labourers (Working Peoples' Coalition newsletter, 24 March 2023).

Bibliography

Reports and Documents

Correspondence between the Directors of the East India Company and the Company's Government in India on the subject of slavery, *Accounts and Papers*, vol. 16, section 15-11-1837 to 16-8-1838, part LI.

Dantwala, M.L. and M.B. Desai (1948), 'Report of the Hali Labour Enquiry Committee (HLEC)', unpublished, Bombay.

Government of Gujarat (GoG) (1966), *Report of the Minimum Wages Advisory Committee for Employment in Agriculture*, Ahmedabad: Education and Labour Department.

—— (1972), *Report of the Committee on Unprotected and Unorganized Labour*, Gandhinagar: Education and Labour Department.

Government of India (GoI) (1948), *Report of the Committee on Fair Wages 1948*, Delhi.

—— (1952), *Agricultural Wages in India*, Agricultural Labour Enquiry, vol. 1, Ministry of Labour and Employment, New Delhi.

—— (1954), *Rural Man-Power and Occupational Structure*, Agricultural Labour Enquiry, Ministry of Labour and Employment, Delhi.

—— (1955), *Report on Intensive Survey of Agricultural Labour, 1951–52*, Agricultural Labour Enquiry, vol. 1 (all-India) and vol. 5 (west India), Ministry of Labour and Employment, Delhi.

—— (1960), *Report on the Second Labour Enquiry, 1956–57, Agricultural Labour in India*, vol. 1 (all-India) and vol. 5 (west India), Labour Bureau, Ministry of Labour and Employment, Delhi.

—— (1969), *Report of the National Commission on Labour*, Ministry of Labour, Employment and Rehabilitation, Delhi.

—— (1991), *Report of the National Commission on Rural Labour*, 2 vols, Ministry of Labour, Delhi.

—— (2014/2015), 'Concept Note on Smart City Scheme', draft, Ministry of Urban Development, Delhi.

Jayakar, M.S. (1925), *Settlement Report on Bardoli Taluk, Surat District*, Selections from the Records of the Bombay Government, no. 647, 25 June.

Lumsden, W.J. (1826), 'Collector of Surat, letter of 9 August 1825 to David Greenhill,

Acting Secretary to the Government of Bombay, Consultation 108 of 1825', Judicial Department, vol. 25–26, Bombay Record Department.

Prescott, C. (1865), 'Survey and Settlement Report of Chikhli Taluka', Bombay Presidency, Revenue Department, Bombay.

'Report from the Select Committee of the House of Lords appointed to inquire into the present state of the affairs of the East-India Company together with the Minutes of Evidence and Appendix' (1830), London.

Report of the Congress Agrarian Reforms Committee (1951), Delhi.

Report on Social Security for Unorganized Workers (2006), National Commission for Enterprises in the Unorganized Sector, Delhi.

Settlement Report on Bardoli Taluk, Surat District (1895), Selections from the Records of the Bombay Government, no. 359, New Series, Bombay.

'Slavery (East Indies): Copy of the Despatch from the Governor General of India in Council to the Court of Directors of the East India Company, dated the 8th day of February 1841 (No. 3) with the Report for the Indian Law Commissioners and its Appendix Enclosed in that Despatch, on the subject of Slavery in the East Indies', ordered by The House of Commons to be printed on 26th April 1841.

'Slavery', *Accounts and Papers*, vol. 16, Session 15 November 1837–16 August 1838, 697 Correspondence between the Directors of the East India Company and the Company's Government in India, on the subject of Slavery.

BOOKS AND ARTICLES

Ambedkar, B.R. (1948), *The Untouchables: Who Were They and Why They Became Untouchables?*, Bombay: Amrit Book Company.

Baines, J.A. (1912), *Ethnography, Castes and Tribes*, Strassbourg: Karl J. Trubner.

Bellasis, A.F. (1854), 'Report on the Southern Districts of the Surat Collectorate', *Selections from the Records of the Bombay Government*, New Series, no. 2, Bombay.

Bhalla, S.S., K. Bhasin and A. Virmani (2022), 'Pandemic, Poverty, and Inequality: Evidence from India', Working Paper no. WP/22/69, International Monetary Fund, April.

Brass, T. (1990), 'Class Struggle and the Deproletarianization of Agricultural Labour in Haryana (India)', *The Journal of Peasant Studies*, vol. 18, no. 1, pp. 36–67.

Breman, J. (1970), 'Meester en Knecht', unpublished PhD thesis submitted to University of Amsterdam, The Netherlands.

—— (1974a) 'Mobilization of Landless Labourers: Halpatis of South Gujarat', *Economic and Political Weekly*, vol. 9, no. 12, pp. 489–96.

—— (1974b), *Patronage and Exploitation: Changing Agrarian Relations in South Gujarat, India*, Berkeley: University of California Press. Reprinted in 1979 by Manohar Publishers and Distributors, Delhi.

—— (1976), 'A Dualistic Labour System? Critique of the "Informal Sector" Concept', *Economic and Political Weekly*, vol. 11, no. 50, part 1, November, pp. 1870–76, parts 2 and 3, December, pp. 1905–08 and 1939–43. Reprinted in Breman (1994), pp. 3–45.

—— (1977), 'Labour Relations in the "Formal" and "Informal" Sectors: A Case Study',

Journal of Peasant Studies, vol. 4, no. 3, April, pp. 171–205 and vol. 4, no. 4, July, pp. 337–59. Reprinted in Breman (1994), pp. 46–130.

—— (1978), 'Seasonal Migration and Cooperative Capitalism: Crushing of Cane and of Labour by the Sugar Factories of Bardoli', *Economic and Political Weekly*, vol.13, nos 31 and 33, pp. 1317–60; and *The Journal of Peasant Studies*, vol. 6, no. 1, pp. 41–70 and vol. 6, no. 4, pp. 168–209. Reprinted in Breman (1994), pp. 193–211.

—— (1979), 'The Market for Non-Agrarian Labour: The Formal Versus Informal Sector', in S.D. Pillai and C. Baks, eds, *Winners and Losers: Styles of Development and Change in an Indian Region*, Bombay: Popular Prakashan, pp. 122–66.

—— (1985a) 'Between Accumulation and Immiserization: The Partiality of Fieldwork in Rural India', *Journal of Peasant Studies*, vol. 13, no. 1, October, pp. 5–36. Reprinted in Breman (1994), pp. 370–407.

—— (1985b), *Of Peasants, Migrants and Paupers: Rural Labour Circulation and Capitalist Production in West India*, New Delhi: Oxford University Press and Oxford: Clarendon Press.

—— (1985c), 'State Protection for the Rural Proletariat', *Economic and Political Weekly*, vol. 20, June, pp. 1043–55. Reprinted in Breman (1994), pp. 291–332.

—— (1988), 'The Renaissance of Social Darwinism', Annual Lecture, The Hague: Institute of Social Studies. Reprinted in Breman (2003), pp. 17–50.

—— (1993), *Beyond Patronage and Exploitation; Changing Agrarian Relations in South Gujarat*, New Delhi: Oxford University Press.

—— (1994), *Wage Hunters and Gatherers: Search for Work in the Rural and Urban Economy of South Gujarat*, New Delhi: Oxford University Press.

—— (1996), *Footloose Labour: Working in India's Informal Economy*, Cambridge: Cambridge University Press.

—— (1997), 'The Village in Focus', in J. Breman, P. Kloos and A. Saith, eds, *The Village in Asia Revisited*, New Delhi: Oxford University Press, pp. 15–75.

—— (1999), 'Silencing the Voice of Agricultural Labourers', *Modern Asian Studies*, vol. 33, no. 1, pp. 1–22. Reprinted in Breman (2003), pp. 51–104.

—— (2003), *The Labouring Poor in India: Patterns of Exploitation, Subordination and Exclusion*, New Delhi: Oxford University Press.

—— (2004), *The Making and Unmaking of an Industrial Working Class: Sliding Down the Labour Hierarchy in Ahmedabad, India*, New Delhi: Oxford University Press.

—— (2007a), *Labour Bondage in West India: From Past to Present*, New Delhi: Oxford University Press.

—— (2007b), *The Poverty Regime in Village India: Half a Century of Work and Life at the Bottom of the Rural Economy in South Gujarat*, New Delhi: Oxford University Press.

—— (2010a), 'India's Social Question in a State of Denial', *Economic and Political Weekly*, vol. 45, no. 23, pp. 42–46.

—— (2010b), 'Neo-Bondage: A Fieldwork-Based Account', *International Labor and Working Class History*, no. 78, Fall, pp. 48–62.

—— (2010c), *Outcast Labour in Asia; Circulation and Informalization of the Workforce at the Bottom of the Economy*, New Delhi: Oxford University Press.

—— (2013a), *At Work in the Informal Economy of India: A Perspective from the Bottom Up*, New Delhi: Oxford University Press.

—— (2013b), 'The Practice of Poor Relief in Rural South Gujarat', in J. Breman and K.P. Kannan, eds, *The Long Road to Social Security: Assessing the Implementation of National Social Security Initiatives for the Working Poor in India*, New Delhi: Oxford University Press, pp. 293–334.

—— (2015), 'Down and Out in Ahmedabad', *Economic and Political Weekly*, vol. 50, no. 12, 21 March.

—— (2016), *On Pauperism in Past and Present*, New Delhi: Oxford University Press.

—— (2019), *Capitalism, Labour and Inequality in India*, Cambridge: Cambridge University Press.

—— (2020), 'The Pandemic in India and its Impact on Footloose Labour', *The Indian Journal of Labour Economics*, vol. 61, pp. 901–19.

—— (2021), 'Classes of Labour in India: A Review Essay', *Global Labour Journal*, vol. 12, no. 2, May, pp. 139–49.

—— (2022), 'Coolie Labour and Colonial Capitalism in Asia', *Journal of Agrarian Change*, August, pp. 1–14.

Breman, J., I. Guerin and A. Prakash, eds (2009), *India's Unfree Workforce: Of Bondage Old and New*, New Delhi: Oxford University Press.

Breman, J., K. Harris, C.K. Lee and M. van der Linden, eds (2019), *The Social Question in the Twenty-First Century: A Global View*, Oakland: University of California Press.

Breman, J. and K.P. Kannan, eds (2013), *The Long Road to Social Security: Assessing the Implementation of National Social Security Initiatives for the Working Poor in India*, New Delhi: Oxford University Press.

Breman, J., P. Kloos and A. Saith, eds (1997), *The Village in Asia Revisited*, New Delhi: Oxford University Press.

Breman, J. and G. Shah (2022), *Gujarat, Cradle and Harbinger of Identity Politics: India's Injurious Frame of Communalism*, New Delhi: Tulika Books.

Broomfield, R.S. and R.M. Maxwell (1929), *Report of the Special Enquiry into the Second Revision Settlement of the Bardoli and Chorasi Talukas*, Bombay: Government Press.

Calman, L.J. (1987), 'Congress Confronts Communism: Thana District, 1945–47', *Modern Asian Studies*, vol. 21, no. 2, pp. 329–48.

Dave, J. (1946), *Halpati-Mukit: Halipratha ane Mukitadanni Hilachal*, Ahmedabad: Navjivan.

Davis, M. (2000), *Late Victorian Holocausts: El Nino Famines and the Making of the Third World*, London and New York: Verso.

Deaton, A. and V. Kozel (2005), *Data and Dogma: The Great India Poverty Debate*, New Delhi: Oxford University Press (on behalf of IBRD, The World Bank).

Desai, D. (1942), 'Agrarian Serfdom in India', *Indian Sociologist*, July–August.

Desai, I.I. (1971), *Raniparajna Jagruti*, Swatantra Ithihas Samiti, no. 3, Surat.

Desai, K.I. (1979), 'Tribals in a Non-Tribal Setting; A Sociological Study of Tribals in an Urban Community', unpublished PhD thesis submitted to University of Bombay, Bombay.

Desai, M. (1929), *The Story of Bardoli*, Ahmedabad: Navjivan.

Desai, M.D. (1974), *Employment, Income and Levels of Living of Agricultural Labourers: A Study in the Surat District*, Vallabh Vidyanagar, Anand: Agro-Economic Research Centre, Sardar Patel University.

Desai, N. (1990), *Women's Work and Family Strategies in a Rural Community in South Gujarat*, New Delhi: Indian Council of Social Science Research.

Dhamne, P.S. (1956), *Summary of the Report on Forced Labour*, Government of India Press.

Dirks, N.B. (2001), *Castes of Mind: Colonialism and the Making of Modern India*, Princeton: Princeton University Press. Reprinted in 2002 by Permanent Black, Ranikhet.

Epstein, T.S. (1967), 'Productive Efficiency and Customary Systems of Rewards in Traditional South India', in M. Lipton, ed., *Themes in Economic Anthropology*, A.S.A. Monograph Series, no. 6, London.

Gandhi, M.K. (1927a), 'Face to Face with the Pauper', *Young India*, 31 March.

—— (1927b), column in *Navjivan*, 15 June.

Gidla, S. (2017), *Ants among Elephants: An Untouchable Family and the Making of Modern India*, New York: Farrar, Straus and Giroux.

Gooptu, N. and J. Parry, eds (2017), *Persistence of Poverty in India*, London: Routledge.

Guérin, I. (2013), 'Bonded Labour, Agrarian Changes and Capitalism: Emerging Patterns in South India', *Journal of Agrarian Change*, vol. 13, no. 3, pp. 405–23.

Hardiman, D. (1981), *Peasant Nationalists of Gujarat: Kheda District 1917–1934*, New Delhi: Oxford University Press.

Harvey, D. (2012), *Rebel Cities: From the Right to the City to Urban Revolution*, London and New York: Verso Books.

Hauser, W. (1994), *Sahajanand on Agricultural Labour and the Rural Poor*, New Delhi: Manohar Publishers and Distributors.

Hauser, W. (2006), *Culture, Vernacular Politics and the Peasants*, New Delhi: Manohar Publishers and Distributors.

International Labour Organization (ILO) (2009), *The Cost of Coercion*, Global Report on the Follow-Up to the ILO Declaration on Fundamental Principles and Rights at Work, Geneva.

Jodhka, S.S. (2002), 'Nation and Village: Images of Rural India in Gandhi, Nehru and Ambedkar', *Economic and Political Weekly*, vol. 37, no. 32, pp. 3343–53.

Jose, S.P. (2022), 'The Informalization of India's Labour Reforms', *Economic and Political Weekly*, vol. 57, no. 46, pp. 53–59.

Katiyar, S., A. Vijeta and A. Rose, (2021), *Impact of the Second Wave of COVID 19 on Seasonal Migrant Workers in West India and Their Response to the Infection*, Ahmedabad: Prayas.

Keatinge, G. (1921), *Agricultural Progress in Western India*, London: Longman.

Khela, S. (2012), *A Rogue and Peasant Slave: Adivasi Resistance, 1800–2000*, New Delhi: Navayana Publishing.

Kosambi, D.D. ([1956] 1976), *An Introduction to the Study of Indian History*, Bombay: Popular Prakashan.

Kothari, U. (1990), 'Women's Work and Rural Transformation in India: A Study from Gujarat', unpublished PhD thesis submitted to University of Edinburgh, Edinburgh.

Lal, R.B. (1977), 'Bonded Labour in Gujarat (Does It Exist in Gujarat?)', unpublished Ms., Tribal Research and Training Institute, Gujarat Vidyapith, Ahmedabad.

Lerche, J. (2007), 'A Global Alliance Against Forced Labour? Unfree Labour, Neo-

Liberal Globalization and the International Labour Organization', *Journal of Agrarian Change,* vol. 7, no. 4, pp. 425–55.

—— (2012), 'Labour Regulations and Labour Standards in India: Decent Work?', *Global Labour Journal,* vol. 3, no. 1, pp. 16–39.

—— (2013), 'The Agrarian Question in Neoliberal India: Agrarian Transition By-passed?', *Journal of Agrarian Change,* vol. 13, no. 3, pp. 382–404.

Lewis, O. (1966), *La Vida: A Puerto Rican Family in the Culture of Poverty,* San Juan and New York: Random House.

Lorenzo, A.M. (1947), *Agricultural Labour Conditions in Northern India,* Bombay: New Book Company.

Marx, K. (1976), *Capital,* vol. 1, translated by Ben Fowkes, London: Penguin.

Mehta, D. (1975), Oral history interview of Shri Dinkar Mehta by Dr. Hari Dev Sharma for the Nehru Memorial Museum and Library, Ahmedabad, 27 July.

Mehta, J.M. (1930), *A Study of the Rural Economy of Gujarat,* Baroda: Baroda State Press.

Miles, R. (1987), *Capitalism and Unfree Labour: Anomaly or Necessity?* London and New York: Tavistock Publications.

Mukhtyar, G.C. (1930), *Life and Labour in a South Gujarat Village,* Bombay: Longmans Green & Co.

Parry, J. (2021), 'Response to Jan Breman's Review of "Classes of Labour: Work and Life in a Central Indian Steel Town"', *Global Labour Journal,* vol. 12, no. 2, May, pp. 150–60.

Parry, J.P., J. Breman and K. Kapadia, eds (1999), *The Worlds of Indian Industrial Labour,* Contributions to Indian Sociology: Occasional Studies 9, New Delhi: Sage Publications.

Patel, J.M. (1964), 'Agricultural Labour in a South Gujarat Village', in V.S. Vyas, ed., *Agricultural Labour in Four Indian Villages,* Vallabh Vidyanagar: Sardar Patel University, pp. 92–119.

Pocock, D. (1973), *Mind, Body and Wealth: A Study of Belief and Practice in an Indian Village,* Oxford: Basil Blackwell.

Polanyi, K. (1944), *The Great Transformation: The Political and Economic Origins of Our Times,* Boston: Beacon Press.

Prayas Centre for Labour Research and Action (PCLRA) (2018), *A Bitter Harvest: A Study of Sugarcane Harvesting Workers of South Gujarat,* Ahmedabad.

Rabitoy, N. (1975), 'System v. Expediency: The Reality of Land Revenue Administration in the Bombay Presidency, 1812–1820', *Modern Asian Studies,* vol. 9, no. 4, pp. 529–46.

Ramachandran, V.K. (1990), *Wage Labour and Unfreedom in Indian Agriculture: An Indian Case Study,* Oxford: Clarendon Press.

Ramamurti, B. (1954), *Agricultural Labour: How They Work and Live,* Delhi: Ministry of Labour, Government of India.

Roy, S. and R. van der Weide (2022), 'Poverty in India Has Declined Over the Last Decade But Not As Much As Previously Thought', Policy Research Working Paper, World Bank, Washington D.C.

Rudra, A. *et al.,* eds (1978), *Studies in the Development of Capitalism in India: Essays,* Lahore: Vanguard Books.

Sarkar, S. (1983), *'Popular' Movements and 'Middle Class' Leadership: Perspectives and Problems of a 'History from Below'*, Calcutta.

Sarkar, T. (2022), *Hindu Nationalism in India*, Ranikhet: Permanent Black.

Scott, J.C. (1990), *Domination and the Arts of Resistance: Hidden Transcripts*, New Haven: Yale University Press.

Sethi, A. (2011), *A Free Man*, Noida and London: Random House India.

Shah, G. (1974), 'Traditional Society and Political Mobilization: The Experience of Bardoli Satyagraha (1920–1928)', *Contributions to Indian Sociology* (NS), no. 8, pp. 89–107.

—— (1978), 'Agricultural Labourers: Are They Bonded?', unpublished Ms., Centre for Social Studies, Surat.

Shah, P.G. (1958), *The Dublas of Gujarat*, Delhi: Bharatiya Adimjati Seva Sangh.

—— (1959), 'A Serf Tribe', *Journal of the Gujarat Research Society*, vol. 21, no. 1/81, January, pp. 42–58.

Shanta, S. (2022), 'Made to Live our Trauma Again: Bonded Labourers "Beaten Up, Raped", Talk of Police Inaction', *The Wire*, 6 February.

Shukla, J.B. (1937), *Life and Labour in a Gujarat Taluka*, Calcutta: Longmans, Galla and Co.

Srinivas, M.N. (1959), 'The Dominant Caste in Rampura', *American Anthropologist*, vol. 61, no. 1, pp. 1–16.

—— (1987), 'Development of Sociology in India: An Overview', *Economic and Political Weekly*, vol. 22, no. 4, 24 January, pp. 135–38.

Teltumbde, A. (2018), *Republic of Caste*, New Delhi: Navayana Publishing.

The World Bank (2022), *Poverty and Shared Prosperity: Correcting Course*, Washington, https://www.worldbank.org/en/publication/poverty-and-shared-prosperity, accessed 10 October 2022.

Thorner, A. and D. Thorner (1962), *Land and Labour in India*, London: Asia Publishing House.

Thorner, D. (1976), *The Agrarian Prospect in India*, second edition, Madras: Allied Publishers.

—— (1978), 'Capitalist Farming in India', in A. Rudra *et al.*, eds, *Studies in the Development of Capitalism in India: Essays*, Lahore: Vanguard Books, pp. 37–42.

—— (1980), *The Shaping of Modern India*, edited by A. Thorner, New Delhi: Allied Publishers.

Tinker, H. (1974), *A New System of Slavery: The Export of Indian Labour Overseas, 1830–1920*, London: Oxford University Press.

Tocqueville, A. de (1968), *Alexis de Tocueville's Memoir on Pauperism*, translated by Seymour Drescher, New Haven: Yale University Press.

United Nations (2015), *The Millennium Development Goals Report 2015*, New York: United Nations.

Visaria, L. and H. Joshi (2021), 'Seasonal Sugarcane Harvesters of Gujarat: Trapped in a Cycle of Poverty', *Journal of Social and Economic Development*, vol. 23, no. 1, pp. 113–30.

Vishwanath, L.S. (1985), 'Gujarat Kisan Sabha, 1936–56', *Economic and Political Weekly*, vol. 20, no. 28, pp. 1197–2000.

Weber, M. ([1892] 1984), *Die Lage der Landarbeiter im Ostelbischen Deutschland* (The Condition of Agricultural Labour in Eastern Germany), edited by M. Riesebrodt, Tuebingen: Mohr-Siebeck.

—— (1893), *Die Ländliche Arbeitsverfassung*, in *Verhandlungen des Vereins für Sozialpolitik, Band 58* (Proceedings of the Association for Social Politics, vol. 58), Leipzig.

—— (1922), 'Wirtschaft und Gesellschaft', in *Grundriss der Sozialoekonomik*, III: *Abteiling* (*The Theory of Social and Economic Organization*, Part III: *Economy and Society*), Tuebingen: Mohr-Siebeck.

—— (1924), 'Entwicklungstendenzen in der Lage der Ostelbischen Landarbeiter', in *Gesammelte Aufsätze zur Sozial und Wirtschaftsgeschichte*, Tüebingen: Mohr-Siebeck; English translation by K. Tribe, 'Development Tendencies in the Situation of East Elbian Rural Labourers', *Economy and Society*, vol. 8, no. 2, 1979, pp. 177–205.

Williams, E. ([1944] (2014), *Capitalism and Slavery*, Chapel Hill: The University of North Carolina Press.

Yadav, Y. (2021), *Making Sense of Indian Democracy*, Hyderabad: Orient Blackswan.

Index